THE PATTERN O

A Textbook to Basi...
Complementary Medicine

About the Author

The author, Dr Aubrey Thomas Westlake, was educated at Sidcot, a Quaker school in the Mendips; and subsequently underwent medical training at Birmingham and Cambridge Universities and at St Bartholomew's Hospital, London. He qualified in 1918, MRCS (Eng), LRCP (Lond) and later BA, MB, B CHIR (Cantab). This was followed by general orthodox practice in Bermondsey for eighteen years, with the famous Dr Alfred Salter MP, from which the author retired just before the Second World War.

He was Vice President of the British Society of Dowsers for some years, and is now an Hon. Life Vice President. He is an Hon. Fellow of the Radionic Society, was Vice President of the Society for the Study of Radiesthesia and has been President of the Psionic Medical Society since 1978.

He only retired from private medical practice in 1984, at the age of 91, which has given him the time to finish writing his autobiography. Dr Westlake has also written two other books, *Health Abounding. A Social Credit National Health Service* and *Life Threatened. Menace and Way Out*.

To my late wife
for her loving help and encouragement
over the fifty-two and a half years
of our married life

The Pattern
of Health

*A search for
a greater understanding
of the life force
in health and disease*

THIRD EDITION

by

Aubrey T. Westlake

B.A., M.B., B.Chir. (Cantab),
M.R.C.S., L.R.C.P., F.I.Psi.Med.

ELEMENT BOOKS

'Without exaggeration one can well maintain in the course of medical development there has scarcely ever been an epoch which offers to the historically minded physician such decided stimulation to retrospection into the past as the contemporary. Never has the poetic expression of the truth *"Multa renascentur, quae iam cecidere"* (Many things which had died will know re-birth) held to such an extent as in our time. We are witnesses of the constant, obvious resurrection of old ideas occurring in the doctrines of disease and methods of treatment, admittedly in new vestments and essentially on higher planes of knowledge.'

> Dr Max Neuberger: *The Doctrine of the*
> *Healing Powers of Nature throughout the Course*
> *of Time,* translated by Dr Linn Boyd. 1946

'Man is what he is by virtue of body, etheric body, soul (astral body) and Ego (Spirit). He must in health be seen and understood from the aspect of these his members; in disease he must be observed in the disturbance of their equilibrium; and for his healing we must find the remedies that can restore that balance.'

> Steiner, from *Fundamentals of Therapy*

'God created man in his own image, in the image of God created he him, male and female created he them'.

> *Genesis* I v 27

Acknowledgements

I should like to take this opportunity to thank all those many good friends who in their very various ways made this 'search' possible. Most of these will be mentioned by name in the text, but if, inadvertently, anyone has been overlooked I trust this acknowledgement will remedy any omissions. In particular I should like to express my appreciation of the invaluable assistance of Henry Finlayson, but for whom I doubt whether this book would ever have been completed.

I am also indebted to Mr and Mrs George Sandwith, whose unique field researches into the ancient magics, as set forth in their book *The Miracle Hunters,* not only encouraged me in my research, but provided a welcome corroboration of the reality of the Life Force.

I am also grateful to Messrs Max Freedom Long, J.E.R. McDonagh, and the late Wilhelm Reich for their consent to quote from their published books: to Miss Nora Weeks for permission to quote from the writings of the late Dr Edward Bach, and to the Rudolf Steiner Nachlass Verwaltung to quote various passages from the works of the late Rudolf Steiner; to the publishers Messrs Peter Davies Ltd to quote from *Modern Miraculous Cures* by François Leuret and Henri Bon and to Hodder and Stoughton Ltd to quote from *A Scientist of the Invisible* by A.P. Shepherd.

Contents

Foreword

I am delighted that this book by Aubrey Westlake is being kept in print. Firstly, because it was my first real introduction to complementary medicine; although Brian Inglis was, of course, the first in this field, he could not speak with the voice of personal experience as a therapist.

My teacher in the Gurdjieff work, Vincent Stuart, who first published *The Pattern of Health* asked me, because I was the only doctor in the group, to visit Aubrey and see if I could make anything of these alternative therapies and possibly find out how they worked.

Being, at that time, a little disillusioned with orthodox medicine and open to other possibilities, I was very interested to see patients with advanced cancer, in apparent good health and living well beyond their expected time under his treatment and was impressed with what he had to say. I was also impressed by the healing patterns his group had evolved, and started to use some of the therapies that he mentioned, like Bach Remedies, in my own practice.

From the meetings that I had with Aubrey, an understanding of the energies used started to grow in my mind, and subsequently this has vastly changed the course of my life; I am therefore very grateful for this book and feel sure that others will also benefit from it. The healing patterns he has described deserve some research.

It is a book that contains seeds for the future which have yet to burst into growth.

Dr Alec Forbes, MA, DM, FRCP

Foreword to the Third Edition

The trend of events and the need of the times have called for a third edition of this book. It is now twenty-four years since it was first published, and instead of becoming out of date, its theme – the search for a greater understanding of the Life Force in health and disease – which then seemed of little significance, has now become a matter of urgency, pressing and crucial.

For, during this comparatively short period, mankind has really pried open Pandora's box with a vengeance, flooding the whole world so thoroughly with a horrific miasma of contamination and pollution, that only Hope now remains.

What is this hope? It is that we shall be given the essential perception and understanding of the nature of true healing; and that health be seen as the resultant of a continuous creative act of that healing, brought about by the supersensible force – the Life Force – which transforms and transmutes the inimical into wholeness and harmony. For this hope, for this healing, the whole world is now crying out.

When *The Pattern of Health* was first written it could not have been foreseen that its survey would be of such importance twenty-four years later, but as it turns out it did, in fact, contain a large number of clues which have become essential in the current search for health and healing – a search which has grown concomitantly with the letting loose of the disintegrating forces of modern scientific technological development. This search is now popularly known as Fringe or alternative Medicine, embracing all forms of therapeutics and 'clinical techniques not taught in the orthodox medical schools' – to quote Brian Inglis's definition.

This is partly a reaction against and a dissatisfaction with modern scientific medicine which, with the ever increasing use of synthetic drugs and other developments, is adding to the internal pollution of the human organism, thereby not only interfering with the true healing processes but actually very often producing disorder instead of harmony. But the main reason is a realization that the whole of modern medicine is disease-orientated, dealing mainly with symptoms rather than basic causes. On the positive side is the unrivalled skill and technique of modern medicine in salvaging the apparently hopeless and in dealing with emergencies; and it may be that while the present state of disorder and disintegration maintains, this is the only practical way of dealing with the enormous mass of chronic ill health and disease. But in this case it must not, and cannot be expected to provide fundamental healing leading to health and wholeness, as this involves new attitudes, new thinking and a radical change of outlook.

So we come to a divergence of ways. The way of materialistic medicine with world-wide prestige and general acceptance, and the way of what may be called full healing of body, mind and spirit, the science and art of which is only just beginning to emerge and take proper shape and pattern; but it is this which can be the hope of the future and its veritable salvation. It is a way which should especially appeal to modern Youth looking and seeking honestly and sanely for new concepts and ways of thought, for this healing is that of the whole man and his environment. If this seeking could find this path – the signposting of which is the *raison d'être* of this book – then indeed the words of Christ 'I am come that ye might have life and have it more abundantly' could become, not only a promise, but a vital and living reality.

There have, of course, been further developments of the work recorded in this book, but in so far as it has been possible to reprint most of the original text without alteration it is clear that it still forms a sound and necessary foundation for any student who wishes to delve into these new fields of study and research.

The most important additions since the last edition are: (1) Psionic Medicine which is an integration of Radiesthesia, McDonagh's Unity Theory of Disease, Hahnemann's Miasmic Theory and Homoeopathy, as developed by the late Dr George Laurence for the detection of basic causal factors in disease, and especially prevention of a pending disease and (2) the late Malcolm Rae's discovery of the archetypal patterns of substances, particularly of homoeopathic remedies. Most of what has already been explored holds true. There is also a Foreword to this edition by Dr Alec Forbes.

A truer pattern of health is gradually emerging, so the first edition was rightly named, and the further exploration is a task for the future. Like the Norsemen of old, and later Columbus, we have at present only discovered a little of the coast line of a whole new and infinitely fascinating continent.

FOREWORD

The exploration will lead directly into new dimensions of reality and present a challenge to all those of a youthful spirit and an open uncluttered mind, for the approach, and here I quote from my book *Life Threatened:* 'the approach must be threefold – as a believer in the spiritual world, as a scientific devotee of truth, and as a poet in search of the miraculous; for to fully appreciate these realms sincere belief, exact sense perception, and a freely working fantasy are all required.'

Aubrey T. Westlake
Godshill, Fordingbridge, Hampshire
February 1985

Introduction

This book is an account of a search for a greater understanding of the true nature of health and disease and particularly of health. It may indeed be said to form a sort of pilgrimage which led into unknown regions of medicine and allied subjects, where it was difficult to keep a sense of direction, to find the right path, and to distinguish between the truth and error.

As the search went on it was found that the concepts of health and disease seemed to alter; indeed I was finally led right out of the material field into regions where I had to abandon my preconceptions and reorientate my ideas. But it was at this point that light began to be thrown on the whole subject, and a consistent and coherent picture of health and disease began to emerge.

As will be seen, the thread which enabled me to find my way through the maze was provided by one clue, the supersensory force – Vis Medicatrix Naturae (the healing power of Nature) – a force which has kept on being discovered in all its various forms by so many workers both in the past and in the present, and which has been given so many different names and yet is, in my opinion, one and the same vital force or aspects of it.

During the exploration, reports, as it were, were sent back from time to time as to the findings up to date. These are the papers which were read to various societies, and which form a more or less progressive, chronological series, as listed in the References. The present narrative is largely compiled from these 'original notes', but arranged in a form in which the development of the idea of health and disease can be followed, as it in fact emerged, along with a great many other most interesting collaterals.

A great deal of the confusion and misunderstanding in this whole subject has undoubtedly been due to the fact that there is a problem of nomenclature. The need to think in new ways about these pre-matter problems and concepts has meant that words, of necessity used, are not only inadequate, but convey meanings never intended. This difficulty has still to be overcome.

In this scientific age a vast amount of human knowledge and

experience, which lies at present outside a strictly scientific approach (as usually understood), is dismissed as superstitions and wishful thinking, or even as downright chicanery. This applies particularly to the whole of the psychic and occult fields, which down through the ages have been a happy hunting ground for the charlatan, the quack, the credulous, and, not least, the sceptic. The medical field, once one gets outside the strictly orthodox, is no exception, and this makes doubly difficult an investigation of theories and therapies, which smack in any way of magic or the miraculous. And indeed, unless one is firmly anchored in reality, one tends to 'take off' and gets lost in clouds of self-deception.

To guard against this it is very necessary to keep one's feet very firmly and literally on the ground. In my own case to do so I have engaged in farming, in running a holiday centre, and in local government, with all the very definite and concrete problems which such activities entail. While so engaged, I have still found time for the essential exploration, because modern medicine must recover anew an integretion with religion and philosophy.

For medicine during the long period of the Indian, Chinese, Greek and Arabian civilizations, culminating in the great Persian physician Avicenna (980-1037), had its roots in religion and philosophy; it remained one with the other sciences, and disease was approached through the front door of health. But with the coming of the Renaissance medicine first threw off religion, and, two centuries later, philosophy as well, becoming increasingly materialistic as it became purely scientific.

This was probably an inevitable phase and a necessary development, if progress was to be made, but the mere collection of facts and the increasing fragmentation of knowledge is now leading to a barrenness of ideas in which no guiding principles are discernible. This whatever the technical achievements may be, and they are many, is, for medicine, materialistic nihilism, and contemporary medicine is showing signs of having arrived there.

The time is over-ripe for a new integrative philosophy of medicine based on a fundamental conception of health. Disease would then be considered, as it once was, as a deviation or imbalance from a norm.

Thus I am sure that the renewed interest in Vis Medicatrix

Naturae, and particularly in its measurement, and thus control, by Radiesthesia, derives from the fact that it points the way to the new integration, in which medicine will be equally scientific, philosophic and religious.

Already we see this change taking place in physics, and in medicine we have the beginning of a move away from pathology and chemistry, which have dominated medicine for the last hundred years, to a world of function and radiation, and to even more intangible realms, which, until very recently, have been right outside the scope of science. This change, curiously enough, would have been more rapid but for the discovery of the antibiotics.

The really interesting thing about the new medicine which is emerging is that, while it will deal with increasing competence with the physical, to do so it will have to include the metaphysical. It is becoming evident that a true understanding of the physical is only possible in terms of metaphysics, and vice versa. This will constitute a major revolution in modern thought.

This said, I can only hope that the reader will be content to accompany me on my pilgrimage, and that he will grant that I have managed with the help of my master clue to traverse the labyrinthine jungle of scientific intangibles to the beginnings of the firm ground of understanding and integration, without too badly losing my sense of proportion or my way, or becoming too 'airborne' or other-worldly.

CHAPTER ONE
How it all Began

It may sound surprising, in these days when specialization starts at 11+, that I left school at eighteen without any definite idea of what I wanted to do, beyond a rather vague notion that I wanted to study Health.

This at first seemed promising, but on going into it I soon found like Dr J. T. Wrench, the author of the famous *Wheel of Health*, that such a study in the year 1911 was not only impossible but also slightly impious. To study Health, it seemed, one had just to study Disease, which seemed a contradiction in terms.

But, if doctors did not study Health, who did?

The Nature Cure advocates seemed to come nearest to what I was looking for, but on investigation it appeared that health for them was largely a question of food fads of one sort or another, with little or no scientific basis for their assertions.

The outstanding figure in this field at that time was Eustace Miles with his famous restaurant in Chandos Street, and I very nearly became one of his assistants. But fortunately the arrangement fell through, for as it turned out, it would not have led to a true study of Health.

Eventually Professor Sims Woodhead (Professor of Pathology at Cambridge) persuaded my father that to study medicine was the right thing to do, for, as he said, 'after he has qualified he will be at liberty to study anything he likes, and at least he will have professional standing and a sound knowledge of what health is not', which, in the event, proved to be very sound advice.

So it was decided, and in 1913 I entered St. John's College, Cambridge, as a medical student and my pilgrimage had begun.

Through my student days at Cambridge, including the period during the war at the 1st Eastern General Military Hospital and subsequently at St. Bartholomew's Hospital, London, until my qualification in 1918, I was necessarily busy imbibing all I could about disease and its treatment. All heterodox views were of necessity in abeyance, and they remained so during my time with

I

the Friends' War Victims Relief Committee as a doctor in France at the end of the war.

Peace found me again at a loss as to what to do. I had not forgotten my first love but it was very obvious that it was now necessary for me to make a living, so I went up to London to see if I could get a resident post at a Children's Hospital. I did not get it but instead I got a partnership with a firm of doctors in Bermondsey, where I was to remain for the next eighteen years, to get married and bring up a family of five.

The manner in which this came about is worth recounting as showing the extraordinary way in which 'Destiny' works.

As fate would have it, a day or two previously I had gone to see the Secretary of the Quaker Peace Council and mentioned in the course of conversation that I was looking for a job. Next day a man who was a conscientious objector looked in to see the secretary who chanced to say she had seen me and that I wanted a job. The following day the man went down with appendicitis and sent for the famous Bermondsey doctor, Alfred Salter, who attended C.O.s medically. Dr Salter demurred as he had made it a rule, in view of his heavy commitments, not to see anyone outside Bermondsey, but, as the man was a special friend of his, he relented and went to see him.

During the visit the patient mentioned in passing that I was looking for a job and asked Dr Salter if he knew of anything for me. Dr Salter said his partnership was in need of a locum, and he asked how he could get in touch with me.

In the light of subsequent events it became very clear to me why I had missed the hospital job. In this curious and roundabout way Destiny had brought me to what proved to be a full and satisfying life as a panel doctor in a densely populated district of S.E. London, the best possible training ground in the profound questions of life and death, health and disease. In few other ways could I have got the variety of clinical experience essential for exploring unorthodox fields of medicine.

But here again in this busy practice there was little or no time to think about health. I was far too busy dealing with disease in all its manifold forms. But from time to time I felt, as I had even in my student days, that in the orthodox field things were far from satisfactory, as we seemed most of the time to be dealing with the alleviation of symptoms and never getting down to causes.

It was at this point that I began to entertain certain conceptions which were later to find expression and fulfilment in what I can only call the true preventive medicine.

One thing which had struck me in the course of my medical studies was the contingent nature of many of its findings. It seemed to me that a great deal of medical diagnosis, more often than not, was just shutting the stable door after the horse had been stolen; in other words, that usually a diagnosis was possible only when destructive changes had already taken place in the tissues. The best one could do then, by treatment, was to alleviate symptoms or remove the diseased part of the organism. Little appeared to be known of basic and primary causes, and it seemed impossible to diagnose departures from the normal in the very earliest stages. The average doctor was mainly engaged in baling out leaking boats.

I felt that there should be some more exact and subtle method of finding out precisely what was the matter and of applying early remedies. Hence, when about 1925 I first came across Abrams' work I felt at once that here was the sort of thing I had been seeking, and I read such books as I could about him.

Dr Albert Abrams, born in 1863, was a noted San Francisco physician. After qualification in America he studied in Europe under such famous masters as Virchow, Wasserman and von Helmholtz. Subsequently he specialized in nervous diseases, and was regarded as among the foremost neurologists of the day. Indeed, he was described by Sir James Barr as 'by far the greatest genius the medical profession had produced for half a century'.

He conceived the idea that, as all matter is constantly emitting radiation, which is as specific for normal human tissue as for matter in other forms, it should be possible to detect a change in the radiation of tissue damaged by disease or accident.

But the difficulty was to detect such radiation, as he found that there was no instrument delicate enough to meet his requirements. He spared neither time nor money in the search for such an instrument but with no success. A chance observation in the percussion note over a special area of the abdomen in a patient with cancer when that patient was facing west, and only west, gave him the clue he was looking for. Subsequently it came to be known as the Electronic Reaction of Abrams, or E.R.A., for short.

This started him off on a long and intensive series of experiments, for it occurred to him that a similar reflex might be detected in the body of a healthy young man when in close contact with a cancer specimen. He found this to be so. This observation together with the fact that the 'radiations' could pass along a wire, and a blood spot could be substituted for the actual patient, resulted, after further experiments, in the evolving of an instrument called a 'Reflexoscope', which, when used with a healthy human being as detector, was capable of differentiating between cancer, syphilis and tuberculosis, the characteristic reaction in each case being clear and definite.

Later still, holding that 'the beginning of disease is a disturbance of electronic equilibrium within the molecule', he sought the means of restoring the lost equilibrium. To this end he got Hoffmann, the inventor of the Zeppelin Detector, to produce a treatment instrument, which he called the Oscilloclast.

This device was the famous Abrams' Box which the Horder Committee investigated in 1925 and left in the air. Still, the committee reported that 'the fundamental proposition underlying the so-called E.R.A. is established to a very high degree of probability'.

From Abram's Box were derived in due course the Drown diagnostic and treatment instrument and, later, de la Warr's and, indeed, the whole science and art of Radionics, as it is now called. But all this I only learnt much later, as I shall recount in due course.

At the time, feeling that Dr Abrams was somehow right, I had serious thoughts of buying an Oscilloclast to use for treatment. My wife indeed sold some excellent shares of hers to make this possible. But, alas, it never materialized! The claims of a more than busy panel practice, and a private practice with fees never more than 2/6 a visit, made further investigation of this sort out of the question. And so things remained until 1937. Twenty years after qualifying I was no nearer knowing how to study the fundamental problem of health and disease than I had been as a youth of eighteen.

But, as I have already said, my medical work in Bermondsey taught me a great deal in other ways. I developed a great admiration and, indeed, affection for the Bermondsey people. They were good sound English stock, the very salt of the earth, which on the physical level was undoubtedly helped by the fact that they spent the greater part of their wages on food, fresh, cheap, good food from the street markets. One felt that medical work among them was infinitely worth while. Their implicit trust that one was doing one's utmost for them made one give of one's very best. They were both considerate and grateful. Under such circumstances one could produce results which were due to more than the drugs one used.

In those days Bermondsey, though poor and slummy, was a very definite community in the full sense of the word. It was only later, when the people had become demoralized by party politics and the old social life had been destroyed by flats and flat life,* that they began to lose those qualities which had made medical work among them so rewarding and satisfying.

Bermondsey taught me the true meaning of being a general practitioner in the sense of a family doctor, for one was much more than just a medical attendant, one was also a friend, a guide and a counsellor in all the problems of family life, very often under the most adverse conditions. I can say in all sincerity that I would not have missed those contacts and that experience for a very great deal. Nevertheless, I am thankful the experience was gained in the inter-war years, as I doubt very much whether I should feel the same in modern Bermondsey, under the National Health Service and a misconceived Welfare State.

But one can have too much of a good thing, so when the opportunity came in 1938 for me to leave my Bermondsey practice for semi-retirement on my estate on the border of the New Forest I took it thankfully and hopefully, though also with regret.

Destiny indeed was very kind to me, as it is not given to many

* See my paper 'Flats: the destruction of the English Working People', *Town and Country Planning*, Feb. 1961.

medical men to have such a sound medical experience as Bermondsey gave me and yet to have the opportunity and time to explore outside the trodden paths and current mystique of research.

This move, which to begin with meant severe financial stringency, opened up rich possibilities for the realization of my youthful dreams, though not perhaps in quite the way I had imagined.

I was now free to explore the health approach to medicine as well as the possibility of detecting the basic and fundamental causes lying behind the manifestation of disease.

The health approach involves, I was to discover, the recognition that health of soil, plant, animal and man are inextricably interlinked. This has been well stated by Dr J.E.R. McDonagh, whom, however, at that time I knew only as the discoverer of S.U.P.36, a drug which gave excellent results in grave infections and was only superseded later by the antibiotics. His great contribution to medicine I shall describe later on in Chapter XI.

Dr McDonagh put it this way: 'The problem of health and disease has been approached, as it were, by the back door instead of the front door. Had the order been reversed, it would have been realized long ere this that the health of plants depends upon life in the soil, and that of animals and man upon the quality of the vegetable and animal food upon which they live. The way in which protein derived its sustenance would have been known, and also the way it deals with the food before passing it on to the various structures and tissues and organs. This knowledge would have led to an appreciation of the fact that the maintenance of this harmony between soil, plant, animal and man is the only means by which the protein is able to protect its host against invaders. The natural corollary would have followed that food of inferior quality is the most important cause of disease.'

It would have followed, as Dr McDonagh has pointed out, that the ecological branch of science would have included in one whole, instead of separate, watertight compartments, pedology, agronomy, veterinary science, and medicine.

Or, again, as Dr Innes Pearse and Miss Crocker, of the famous *Peckham Experiment*, observe, 'health is totally distinct from sickness where subject to disorder (sub-health), the individual obeys the laws of pathology. In health man observes a different natural law, the law of function, for health means living a full functional existence, in which development proceeds according to potentiality.'

But all this I only came to appreciate very gradually through the work of the Soil Association (of which I was a foundation member), and through the efforts of my son in farming organically our small holding of thirty acres.

Exploration of the other aspect – the detection of basic causes – was to lead me far afield into fascinating and far reaching realms of thought and practice, and, in particular, into the fertile field of radiesthetic medicine.

But before recounting my wanderings in these new fields of medicine, it may be as well to round off this phase of my medical life.

I had for some years been a member of the Social Credit Party. I joined it because I had become convinced that, unless we could have a sane economic system in this country, such as Social Credit might open up, we should stagger from one crisis to another, and little by little we should become State-ridden, with the individual progressively losing what freedom he still had left. I might add that what I felt was true then is even more true now. Everything that has happened since has only served to convince me of the vital necessity for a sensible monetary system.

In 1941 John Hargrave, the leader of the Social Credit Party, asked me to write an outline for a Social Credit National Health Service. Such a colossal task appeared to me to be quite beyond my capacity and ability. But I was most definitely assured that with my medical and general experience I was competent to write at least an outline, and so I set to work to see what I could do.

In a sense there was more than ample material to help me, as this was the time when comprehensive medical services were very much to the fore and under discussion by all the relevant bodies, including the Government in its famous White Paper, the basis of the eventual National Health Service of 1948. In my view they all failed in that they were, without exception, national medical services for the better diagnosis and treatment of *disease*, and had little to say about true prevention, and nothing at all about health as a positive thing, as distinct from the absence of disease.

The fact was, I suspect, as I had found back in 1912, that hardly anyone knew anything about health or what it was, and indeed I myself was only at the very beginning of an understanding. However, I found that enough was known to make possible the writing of an Outline, and this was published in 1942. Such was its unexpected success that an amplified and much revised and improved second edition was published in 1944, under the title of *Health Abounding*, published by the Social Credit Party.

This booklet set forth, among other things, a medical service which dealt with the three aspects – the curative, the preventive and the perfective – this last dealing in outline with everything known at that time which made for positive and radiant health.

Although I know, of course, that it was impossible, I have always thought that it was a great pity that the Labour Government did not base its National Health Service, which it introduced four years later, on this Social Credit Outline, for, if it had, it would have provided a real *health* service for the nation. But the fact is, unfortunately, that the nation was not ready for a health service. Whether the Outline had any influence in official quarters I do not, of course, know, but I hope it made someone think. In any case, it provided me with a survey of my knowledge up to that time and thus a starting-off place for my wanderings. It was quite clear to me that one had to go exploring if one wanted to know anything about the true nature of health and, as a consequence, the true nature of disease.

Since then, following the clue of the Vis Medicatrix Naturae wherever it led, I wandered far afield, and the many various and exciting things I contacted, and of the many outstanding personalities I was privileged to meet I shall recount in the following chapters.

CHAPTER TWO

Dr Bach and his Flower Remedies

My first firm contact with the new fields of medicine I was destined to explore came about in the following way. Staying on my estate in one of the camping chalets was a woman, Mrs Olive Wilson, with her young son. In the course of conversation she told me her son had been cured of meningitis by a remarkable doctor – a Dr Bach – who had only used remedies which he himself had found and prepared in a special way from wild flowers.

This intrigued me very much, as from my then medical knowledge I could not imagine how flower preparations could possibly influence, let alone cure, such a serious pathological condition as a meningitis, and so I asked her to tell me more.

It happened that she had worked with the doctor and had had instruction from him in the preparation of his remedies, and had subsequently used them herself in treatment with the greatest success.

The story of his life and discoveries as she unfolded it to me was hard to believe, and yet it was true.

Dr Edward Bach, born in 1880, was a well-known Harley-street bacteriologist and a brilliant research worker. Suddenly for no apparent reason he threw up all his work and his lucrative practice, and retired to the wilds of Wales, there to hunt intuitively for the flowers and trees which had special vital healing force.

These flowers, prepared in a special way either by strong sunlight or boiling, could deal effectively, so he claimed, with the disharmonies of the personality and with all the emotional states lying behind the physical, and thus restore peace and inner happiness to the sick and distressed, thereby curing all diseases in a simple but fundamental way.

For example, if you suffered from known fears, you took Mimulus; if you had had a shock of any sort, the remedy was Star of Bethlehem; indecision was treated with Scleranthus; lack of

9

faith with Gentian; obsessional thoughts with White Chestnut; and panic or any urgency with Rock Rose.

As with all pioneers, his path was by no means easy. His medical colleagues thought he was slightly mad, and his friends were filled with regrets for what they felt was a sheer waste of his brilliant talents.

But Dr Bach had no doubts and no regrets. He knew he was on the right path, and after Wales he went to Norfolk and from there to Sotwell, near Wallingford, where he settled down for the remainder of his life with his lay co-workers – the late Miss Nora Weeks and Mr Bullen – and where the work is still carried on.

He finally found thirty-eight remedies in all, chiefly from the common flowers or trees of the hedgerows. But the obtaining of any given remedy was a very severe strain, as previous to finding the flower which gave it, he experienced *in toto* both the physical and emotional states of which it was the antidote. This took such a toll of his physique that he died in 1936 at the comparatively early age of fifty-six.*

Mrs Wilson left me in no doubt that she had regarded Dr Bach as a very remarkable man and a quite exceptionally gifted physician, and his discoveries one of the great advances in fundamental healing.

All this I found it hard to accept. Dr Bach's claim that treatment of the emotional state or states is all that is necessary to cure the patient, or, in his own words, 'only through tranquillity of mind and soul can a human being reach bodily health', seemed too far-fetched, and at first I was frankly sceptical. But Mrs Wilson assured me that I need not accept her word nor, indeed, Dr Bach's, all one had to do was to try the method and the results would convince one of the truth of his claims.

So I proceeded to try the remedies. To make the test as conclusive as possible I eliminated all other therapeutic factors so that with only one factor operating – the Bach remedy – if anything happened it would presumably be due to the remedy and to nothing else. I treated a variety of conditions in this way, and much to my surprise I became completely convinced that the remedies acted as Dr Bach had claimed; anyhow, in acute conditions.

* See *Dr Bach – Physician*, a biography of Dr Bach by Miss Nora Weeks.

The following are some of the remarkable and dramatic results which I obtained:

1. A man aged 29. Fear and worry about keeping his end up at his job, producing symptoms suggestive of a duodenal ulcer. Given Mimulus and Agrimony. Improvement in twenty-four hours. All physical symptoms had disappeared within the week, and after a fortnight no need to continue treatment. Remained well.

2. Woman aged 51. Complained that as night came on she began to get panicky and felt that she would die through being unable to get her breath. She dared not sleep. After a while she would be compelled to go out of the house, at any time, in any weather, and walk and walk until exhausted. This had been going on for six months until she was frantic, and no treatment had had any effect. Given Rock Rose, Star of Bethlehem, Cherry Plum and Walnut. The first night after starting the remedies she slept all night, except for brief wakings. Normal nights for a week and then a slight return of symptoms which soon cleared up with a change to Mimulus, Star of Bethlehem and Cherry Plum. No further trouble, and remained perfectly normal.

3. Girl aged 2¼. Mother never got a good night's sleep as child wanted to tumble around all the time and never seemed to tire. No sleep in the daytime. Child very daring and determined and knew her own mind. Given Agrimony and Star of Bethlehem. Greatly improved and then relapsed, so given Vine and Impatiens in addition. Twenty-four hours later the child suddenly became ill, flushed and feverish, rapid pulse and vomiting, lay lifeless in mother's arms. Parents very alarmed. But after a short while the child started to recover, and when I saw her last, one and half hours later, she was lively and full of energy. I thought at the time it was some sort of crisis. In any case, from that time the child started to sleep quite normally and there was no more trouble.

4. Girl aged 2. Fell and cut her lip, which had to be stitched. During the rest of the day hungry and thirsty but would not touch a thing. Very restless. Saw her in the evening and prescribed Mimulus and Star of Bethlehem. As she would not drink them they were put in some water, in which her hands and face were bathed (Dr Bach said this was equally effective as taking by mouth).

She fell asleep almost at once and slept all night. On waking was slightly sick but asked for food. Her mother tried to give her milk, but on seeing the spoon she cried bitterly and refused the milk; evidently very frightened and fearful. She was again bathed with the remedies. Ten to fifteen minutes later she again asked for food and, to the amazement of her mother, ate a proper breakfast with no coaxing or fuss at all, apparently forgetting all about her lip and fear of pain. At 12.30 p.m. she was given another dose of remedies and ate a good dinner. No further trouble, and stitch removed five days later.

5. Woman aged 70. Was called to see her at 10.30 p.m. as condition seemed alarming. She was in a very agitated, distressed condition, panicky and fearful. She said she had completely lost her memory and this fact was producing her panic. As she was afraid she would not recover her memory, this made her more afraid, and so on. As I had the remedies with me I gave her Rock Rose, Clematis and Star of Bethlehem, this latter as, though there was no history of shock, I thought the condition must have been caused by a shock of some sort. A few minutes after taking the remedies she turned to her daughter and said: 'Wasn't I doing this,' and then, gradually, exactly like an incoming tide, her memory began to return, ebbing and flowing, but at each flow more was uncovered until finally, at the end of a quarter of an hour, she recovered the memory of the original shock which had set the whole thing off. She then became, as far as I could judge, her normal self, self-possessed, calm and rational. It was a most dramatic change in such a short time. She went to bed, slept well, and was perfectly fit and normal in the morning, and remained so.

6. Boy aged 8½. He had had a bad kick in left frontal region the previous morning in a fight. Lay about all day, pale and listless. Had had a very restless night. Complained about his head, started to vomit, and could keep nothing down. I saw him in the afternoon thirty-six hours after the kick. He was very flushed, and looked feverish, but temperature was normal. Complained of a severe headache. He was drowsy and slept in snatches as the pain in his head woke him up every twenty minutes. He was restless and looked ill, but the vomiting had stopped. I diagnosed slight concussion and gave Rock Rose, Clematis, Star of Bethlehem

and Beech. In the light of a similar case which it happened I had had a day or two previously, I ventured to prophesy that he would be well in the morning. It was clear I was not believed. He went to sleep about 5.0 p.m. and slept peacefully for 3 hours. Later he went to sleep again and had an excellent night, waking feeling perfectly well, except for slight irritability and touchiness for which I gave Impatiens, Oat and Beech. He got up, remained well, and there were no after-effects,

7. Baby aged 6 months. This baby had always been good, seldom cried, and gave no trouble, but of late had been too good. It just lay in its cot and seemed interested in nothing, not even food. It had been carefully examined and specialist's opinion obtained, but nothing could be found to account for the condition. Yet it was obviously slipping away, and for some reason did not seem interested in living. The mother was the more alarmed, as she had had a friend who had had a baby like this, which, in spite of every medical attention, had faded away and died for no apparent reason. I gave the child Rock Rose and Clematis. Almost at once the baby responded. One could almost see it coming back to life. Within a few days it was a normal, healthy baby, eating well and showing an interest in everything, and crying lustily on occasions. It did not look back from that point.

8. Woman aged 44. Very severe migraines, usually lasting twenty-four hours, during which time she was dead to the world. Started at fourteen, and had attacks every two or three months, but lately they had increased to once or twice a week. Bach treatment given for two months, after which she became completely free from attacks and a different woman. I ought to add that in this case there was a very difficult psychological situation which was dealt with at the same time. Remained well.

Here then, on the first stage of my wanderings, I was confronted with the undoubted and astonishing fact that there was a force or power within certain plants which would heal in a fundamental way. What was that power? That was what I had to find out, if I could.

In these early cases the remedies were chosen as suggested by Dr Bach by an assessment of the emotional state or condition, but I found later, especially in complicated and chronic conditions,

that it was very difficult to assess the emotional state of the patient.
I think this is partly due to the fact that our very training as
doctors makes it more difficult to assess what, to a layman, presents
little or no difficulty. We know too much.

I found that I could get over this difficulty by using myself as an
indicator. This was the technique. I took the patient's left hand in
my right and then, after a short interval to get 'attuned', working
blindly I took up each remedy in turn in my left hand, running
through the whole thirty-eight. On some I got a reaction, i.e. a
sort of tingling sensation which started at the back of my scalp,
and, if strong, would go all over me. If and when I got this reaction on a bottle, I put it aside. At the end I looked to see which
bottles I had put on one side, and I took it that they were what the
patient needed. The numbers chosen might vary from one to six;
seldom more. I was not sure how accurate this method was, but
it seemed to work, judging from the fact that one could work
from the remedies obtained into diagnosing the emotional state
of the patient, and this diagnosing was strangely accurate. This,
so to speak, was proof in reverse.

I found that the fact that one could do this was of great help on
numerous occasions, as indeed it still is, as the indicated Bach
remedies gave me an insight into the patient's emotional make-up,
which otherwise I might not have obtained, especially if it was
something the patient was reluctant to reveal, but it was nevertheless important for me to know.

One of the most spectacular cases in which this method worked
was a child aged about six, who was brought to me because she
was 'a queer little thing', according to her parents. She seemed
retarded both mentally and physically, though she was certainly
not mentally deficient; far from it. I 'bached' her, as I called it, and
got a terrific reaction on Clematis. This was given to her, and
from that time she began to become normal in every way, and
never looked back. It was the turning point in the child's life. I
only saw her the once, but that once was sufficient.

I could not always get results; sometimes I seemed 'dead';
there was no reaction. I was not able to find out what conditions
made for a 'live' reaction, and in these circumstances I fell back
on the intellectual plus, I hope, intuitive assessment.

From those early days to the present time I have continued to use the Bach remedies, and I have found them a quite invaluable and ever-ready standby. But with wider experience of the remedies I am not convinced that they will cure a patient by themselves.

There is a certain amount of evidence to show that, although the emotional state may be altered, the physical, pathological changes may have gone too far to follow suit, and therefore direct treatment of the physical may be needed as well. Also, as I shall describe later on in the book when dealing with 'Pattern',* I departed from the simple use of the Bach remedies as taught by Dr Bach, and introduced a more complicated concept for using them. But I would not advise any novice to take this up until he has mastered the simplicity of Dr Bach's method of using the remedies.

Miss Nora Weeks and her co-worker Mr Bullen, stated this most cogently in the *Bach Remedy Newsletter,* of June 1960. They said: 'Throughout the years since Dr Bach's death in 1936, we have endeavoured to keep to the principle of simplicity. Many and many a time there have been suggestions of adding to the number of remedies, of altering this or that; but beauty and simplicity can be so easily distorted, become complicated and marred, and we have considered it a privilege to maintain this work as it was first conceived so that people can say with confidence: "I am afraid, I will take Mimulus; I am irritable, I will take Impatiens".'

As a user of the remedies for forty-five years I can affirm that, generally speaking, it is just as simple and just as sure as that, surprising as it may sound.†

* See Chapter XII, p. 123.

†In addition to the 38 remedies Dr Bach discovered, he also made a mixture of five – the famous Rescue Remedy, invaluable, especially in emergencies. My wife also discovered what we called 'The Radiation Remedy', a mixture of seven remedies, especially invaluable in over exposure to any form of radiation, such as Xrays and nuclear fallout.

CHAPTER THREE

I Come to Medical Dowsing

Curiously enough, an attack of food poisoning in 1938, from which I did not properly recover, was the means whereby I was again put on the trail. For, having tried the usual orthodox remedies and derived no benefit, I tried Nature Cure by one of its sanest exponents, but also with no better results, except that, as a last resort, the Nature Cure practitioner referred me to Dr Hector Munro, who, he said, had extraordinary methods of diagnosis.

I duly went to see Dr Munro and found that all he did was to run his hands over my abdomen, where my trouble lay, but without actual contact. It seemed he was 'sensing' with his hands, for after a pause he told me I had nothing to worry about, and that with appropriate treatment I should soon be well again even though the condition was so chronic. Seeing my astonishment he asked me whether I would care to know more about this sort of work, and, if I would, whether I would care to come and join a group of doctors who, he said, were studying Radiesthesia or Medical Dowsing.

Much intrigued, I said I should be delighted to join, and in due course I was admitted as a member and started to attend the monthly meetings of the Medical Society for the Study of Radiesthesia. In this way I was introduced to an exciting and fascinating world of healing and to the medical men who were the pioneers of the new medicine.

Years later, when I became editor of the journal of the Society, *Radiesthesia*, I had the melancholy task of preparing their memoirs, as all the original group died between 1946 and 1952. A full account of their life and work will be found in *Radiesthesia IV*.

But at this time I had the great privilege of getting to know each personally and to see them at work in their various ways – and a most remarkable group they were.

There was Dr Ernest Jensen, the Harley-street physician –

kindly, erudite, open-minded, with a great sense of humour and devoted to his work; Dr Ernest Martin, the first doctor in England to use the pendulum for diagnosis and treatment, and a foremost worker in the external field of radiation; Dr Dudley Wright, surgeon, physician, dietician, farmer and gardener – ever open to new ideas, tolerant and sympathetic; Dr Hector Munro, a natural psychic, and a doctor to whom no trouble for his patients was too great; and many others, all of whom it was a pleasure to know and to associate with.

The doyen of them all was undoubtedly Dr Guyon Richards, who was not only the founder and president of the Society but had done an enormous amount of original research work on Radiesthesia, which he had set forth in his main work *The Chain of Life*. Incidentally he successfully diagnosed and treated my chronic condition, which no one else had been able to do. Indeed, looking back, I do not see how anyone else could have done so without the aid of Radiesthesia.

What did I find out and learn from such men? What was the Radiesthesia I had so unexpectedly come across? I found that once again I was contacting a force or power of a nature similar to that I had found in the Bach remedies, but this time the faculty of dowsing was being used to analyse and measure the force in the disease pattern, i.e. the diagnosis, and in the same way to determine the remedies which would correct this pattern, i.e. the treatment.

I learnt that forty to fifty years ago it was discovered, mainly by Frenchmen, that dowsing could be used not only for finding water, the traditional substance, as well as minerals and oil, but it could also be used for medical purposes, for diagnosing patholo-gical conditions and for determining the appropriate remedies – hence the term Medical Dowsing.

This early work was later developed by other research workers such as Turenne, Lesourd and others who added a great deal to the special technique required for medical purposes. This again had been added to and adapted by the English pioneers who formed the nucleus of the Medical Society for the Study of Radiesthesia. I found at the time I came into the Society that there were two main schools of thought, the radiesthetic and the radionic, both using the same faculty of sensitivity. The chief difference lay not in the phenomena investigated but in the means employed.

Radiesthetic work was done mainly with a pendulum, using a simple rule to detect departures from a norm. Radionic work used instruments or machines such as had been developed by Dr Drown in America and de la Warr here, in England, from the 'Box' of Dr Abrams, as I have already explained.

Both of these used 'rates', i.e. sets of figures at which the ten calibrated dials of the instruments were set for the detection of various pathological conditions. In both cases a sample of the patient is employed – usually a blood spot or sample of hair, though urine or saliva is equally good.

I shall not attempt to describe the actual techniques used, as these are readily accessible either in *Radiesthesia IV* or in such a book as *An Introduction to Medical Radiesthesia and Radionics* by V. D. Wethered. But I should like to say a word about Bovis and his Biometer.

Monsieur Bovis claimed that it was possible to measure radiations from various substances, and more especially from the human body. To do this he invented a special rule with a graduated scale and a moving slide. This he called the Biometer. With it, and using a pendulum, the general physical vitality of a person can be measured from the tip of the thumb, the normal reading being between 120 and 140 degrees Bovis. A 'psychic' measurement can also be made but this time using the ball of the thumb. A blood spot can be used in place of the thumb if the person is not available.

I was able to obtain these measurements as I found that my wife was a first-class sensitive, able to get gratifyingly accurate results with the pendulum – thus making up for my deficiency. Her dowsing ability has indeed been quite invaluable to me, as without her willing co-operation and skill in this field I should not have progressed as far as I have, especially in the later research work.

In fact I did not possess a Bovis Biometer, but Mr Benham, the dowsing physicist, made us a very simple adaptation of it, and with it my wife was able to obtain the Bovis measurements. She found she could use it also for other radiesthetic purposes, such as picking out Bach remedies and other simple remedies required for patients, and deciding whether a given food was suitable or not.

These Bovis measurements, both physical and psychic, I found to be of very great help in my clinical work, as the physical gave, firstly, the measurement of the physical energy of the patient, from which it is possible to follow the results of treatment, and, secondly, it enabled me to differentiate between physical and psychological depletion. For example, a patient complains of weakness and fatigue; if the physical reading is low I take it that the case is one of actual physical depletion; whereas, if the reading is normal, that the depletion is probably due to psychological or psychic factors.

The main use of the psychic measurement I found was to give an indication of the type of treatment which could be used. If there was a reading of over 250 Bovis, I knew I was dealing with a sensitive, and therefore, if Bach, homoeopathic or similar remedies were used, they were likely to be effective.

But to return. The main difficulty in Radiesthesia seemed to me to be the interpretation of the findings, as every worker in this field used his own technique, and thus it was almost impossible to compare findings.

In Radionics the difficulty had been largely overcome, as a standardized technique was used by all operators though the 'rates' were different, depending on whether a Drown or a de la Warr instrument was used.

I was all agog to plunge into this new and fascinating field as I had done in the case of the Bach remedies, but, alas, to my consternation and sorrow I found that I did not appear to have the dowsing faculty but fortunately, as I have already said, my wife could, most skilfully.

By great good fortune, first as his patient and then as his colleague, I was able to study Dr Guyon Richards' technique and methods at first hand. Later he was good enough to cooperate with me in the investigation of patients for whom radiesthetic diagnoses and treatment were indicated. Thus I learnt much from this talented pioneer, and was able in some measure to assess his outstanding work in the radiesthetic field.

In particular, I learnt the radiesthetic use of homoeopathic remedies which is somewhat at variance with the strict canons of Homoeopathy, but which seems to me a great advance.

Many years previously I had investigated Homoeopathy with a view to using it in my practice, but I found that I did not have the type of mind needed to work it successfully, and so I proceeded no further. I now found that radiesthetically not only could the correct remedies needed by the patient (rather than the disease) be ascertained, but also the exact potency. Hitherto this essential point in treatment could only be ascertained by intuition, guesswork, trial and error or by long experience. Further, it was found radiesthetically that very seldom was there 'a simillimum' in the classic homoeopathic sense of the single remedy but, rather, a group of remedies which together acted as 'the simillimum'. This, homoeopathically, was polypharmacy and was counted as a heresy. Nevertheless, it was found to work.

In the first flush of enthusiasm I thought that at last I had found the answer to my search for a more accurate and subtle method of diagnosis and treatment. In the hands of Dr Richards and other brilliant medical exponents of Radiesthesia it all looked so straightforward and conclusive, but time and further experience were to modify my original naive judgement. It was not in fact as easy as it looked.

Take, for example, the following case which I reported to the Medical Society for the Study of Radiesthesia in 1945.

The interest of the case lay in

(1) that it provided an unintentional experiment in comparative radiesthetic diagnosis, as during the course of the illness three independent radiesthetists were asked to co-operate, all of them competent, skilled and experienced operators. The one designated A used a de la Warr instrument, while the other two, B and C, used the pendulum, though with very different techniques.

Unfortunately, their diagnoses not only did not agree, but, what was perhaps worse, I found it almost impossible at times to correlate their findings with the clinical condition.

(2) For the greater part of the illness I kept a record of the Bovis physical measurements (recorded by my wife), which

almost exactly followed the clinical condition and were a very great help in assessing the situation.

Let me quote the last part of my report on this case: 'At this point I thought it would be interesting to see what the de la Warr instrument findings would now reveal, and accordingly on September 13th I got a report from A. This showed much the same condition as before, except actual TB instead of TB toxins.

'As the condition continued to deteriorate, I thought it would be well to obtain a third radiesthetic opinion (pendulum) C. This was that there was cancer in the bronchial and lymph glands of the chest.

'A final test by B (pendulum) showed nothing serious! Nevertheless, the patient was going down hill rapidly, and a test by C on September 24th showed a slight improvement in the general condition, but an extension of the cancer.

'However, the patient's condition continued to deteriorate, and a final test on October 5th by C showed the condition much the same, but on October 6th the patient died suddenly.' Unfortunately, no post mortem was possible, and so it was not possible to decide which radiesthetist was right. My own clinical diagnosis had been carcinoma, and I saw no reason to alter it.

I suggested that the lesson of this case was that, until it was possible to get more correlation and agreement between various instruments, methods, operators and clinical findings in particular, little headway would be made, and we should deserve the scepticism of the doubters and critics.

Another case at this time which rather shook me was one of advanced cancer of which I had the supervision. As a last desperate hope she was having treatment as indicated by a de la Warr instrument. It happened that between the sending of a blood spot and the receipt of the report on it the patient died. This fact was unknown to the operator but known to me. Imagine my amazement when I received the following report: 'There is an improvement in the patient's condition.'

I made the following comments in a letter asking for further light on what to me was an extraordinary situation:

1. 'How was it possible at all to get readings if the patient was dead, much less to get readings showing an improvement?'

2. 'If readings were obtained, as they were, it would appear that they had no basis in fact, the patient being dead.'

3. 'If this is so, how is one to know that one's readings, while the patient is alive, have any basis in fact?'

4. 'The only conclusions one can legitimately draw are (a) that the readings are unreliable; that is that they may be accurate but there is no means of knowing when they are, or (b) that they are not readings of physical states at all.'

The answer to these comments was: 'In some cases radionic analysis deals with a body other than the physical – the etheric or astral – and in that case death will have no effect on the readings except that one might find some improvement or, at any rate, no deterioration in the condition.'

This case seemed to me to raise problems of fundamental importance both of theory and practice. How important I was only to learn years later when I came to understand more of what was involved.

But another example, which happened about the same time, was more encouraging, as quite by accident a good test case was provided.

It happened that I had posted my own blood spot to operators of a de la Warr instrument. That same evening I had a motor accident in which I ran down two men, seriously injuring one of them, and, as a result, I myself had severe physical shock. Next day the blood spot was tested on the instrument, and among other things shock came in very strongly, with its remedy vanadium. The operators said that they had seldom recorded such a strong reaction and were very puzzled about it and its strength, for it was not until later that they had learnt the real cause of this perfectly correct reading. This, I think, was an excellent test case.

Such was my introduction to the intriguing mystery of Radiesthesia.

Reviewing what I had seen and learnt it was clear to me that, while I was prepared to accept a great deal, I could not at that time accept the correctness of all radiesthetic and radionic readings. For example, from my own personal experience and observation of such skilled operators as I met in the Medical Society I was convinced that, while on many occasions they were brilliantly accurate, I was equally certain that on others they were right off the mark. Yet it was clear that to them all their readings were equally correct, and maybe this was a psychological necessity. If once they started to question the correctness of their readings and findings an element of doubt might well be introduced which would tend to vitiate all their work. This I feel to be true in some measure of all operators.*

Thus the question remained as to how an operator can distinguish between when he is correct and when he is not, and this particularly in the early stages of disease when radiesthetic diagnosis is most valuable. There appeared to be no effective method of checking as there is in later stages when there are objective physical signs confirmed by the laboratory, X-ray, surgical and post mortem examinations, or even, as in ordinary dowsing, the conclusive test of the presence of water, metals or oil at the place indicated by the divining rod. And yet I was convinced that the findings arrived at, by whatever dowsing technique, in a large percentage of cases were reliable and correct; but how was one to be certain?

All these and other problems were to occupy a great deal of my time and attention in the following years; in particular the factors which make for reliability and accuracy in radiesthetic diagnosis and treatment. My findings on these crucial points I shall deal with in due course in later chapters, for, as it turned out, I was only at the beginning of my radiesthetic experience and had much to learn. †

* In the light of subsequent knowledge this is probably true of what one may call the lower level of dowsing. On the higher levels the problem does not arise.

†How I came to dowse. Since my wife's death I find I can now do simple medical dowsing. Her mantle seems to have been passed on to me – a most remarkable and blessed fact.

CHAPTER FOUR

Vis Medicatrix Naturae:
From Hippocrates to Reich

About this time Dr Munro lent me his copy of the rare volume of the translation by Professor Gregory of Baron von Reichenbach's famous *Researches*. This fascinated me, and I felt, indeed, like Keats when he 'first looked into Chapman's Homer' (to paraphrase),

'Yet never did I breathe its pure serene
Till I heard Gregory speak out loud and bold,'

because here again was the elusive vital force, but this time investigated by a first-class scientist.

As I read I was struck by Reichenbach's extreme scientific care and exactitude – what I can only describe as his beautiful handling of the experimental material, and the imagination and ingenuity with which he tackled the problems which arose. Like a true artistic scientist, when confronted by such problems, he asked the right questions, devised the right experiment, and, as a result, received the right answer. It is only scientists of the highest order who can do this and so obtain the truth.

This book set me thinking, and I felt it was high time I did a little research myself into this force which did not appear to fit into the modern scientific picture. Was it something new or was it only an unfamiliar form of electro-magnetic phenomena? So far all of us seemed to be curiously confused on the whole matter.

I decided that it might be well to look more deeply into the subject, and I bethought myself of the well-known phrase 'Vis Medicatrix Naturae' – the healing power of Nature – which in ancient times was acclaimed as the power that healed, and made medicine possible, as expressed by the greatest of medieval surgeons, Ambrose Paré, in his famous statement: 'I treat, God cures.' Was there in fact a connection between this and Reichenbach's Odyle, Bach's vital force in flowers, and the radiesthetic phenomena?

An opportunity to explore these possibilities offered itself in the form of an invitation to give the opening lecture at the Scientific and Technical Congress of Radionics and Radiesthesia held in London in May 1950. Needless to say, I felt it not only an honour but also a great responsibility; still, here was the chance I had been wanting, and what better subject than 'Vis Medicatrix Naturae'?

So I set to work to find out whatever I could about it. To my dismay I found that nobody seemed to know nor could anyone tell me how to find out. This seemed very strange, as every physician, in his humble moments, must know that all he can in fact do is to invoke this mysterious force to restore his patient to health. But in these scientific times we seem to have forgotten this elementary fact, so bemused are we by modern 'progress'.

But I persevered, and after a great deal of futile searching it was suggested that I should try the Library of the Royal College of Physicians. Alas, I found that it was only open to Members, and I was only a humble Licentiate. Fortunately, the Royal College of Surgeons was more hospitable and the librarian most helpful. Finally he found me the only treatise which appeared to have been written on the subject, *The Doctrine of the Healing Power of Nature throughout the Course of Time* by Dr Max Neuberger, written in 1943. But even this did not seem quite what I was looking for. So in the end I was thrown on my own resources to think the whole subject out for myself, which was possibly a good thing.

Here then is the gist of what I found out and communicated in due course to a distinguished audience on the morning of May 16th, 1950:

The idea of Vis Medicatrix Naturae certainly goes back to the time of Hippocrates, that is to 400 B.C. Hippocrates seems to have been the first to grasp the conception of the great healing powers of nature, and his long and wide experience made him a firm believer in those powers. For to him, to quote Neuberger, 'disease appeared not purely as πάθος, as a malady, but also, by no means least, as πόνος, that is as an exertion, an effort of the body to establish the disturbed equilibrium of the function. Recovery is thus shown to be the work of nature, whose healing powers alone, or supplemented by medical aid, achieve the aim – Nature is the healer of diseases.'

This, then, is the doctrine so famous in the schools of Physic down through the ages, and this conception has never wholly been lost sight of for twenty-three centuries. At those times when it has been largely forgotten, medicine has tended to lose the human touch and to become materialistic and dogmatic.

On the other hand, carried to the extreme, as it has been at various times, it has tended to a fatal *laissez-faire*, to the scandal of medical science and the essential neglect of the patient.

But what is this healing power or force of nature inherent in the organism? Let me give you two quotations. Firstly, Professor William McDougal, from his famous book *Body and Mind* (Methuen):

'The essential notion, which forms the common foundation of all varieties of animism, is that all or some of the manifestations of life and mind which distinguish the living man from the corpse and from inorganic bodies are due to the operation within of something which is of a nature different from that of the body, an animating principle generally, but not necessarily or always conceived as an immaterial, individual being or soul.'

Secondly, Professor James Ward:

'The fundamental difference between living and non-living matter is that in living matter there is always something else present (which for want of better understanding we may call "the vital force") in addition to the properties found in non-living bodies. This additional "something" endows living bodies with a tendency to disturb existing equilibrium, to reverse the dissipation processes which prevail throughout the inanimate world, to store up and build up where they are ever scattering and pulling down; the tendency to conserve individual existence against antagonistic forces, to grow and to progress, not merely taking the easier way, but seemingly striving for the best, retaining any advantage secured and working for new ones.'

The suggestion is that there is a vital power or force in every organism which not only sustains life but maintains it against all the innumerable adverse factors seeking to destroy it. It is this possession of the Life Force which marks the difference between organic and inorganic life.

But it may well be asked whether in postulating this vital force we are really postulating anything more than the sum total of the already well-known physical and chemical forces active in the rest of the world. The materialists would certainly answer 'No', and I think the scientific world in general would endorse that opinion, though it is not quite so certain as it was.

For example, the writer of the article on Biology in the *Encyclopædia Britannica* is quite emphatic on this point. He says: 'It may be convenient to use the terms "vitality" and "vital force" to denote the causes of certain great groups of natural operations, as we employ the names "electricity" and "electrical force" to denote others; but it ceases to be proper to do so if such a name implies the absurd assumption that "electricity" and "vitality" are entities playing the part of efficient causes of electrical or vital phenomena. A mass of living protoplasm is simply a molecular machine of great complexity, the total results of the working of which, or its vital phenomena, depend – on the one hand – upon its construction and, on the other, upon the energy supplied.'

But my thesis is that we are dealing with 'something more' – that is my working hypothesis – and I shall devote the rest of this treatise to trying to show what I think that 'something more' is.

This question of 'something more' would appear to depend on how we look at the problem. One can assume, as the materialists do, that at a certain stage of complexity a critical change takes place. The analogy is the critical point when water becomes ice or, at the other end of the scale, when it becomes steam; in the same way an inorganic structure, such as a collection of mega molecules, when it reaches a certain critical point of complexity, becomes a living entity.

On the other hand, observing the same phenomena from the supersensible angle, one can equally well say that it is only when an inorganic structure has reached a certain point of complexity that the conditions are right for the life force (e.g. the etheric forces postulated by Steiner) to manifest, and thus for the structure to become 'alive'.

For present purposes I am going to assume that the second of these two points of view is the correct one, and I suggest that the best way to do this is to trace the history of this force, known by so many names, the most intriguing being the Vital Fluid or Divine Water of the medieval alchemists, as we have here a tradition of a force of more than usual integrating and healing potency, of biological energy.

The Italian philosopher Regnano remarks that 'whether one clearly recognizes it or not, it is just this search for the nature of the vital principle which properly constitutes the principal object and final goal of all biological studies in general'.

Paracelsus held that there are two kinds of doctors: 'those who heal miraculously and those who heal through medicines. The physician has to accomplish that which God would have done miraculously had there been enough faith in the sick man.' This seems to me to be a valuable clue. 'Those who heal through medicines' we know – the whole body of modern medicine is an expression of this aspect, and it has not got us much further towards an understanding of the force. But what about the miraculous – here apparently we have the power raised to the nth degree – under these conditions we may learn something which in its ordinary state we miss. This we shall discuss in a later chapter.

But to come back to Paracelsus. Paracelsus, the famous medieval physician, 1490 to 1541, has been a figure of controversy from his own day to this. Regarded for centuries as the arch-charlatan of history, his contribution is at last being appreciated and understood, and he provides a good example of 'multa renascentur, quae iam cecidere'.

The *Encyclopædia Britannica* states that 'Paracelsus founded the "sympathetic system" of medicine, according to which the stars and other bodies, especially magnets, influence man by means of a subtle emanation or fluid which pervades all space' (quoted by Sir William Osler in his *The Evolution of Modern Medicine*, p. 140), and Osler says that 'Paracelsus expresses the healing process of nature by the word "munia", which he regarded as a sort of magnetic influence or force and he believed that everybody possessing it could arrest or heal disease in others. 'As the lily breaks forth in invisible perfumes, so healing influences may pass from an invisible body.'

In Paracelsus' own words, 'the vital force is not enclosed in man but radiates within and around him like a luminous sphere and it may be made to act at a distance. It may poison the essence of life (blood) and cause disease, or it may purify it and restore the health.'

J. B. van Helmont, 1577-1644, a disciple of Paracelsus, 'extended this doctrine by teaching that a similar magnetic field radiates from man and that it can be guided by their wills to influence directly the minds and bodies of others'.

According to van Helmont, and I quote his own words, 'the means by which this secret property enables one person to affect another mutually is the Magnale Magnum . . . but this is not the physical substance which we inspissate, measure or weigh, but it is an ethereal spirit, pure living, which pervades all things, and moves the mass of the universe'. His theory of Archeus postulated an extra-corporeal force practically unlimited in its regulative powers – a vital inherent formative force.

The magnetic tradition was carried on by others, notably Robert Fludd, the English mystic and physician who stated that each body is animated by an invisible power and that man possesses the qualities of a magnet; by Father Kircher, the natural philosopher; Valentine Graterakes, the Stroking Doctor – an Irishman who became famous in England as a magnetic healer – his counterpart a century later was Gassner, an Austrian clergyman; and the famous Swedenborg also subscribed to and practised magnetic healing.

I should perhaps add a word of explanation as to the use of the word 'magnetic'. This was derived from the use of magnets for healing purposes; magnets were drawn over the diseased part and in some cases healing followed. It was therefore concluded that it was magnetism which had flowed from the magnet to the sick person – hence the phrase 'magnetic fluid'. The explanation was wrong but the idea was right, as Reichenbach showed some centuries later.

With Mesmer we come to the modern period and the first

attempt to place magnetic healing on a scientific footing. As Ennemoses says in his *History of Magic*, 'The clear declaration of magnetism as a peculiar power of nature was first made by Franz Anton Mesmer, b. 1734, so that he really is the discoverer and central point in the history of magnetism, between the old centuries and the new ages.'

According to the *Encyclopædia Britannica*, 'He developed the doctrine of a magnetic fluid by postulating a specialized variety of it which he called animal magnetism; he claimed to be able to cure many diseases by its means, teaching also that it may be imparted to and stored up in inert objects which are thereby rendered potent to cure diseases.'

Dr D'Eslon, Mesmer's chief pupil, formulated the laws of animal magnetism as follows:

1. Animal magnetism is a universal, continuous fluid, constituting an absolute plenum in nature, and the medium of all mutual influence between interstellar bodies and between the earth and animal bodies.

2. It is the most subtle fluid in nature, capable of flux and reflux, of ebb and flow, and of receiving, propagating and continuing all kinds of motion.

3. The human body has poles and other properties analogous to the magnet.

4. The action and virtue of animal magnetism may be communicated from one body to another, whether animate or inanimate.

5. It operates at a great distance, without the intervention of any body.

6. It is increased and reflected by mirrors, communicated, propagated and increased by sound, and may be accumulated, concentrated and transported.

Mesmer himself concludes the foreword to his *Dissertation on the Discovery of Animal Magnetism*, published in 1799, with these words: 'I am well aware that this little work raises many difficulties, but it must be borne in mind that they are of such a nature as not to be solved by any amount of reasoning without the assistance of experience. Experience alone will scatter the clouds and shed light on this universal truth: that Nature affords a universal means of healing and preserving man.' Like Paracelsus, he held that 'there is only one disease and only one cure'.

Mesmer's ideas aroused the fiercest controversy in the medical and scientific world, and in 1784 a Royal Commission was appointed to examine his claims. It reported unfavourably, though not denying many of the facts, as summed up in its phrase, 'The imagination does everything, the magnetism nothing.' This, together with a lot of what appeared to be mumbo-jumbo on the part of Mesmer and his followers, tended to discredit the whole matter which had made such an auspicious start.

For example, his famous Clinic, the rage of fashionable Paris in 1775, with its lavish furnishings, costly carpets, its strains of music, its mirrors, and with Mesmer, dressed in a silk robe, himself officiating with his wand, and above all the celebrated *baquet* – a large vat filled with water, iron filings and other substances – seemed the height of hocus-pocus.

But was it? The vat, for example, with its slow chemical action must have been, as Reichenbach subsequently showed, a producer of Odyle, and therefore a potent healing agency, as Mesmer claimed. Perhaps the rest of the 'hocus-pocus' in the same way may also make sense on re-examination. It is time this was carried out.

Be that as it may, Mesmerism later became identified with hypnotism,* and when Braid in 1842 showed that hypnotism could be induced by purely mental and psychological means, animal magnetism became totally discredited, in spite of the work of two staunch supporters (1) Dr John Elliotson, Professor of the Practice of Medicine at University College in 1832, whose devotion to the cause of Mesmerism cost him his professorship, and who for fifteen years was subjected, as Dr Branwell remarks, 'to the unprovoked persecution of his professional brethren, being constantly abused and attacked in the grossest manner possible'; and (2) Dr Esdaile, in India, who in 1845 performed under mesmeric influence a great number of painless and success-

---

* In view of this subsequent identification it is important to note that Mesmer himself was interested not so much in the Mesmeric 'trance' as in the Mesmeric 'crisis' – a very different thing, but one of great importance to a true understanding of Mesmer's work, more especially as its significance has been missed even by modern commentators, e.g. Goldsmith in her book *Mesmer – the History of an Idea*.

ful major operations. But this did not save him from similar attacks and abuse.

The discovery of chloroform gave the coup de grâce to this most fruitful line of research.

Violent and unreasoning prejudice which any actual or supposed association with Mesmerism aroused was one of the main causes of the complete failure in 1861-2 of Baron Karl von Reichenbach, the celebrated chemist and discoverer of creosote, to convince the chief German scientists of the reality of the odic force.

The whole melancholy story is told in full by O'Byrne in his Introduction to *Letters on Od and Magnetism* (Hutchinson), and adds yet another chapter to the unscientific attitude of scientists to any unorthodox thought, especially if it is supposed to smack in any way of the psychic. As O'Byrne says: 'Up to the last days of his life he grieved at the thought of having to die without obtaining recognition for his system, and such was the tragic fate that actually befel him.' One hundred years later he is still waiting for that recognition.

With his death, not only the odic theory but the whole conception of animal magnetism would appear to have been buried and forgotten, the only references, as this one from Garrison's *History of Medicine*, being of a disparaging nature: 'The whole subject was exploited in various mystic forms . . . by Baron von Reichenbach, whose concept of odic force still survives in ouija boards and odic telephones.'

The rising tide of scientific thought and achievement of the latter half of the ·nineteenth century had no place for the supposed mumbo-jumbo of vital and magnetic fluids, animal magnetism, etc., just as it had no use for the vital force or for animism. Science had superseded Nature; indeed, it had improved on her, and all these ideas were relegated to the lumber-room of folklore and superstition.

That his work was thus rejected out of hand in the last century was understandable. It was not in tune with the spirit of the times. Electricity and magnetism fitted exactly the materialistic expansion of the nineteenth century; Reichenbach's work was completely alien to that spirit. But what never ceases to astonish me is that a hundred years later, when we are studying the very phenomena with which he dealt, his fundamental work is largely forgotten or ignored.

And yet Reichenbach deserves a better fate than the neglect to which his work has been condemned, for it seems to me that his conclusions are of fundamental importance and should be taken into the most serious consideration by anyone engaged in research work in Radionics and Radiesthesia, for he was the first to put the whole subject on a scientific basis.

Dr Gregory's testimonial to Reichenbach's scientific qualifications is impressive. 'He has,' he says, 'a turn of mind observing, minute, accurate, patient and persevering in a rare degree. All his previous researches bear testimony to this, and at the same time prove that he possesses great ingenuity and skill in devising and performing experiments; great sagacity in reflection on the results, and, more important than all, extreme caution in adopting conclusions; reserve in propounding theories; and conscientiousness in reporting his observations.'

I do not see that anyone, after he has read carefully the detailed experiments as recorded in his, to give it its full title, *Researches on Magnetism, Electricity, Light, Crystallization and Chemical Attraction in their relation to the Vital Force* (translated by Dr Gregory in 1850), can have any doubt left as to the fact and reality of the odic force or Odyle, nor that we are dealing with a force outside the known ones, chemical, electric and magnetic.

Reichenbach was quite clear on this latter point, for he writes, 'under the term odyle I collect and unite all the physical phenomena occurring in the course of these researches, which cannot be brought under any of the hitherto admitted imponderables, and also the Vis Occulta which produces them. It remains for future investigation to determine whether and to what extent these phenomena will admit of being distributed among, or transferred to, the known forces above mentioned. But in any event we shall never be able to do without the word odyle, or some equivalent term, on the adoption of which men may agree. Such a term will always be required to embrace a mass of phenomena, which cannot with propriety or accuracy be registered save as a peculiar group.'

It is impossible for me to present the detailed evidence, but

33

Reichenbach proved to his own satisfaction and to that of any impartial investigator, that odyle is quite distinct from heat, electricity or magnetism, that it is a new force existing in its own right, though it has an ancient lineage, as we have already seen.

There is, however, an important point which I must mention, and this is, that while odyle is developed alone without magnetism, magnetism is never without odyle. This observation I regard as of great importance, as I am sure it is the reason for a great deal of confusion. If, as I believe, one of the factors involved in dowsing is the sensitivity to odyle – running water develops odyle while static water does not – I think it is more than likely that the results obtained with dowsers in artificial electro-magnetic fields,* may be due to the odyle generated and not to the electro-magnetism. This point could easily be settled by finding what response is obtained when odyle is produced by itself, unaccompanied or screened from any other forces.

I am sure that not enough attention has been paid to the fact that when we think we are dealing with chemical or electro-magnetic phenomena in Radionics and Radiesthesia we are also, necessarily, dealing with odyle as well. I am convinced that this is responsible for some, at least, of the difficulties of our present research work. We are ignoring one of the main factors concerned for, as Reichenbach showed with a wealth of experimental data, we are dealing not only with a special phenomenon like animal magnetism, but with a great force of the universe.

His findings can be summarized as follows:

1. Odyle is a universal property of matter in variable and unequal distribution both in space and time.

2. It interpenetrates and fills the structure of the universe. It cannot be eliminated or isolated from anything in nature.

3. It quickly penetrates and courses through everything.

4. It flows in concentrated form from special sources such as heat, friction, sound, electricity, light, the moon, solar and stellar rays, chemical action, organic vital activity of plants and animals, especially man.

5. It possesses polarity. There is both negative odyle, which

* See *Psychical Physics* by Professor Tromp.

gives a sensation of coolness and is pleasant; and positive odyle, which gives a sensation of warmth and discomfort.

6. It can be conducted: metals, glass, resin, silk and water all being perfect conductors.

7. It is radiated to a distance, and these rays penetrate through clothes, bedclothes, boards and walls.

8. Substances can be charged with odyle, or odyle may be transferred from one body to another. This is effected by contact and requires a certain amount of time.

9. It is luminous, either as a luminous glow or as a flame, showing blue at the negative and yellow-red at the positive. These flames can be made to flow in any direction.

10. Human beings are odyle containers, with polarity, and are luminous over the whole surface, hence the so-called aura surrounding the physical body. In the twenty-four hours a periodic fluctuation, a decrease and increase of odylic power, occurs in the human body.

And there the matter rested until the end of the century, when a change began to take place, partly due to the work of the Society for Psychical Research, founded in 1882, and partly to the very advance of scientific thought itself, starting with the physicists. Emil Boirac is typical of this period. He devotes a considerable amount of his book *Psychic Science* to his own experiments with mesmerism and animal magnetism. Also Dr Richardson, F.R.S., with his conception of 'Nervous Ether' – a finely diffused form of matter pervading the whole body and surrounding it in an enveloping atmosphere.

The two wars also shook scientific dogma and made possible the rebirth of many things which, it appeared, science had buried once for all – hence the rise in the last thirty years of Radionics and Radiesthesia.

In spite of a bias to explain things in terms of known physical forces – a legacy from the nineteenth century – it is, I think, true to say that research workers in these fields are finding it necessary to postulate forces at present not recognized by orthodox science.

But the electro-magnetic theory at the moment still holds the field, as typified by Lakhovsky and Professor Tromp.

Lakhovsky, for example, in his well-known book *The Secret of*

Life, holds that, while the mechanical, chemical explanation is insufficient to explain life, it is explained by the phenomena of auto-electrification in human beings. 'My theory demonstrates,' he says, 'that the cell-organic unit in all living beings, is nothing but an electro-magnetic resonator, capable of emitting and absorbing radiation of a very high frequency. These fundamental principles cover the whole field of biology.'

And Professor Tromp in his recently published monumental and erudite *Psychical Physics* states that his main object 'is to give an explanation of dowsing, radiesthesia, etc., by an analysis of external electro-magnetic fields on psychic and physiological phenomena in living organisms'. It is clear that, though he admits the whole subject to be incredibly complicated, he feels that all the phenomena *can* be explained by the influence of electro-static, electro-magnetic and magnetic fields on, in and around living organisms. Whether we agree or not, and I for one do not, I think this, in a way, is all to the good, as a thoroughgoing investigation along these lines, such as Tromp proposes in his laboratories of psychical physics, will at last reveal what still resists explanation in terms of known forces.

Three contemporary research workers have carried the whole matter much further in the direct tradition of which I have been speaking. I refer to the work of Eeman, Brunler and Reich.

Eeman's work I shall discuss in a later chapter, but the work of Dr Brunler forms a link between that of Reichenbach and that of Dr Reich, for Brunler postulates from experimental data that everything radiates, and that, with such rays, is coupled what he calls the di-electric radiation or Bio-cosmic energy. This energy can be conducted, and all electrical non-conductors are good conductors, such as mica, cotton and silk. It can also be stored, and it is this which plants use in their growth. In human beings the di-electric currents flow in and out of the body and form the aura; and it is this energy which is detected and used by radiesthetists and magnetic healers. According to Brunler, the Bio-cosmic or di-electric waves depend on the kinetic energy of the neutrons − $\frac{1}{2}mV^2$, the neutrons carrying no electro-magnetic charge.

He equates this force with the Ether of space, which is all-pervading, fills our atmosphere, and underlies and interpenetrates all matter. It is vital energy – the alpha and omega of life and death.

Finally, we come to the work of Dr Wilhelm Reich. Dr Reich's work is especially interesting as, unlike any other worker in this field, he started out from an entirely different standpoint, namely, from psycho-analysis; he was a disciple of Freud. From psycho-analysis, via sex-economy, the orgasm theory, character analysis, vegeto-therapy, the biological basis of neurosis, he finally came to what he calls medical orgone therapy – a therapy which uses the same fundamental energy, cosmic orgone energy, whether dealing with a neurosis or a cancer. In this he was nearer to the medieval physicians such as Paracelsus and van Helmont, or even eighteenth-century Mesmer, who arrived at the conception of the Vital Fluid from philosophical considerations, and believed in the universal remedy – the Divine Water.

I hold no brief either for Dr Reich's views or his findings; they may or may not be true, or his facts may bear other interpretations as Tromp appears to think. But they are most interesting from the point of view of our present study, as they would appear to draw together into one coherent whole all that we have been discussing.

In the December 1949 issue of the *Orgone-Energy Bulletin* Reich suggests, like Brunler with his Bio-cosmic Energy, that the Ether of classical science and Cosmic Orgone Energy may well be one and the same thing. 'It is,' he says, 'amazing to find that most of the characteristics of Ether, which have never been observed directly, coincide with many characteristics of the Orgone, which have been observed directly and reproduced experimentally.'

And here I will draw this dissertation on Vis Medicatrix Naturae to a close, as Dr Reich's work is of such importance that it requires a separate chapter to itself.

Let me end with the peroration of my original address to the Congress in 1950:

'It seems a far cry from the Cosmic Orgone Energy to the Vital Fluid with which we started, and yet, to my mind, the search for the nature of that "something more" I postulated at the beginning has now an answer, even though it be only a tentative one. We are, I submit, dealing with one and the same force. It is the Vis Medicatrix Naturae of medical science, the Munia of Paracelsus, the Vital Fluid of the medieval alchemists, the Animal Magnetism of Mesmer, the Odic force of Reichenbach, the Nervous Ether of Richardson, the X force of Eeman, the Bio-cosmic energy of Brunler, the Orgone Energy of Reich, and, to incorporate an Eastern conception, the Prana of Indian metaphysics, and the physical embodiment of the belief of the Vitalists – in one word, it is the Life Force itself.

'If it should prove that this is the same as the Ether of space, surely this would be a stupendous fact! It would mean that the universe is not merely a concatenation of blind chemico-physical forces in which life exists as a forlorn and precarious stranger, but that the universe is a living universe in which to be alive, whether as amoeba or man, is to be at home; and that, in literal fact, we live and move and have our being in an ocean of *living* energy.

'This has always been the mystic tradition, why should it not now be scientific truth?'

CHAPTER FIVE

Dr Reich and Cosmic Orgone Energy

Dr Wilhelm Reich, one of the most remarkable of the psycho-analytic group of Viennese doctors, was born in 1897 in Austria. He entered the Medical School of the University of Vienna in 1918, and took his M.D. in 1922.

He specialized in psychiatric work, worked in close co-operation with Freud, but finally broke away to pursue his own highly original line of research, of which the theme was the bio-energetic function of excitability and mobility of living substance.

From 1934 to 1939 he lectured and did research in orgone bio-physics in Norway, but finally, in 1942, he settled in America, in the State of Maine, where at a place he called Orgonon he had his own laboratories and research centre for the investigation of the science of the Life Energy.

When, in 1948, I first came across his writings I found he was a highly controversial figure, regarded with favour neither by the laity nor the medical profession. I wondered why. The reading of his main book, *The Discovery of the Orgone* with its two parts: Part I, 'The Function of the Orgasm', and Part II, 'The Cancer Biopathy', soon showed me why. To anybody not already familiar with the general thesis the book would appear not only incomprehensible but distinctly bizarre, especially as his views on many subjects, and particularly on sex, led to a head-on collision with orthodoxy and conventional morality.

And yet his research work could not be ignored, as his range was impressive, covering physiology, pathology, bacteriology, psychology, biology, cancer research, physics, meteorology and education, to mention a few. Into all of them he introduced new and revolutionary ideas.

Among all this, the aspect which particularly interested me was his claim to have discovered a fundamental energy which he called Primordial or Cosmic Orgone Energy or Orgone, for short. This, he says, 'indicates the history of its discovery through the orgasm formula, as well as its biological effect, i.e. of changing organic substances'.

The history of its discovery is most interesting. Between 1936 and 1939 Reich did a great deal of experimental work, and discovered and observed what he called the Bion. Bions, he found, were invariably produced when matter is heated to incandescence and made to swell; they were also found, but more slowly, when any matter disintegrates or breaks down. 'Bions,' to quote Reich, 'are microscopically visible vesicles of functioning energy and transitional forms from non-living to living matter. The bion is the elementary functional unit of all living matter. It carries a certain amount of orgone energy which makes it function in a specific way biologically. It is a unit of energy, consisting of a membrane, liquid content and an amount of orgone energy – it can be called an orgone energy vesicle. Bions are constantly being produced, and can develop into protozoa or degenerate into cocci and bacilli; their colour is blue. Every living organism,' according to Reich, 'is a membraneous structure which contains in its body fluids an amount of orgone; it is an orgonotic system.'

Two observations can be made: firstly, that, if what he claims is true, we should appear to be faced with the startling proposition of the spontaneous generation of life – a staggering fact and one which, it was thought, Pasteur had settled once and for all. But I am inclined to think that this is a misreading of Reich's claims. Secondly, that we seem to have a satisfactory explanation of the conception of Vis Medicatrix Naturae as it applies to the individual cell.

Up to this point, although Reich had observed the above reactions of bions and bion cultures, he was not aware that he was dealing with a specific biological energy. But in 1939 he was working with ocean sand and found that from it, by his special technique of bionous disintegration by incandescent heat and swelling he could obtain a pure culture of special blue bions; what he subsequently called Sapa bions, which exhibited an energy with an extraordinarily intense biological field.

In a long series of experiments he identified this with sun energy, which is present everywhere, and this he found to be the same energy as that in the living organism which takes it up from the atmosphere and directly from the sun, or, as he puts it, 'the energy which governs the living is of necessity identical with the atmosphere energy'. He then argued that, if energy is in the atmosphere everywhere, it should be possible to demonstrate it. To do this Reich invented what he called an Orgonoscope and other apparatus for the occular demonstration of orgone.

The question thus arose as to whether it was possible to concentrate the atmosphere orgone. He found that this was so, using two properties of orgone; (1) that organic material attracts and absorbs it, and (2) that metallic material, especially iron, attracts and repels it again rapidly, i.e. reflects it. He therefore built a box, the outside of which consisted of organic material and the inside of metallic. Let me quote: 'Since the former absorbs the energy while the latter reflects it, there is an accumulation of energy. The organic covering takes up the energy from the atmosphere and transmits it to the metal on the inside. The metal radiates the energy to the outside, into the organic material and to the inside into the space of the accumulator. The movement of energy towards the inside is free, while towards the outside it is being stopped.' In other words, we have an Orgone Accumulator.

Before discussing the purpose and use of the accumulator let me summarise at this point the main characteristics or functions of Cosmic Orgone Energy, which it is useful to compare with those of Animal Magnetism and Odyle (see pp. 30 and 34).

1. Orgone Energy is present everywhere, and it forms an uninterrupted continuum. It penetrates everything, though at varying rates of speed. It is basically different from electro-magnetic radiation.

2. As far as life is concerned, the living organism is an organized part of the cosmic orgone, and possesses special qualities we call 'living'. It has an orgonomic potential brought about by the fact that orgone energy flows from a weaker or a lower to a stronger or higher system. Each type or species possesses its specific energy level, i.e. it has orgonotic capacity. All surplus energy is discharged, hence there is an orgone energy metabolism.

In Reich's own words: 'The physical orgone functions are closely interrelated and very frequently identical with bioenergetic orgone functions. As a matter of fact, it is quite impossible and even not permissible to separate them, since the bio-energetic functions of orgone energy in the living organizm are merely variations of the orgone energy functions in the atmosphere and in the universe at large.'

3. Orgone is always and everywhere in motion. Movement, dynamics, functionalism, changeability constitute specific qualities. Within the framework of this mobility there are three main motions: (a) wavy motions, (b) pulsations, and (c) a west-east movement of the atmosphere orgone envelopes.

4. This transmits orgonotic excitation with the speed of light; but light itself is an appearance of orgonotic illumination and is of local character. It also has the property of autogenous illumination. This can be observed in a room of complete darkness, where it appears a bluish-grey, or in a pressure vacuum tube, where the colour is a deep violet or blue.

5. Orgone energy exists in varying conditions and forms, but every type is mobile-dynamic, differing in speed, and never static-mechanical.

6. A concentration of orgone energy in an orgonotic system contradicts the general, unrestricted validity of the second law of thermo-dynamics. There exists not only a process of dissipation of energy in heat but also the reverse process of the building up of energy.

7. Finally, there is a motor force in orgone energy capable of setting a motor in motion.*

But to come back to the Orgone Accumulator: Reich claimed that it could be used for therapeutic purposes over a very wide range of diseases, and was, indeed, the most fundamental healing agency yet discovered. Orgone therapy can be applied in three different ways: (1) the large accumulator, in which the patient sits once or twice daily with or without clothes for periods of fifteen to forty-five minutes; (2) local application, in which case the orgone energy is led from a small accumulator through a flexible tube coming out of the top of the box with a funnel at the free end which is applied to (but not touching) whatever spot it is

---

* Reich never revealed the secret of this – what he called the Y factor – as he considered that such immense and unlimited power must not be allowed to fall into the hands of unscrupulous persons, political or financial. Apart from this all his discoveries were given freely to the world for the benefit of mankind.

desired to irradiate; (3) local orgone irradiation with earth bions – the old-fashioned mud-pack, but using specially prepared bionous earth.

For the last two years Reich had been treating advanced cancer cases by means of the orgone accumulator, with, he claims, impressive results. Indeed, the translator of his books (Dr Wolfe) goes further and says: 'Reich has discovered the etiology of cancer and opened a way for its cure and prevention.' Reich himself says that: 'as far as orgone therapy of cancer is concerned, it has at present reached the point where it deserves to be taken out of the experimental stage and put on a large-scale practical basis.' Why this has never been done I shall recount in the next chapter.

With the stimulating and, indeed, intriguing possibilities Reich's work seemed to provide, I felt I must secure a full-sized orgone accumulator and experiment with it. This I was fortunately able to do, and I obtained a threefold one, i.e. one in which the basic pattern of metal and organic material is repeated three times. I also constructed two 'shooters' for local application, the smaller of the two being portable, a great convenience when visiting patients. Later on I constructed an accumulator in the form of a cone, with a diameter of two feet, to the apex of which I could attach a wire or silk cord which could be introduced into any circuit which I happened to be investigating – the theory being that orgone energy concentrated at the apex and would 'flow' along the wire.

The physical therapeutic results with the large accumulator were disappointing, but I found it gave excellent results when I was using it as a psychological technique, as it seemed to have a 'loosening' effect on a patient's psyche. But otherwise I could not obtain the results claimed by Reich and his associates.

I communicated my negative results to Reich, who seemed very puzzled, but suggested as a possible explanation that the climate of this country is too damp and that a fivefold or even tenfold accumulator would be required to get results comparable to those obtained in dry climates, instead of the threefold one with which I was working. Whether this was the explanation I do not know, as I was never able to obtain a five or tenfold accumulator to experiment with.

On the other hand, the therapeutic results of the 'shooter' (threefold) were excellent, and fully substantiated Reich's claims to relief of pain in, and rapid healing of, wounds, and the fast and painless healing of burns and scalds without scarring.

There is also one set of observations which I think should be recorded, for the benefit of future investigators:

I had been giving a TB patient healing treatment (of which more anon) when it occurred to me, if my assumption was correct, that the same basic force was involved, that the accumulator would be interchangeable with my own healing treatment. I knew already that this sent up his physical rate, measured by the Biometer, by about 20 cm. (100 degrees Bovis), and I expected the accumulator to do much the same. But to my astonishment it did the reverse and appeared to extract energy. For example, his physical measurement before going into the accumulator was 24 (120 degrees Bovis); he was in for about twenty minutes, and then his reading was 23, one hour after 22, and next morning $21\frac{1}{2}$. By the evening he had recovered somewhat, and had gone up to $23\frac{1}{2}$, still $\frac{1}{2}$ cm. below the original reading.

I thought this curious result was possibly peculiar to the patient, or had something to do with his complaint, so I got three healthy volunteers to repeat the experiment. Here is the result of twenty minutes in the accumulator in each case:

	Before	After	3 hours later	Next morning
No. 1	28	$26\frac{1}{2}$	—	—
No. 2	27	$25\frac{1}{2}$	25	27
No. 3	29	26	25	28

It is therefore clear that there is a loss of energy, as measured with the Biometer, which continues after leaving the accumulator, and it takes twelve hours or more for healthy people to come back to normal. At the moment I do not know what is the significance of these findings, except that orgone treatment would appear to be the reverse of healing treatment, a curious result if both are healing agencies and the force is presumably the same.

The result of all I had now come across in my wanderings, and especially this work of Reich's, made me feel, as the reader can well imagine, that I was on the edge of something, the possibilities of which defied imagination – even possibly a veritable Elixir of Life. There appeared to be a new realm of experience opening up, the exact nature of which it was at present hard to define in ordinary terms. Even more startling facts were to come, as I shall recount in the next chapter.

CHAPTER SIX

The Oranur Experiment and the Tragic Sequel

With this discovery of Reich's work my wanderings took a more definite line. The investigations into Cosmic Orgone Energy so energetically and so purposefully pursued by Dr Reich seemed to hold out enormous possibilities in so many fields of research that it seemed to be the line to follow up. This I did in such ways as were open to me; for example, I took the *Orgone Energy Bulletin*, a quarterly edited by Reich and containing most interesting and stimulating articles on orgone research work covering all fields. I also continued to experiment with the medical use of the orgone accumulator, especially the 'shooter' for local application.

I became more and more impressed with the scope and extent of the whole vast field of research which was opened up by Dr Reich, particularly as it seemed to run parallel to the work on atomic energy to which it appeared to be the complementary alternative and antidote that the world was looking for.

One day in October 1951 the quarterly *Orgone Energy Bulletin* arrived more bulky than usual, and I sat down to read it. It was early morning before I finished it and went to bed. What it described was more exciting than any science fiction, and yet it was true! It seemed incredible and right out of this world.

I was so impressed with the fascinating and, indeed, horrific narrative and felt the questions raised were of such urgency, particularly in view of the menace of the atomic bomb, that I asked my fellow members of the Medical Society whether I could address them on the subject. In January 1952 I read them the following paper on the Oranur Experiment.*

The present story may be said to start in 1950, though the experimental period leading up to it covered the four years 1947 to

---

* A summary of Reich's work on 'Orgone Energy versus Nuclear Energy' from the *Orgone Energy Bulletin*, Vol. III, No. 4, Oct. 1951, and the 'Oranur Project', Dec. 1950.

1950, for it was in December 1950 that the Oranur project or experiment proper was launched. It started with the very practical question 'Can orgone energy influence nuclear energy? Could an antidote to nuclear radiation destruction of living systems possibly be found in orgone energy?' From Dr Reich's work over a period of fifteen years there seemed every reason to suppose it would neutralize nuclear energy radiation or mitigate its effects. The project was based on three premises:

(i) That atomic energy represents energy freed from matter through disintegration of the atom, i.e. it is a secondary energy *after* matter – a secondary variation of the primordial energy. Whereas Orgone energy is primordial mass-free cosmic energy *before* matter.

(ii) 'From many observations it had been deduced that orgone energy and nuclear or atomic energy are contradictory functions of nature and are thus antagonistic to one another.'

(iii) To make the interrelation more readily comprehensible two series of functions in various spheres which are antagonistic to each other can be formulated, according to Reich, as follows:

In Ethics	Good	Evil
In Religion	God	Devil
In Biology	Life	Death
In Bio-energetics	Pa bions	T. bions
In Physics	Orgone Energy	Nuclear Energy
In Cosmology	Cosmic Energy before matter	Cosmic Energy after matter

It should be added that 'orgone energy cannot be comprehended if the laws pertaining to nuclear energy are applied to the realm of primordial cosmic funtioning'. But this question itself of thinking in functional as opposed to mechanical terms requires a lecture to itself.

The project was planned and developed along the following lines: On December 15th 20 millicuries of Phos R 32 were ordered. Mice were to be injected with this and the main question to be answered was: Can artificially produced radiation sickness be treated or prevented by orgone energy? This in fact was never carried out.

At the same time careful preparations and precautions were taken to ensure protection against radiation and full information was obtained about handling radiating material. All of which proved completely useless. During the preliminary period the normal background count of orgone energy concentration was taken with a Geiger-Müller counter and survey meter; this was found to be between 30-50 c.p.m. over the whole experimental area.

To save time it was decided to order two milligrams of pure radium, and instead of injecting fluid radioisotopes, to irradiate some of the mice with radium. The radium in two one milligram units each contained in $\frac{1}{2}$-inch lead containers arrived on January 5th. One was used as a control and put in a hut 200 feet away and the other was put at 11.30 a.m. into a small onefold orgone charger and placed in a twentyfold orgone energy accumulator standing in the orgone energy room. The background count just before was 40-50 c.p.m., i.e. normal for the building. This was the start of the tremendous and awe-inspiring events about to take place.

Two mistakes were made at this point, but if they hadn't been the entire Oranur effect would have been missed.

(a) The background count was not done as soon as the radium had been put in the accumulator.

(b) Feeling safe about the distance of the radium from the outer wall of the laboratory the radium was left in the accumulator for five hours.

At 1.0 p.m. the background count was up to 70-80; this for some reason was not reported and when Dr Reich came down at 4.30 the count had gone up to 80 c.p.m. 50 feet away from the radium and several hundred c.p.m. on the outside of the orgone energy room. Let us continue the dramatic story in Dr Reich's own words:

'The workers were immediately ordered out of the hall. The inside of the OR room was unbearably charged. The walls felt "glowing" 10 to 16 feet away from where the Ra needle was located. The portable survey GM meter "jammed" when I approached the 20× accumulator. There seemed no sense in counting c.p.m. at that moment. The first thing to do was to take the Ra needle out of the charger in order to calm down the OR reaction.

'The radium was deposited within the small charger in a garage some 150 feet away from the metal room. We aired the building right away and hoped that this would remove the high OR charge quickly, to no avail. It still is "active" at this date (May 1951). The radium itself did not produce any of the effects described above when it was taken outside into the garage. Whereas every one of us could feel the heaviness of the air, the oppression, the pulling pains here and there in the body, headaches and nausea right away within the OR energy building, no such sensations were felt outside in the vicinity of the radium as close as one foot. Furthermore, to our great astonishment, ventilation did not seem to remove the oppressive air from the laboratory building. After one hour ventilation, it was still impossible to enter the OR energy room, the radium having been removed long ago. This was new. Usually fresh air would remove any orgonotic overcharge. However, the high background count in the hall came back to nearly normal soon after the removal of the Ra needle. It sank to 60 c.p.m. after half-an-hour's ventilation.

'It is essential to acquaint the reader more fully with the subjective sensations which all of us experienced long after the removal of the radium; sensations which came back intensely and typically, and even more intensely as the days passed, whenever we came near the orgone energy laboratory, especially the OR energy room with no NR material in it. The OR researcher is professionally required to be free of blocking of his perceptions. He relies on his impressions and sensory reactions to a great extent as guiding posts into new territory, and what he thus finds he controls with objectively operating devices. Both the subjective and the objective experience are essential and must go together. An emotionally blocked or "dead" researcher would be completely useless in OR research. He would only endanger himself and others.'

All the workers were affected and became ill to a greater or lesser extent. In other words the hitherto beneficent orgone energy seemed to have changed itself into a dangerous, deadly power, what they came to call DOR (Deadly Orgone); how dangerous they were yet to find out. All work in the building had to be stopped immediately. No one was permitted to enter it. Those who had work to do in the laboratory outside, only did so for two or three minutes at a time.

In spite of all this the experiment was repeated daily from January 5th to January 12th for one hour each day. But on the 12th the radium remained only ½ hour as the results were so severe. Let Dr Reich take up the tale:

'Three experimental observers remained outside the laboratory within about 100 yards. One assistant rushed the experimental piece of radium into the OR energy room and into the 20 × charger. We desisted from measuring with the GM survey meter this time, in order to avoid unnecessary additional exposure. A few minutes later, we could clearly see through the large windows that the atmosphere in the laboratory had become clouded; it was moving visibly, and shone blue to purple through the glass. As we walked up and down some 100 to 250 feet *outside* the laboratory, all three of us had the same experience, but no one at first dared to mention it. I felt severe nausea, a slight sensation of fainting, loss of equilibrium, clouding of consciousness, and had to make an effort to keep erect on my feet. I saw Dr S. Tropp, who was with me, getting very pale. He had not said anything, and I had not told him how I felt. Then I asked him how he felt, whether he felt what I felt. He immediately admitted to feeling very ill and faint, with pressure in the forehead, nauseated, cramped in the stomach, and weak. Then I confirmed his experience by mentioning my own reactions. We had both hesitated to tell about it since we were so far outside the experimental hall in the fresh, clear dry air of a late afternoon in midwinter. Thereupon, we interrupted the experiment and put the radium away to half a mile distance from the laboratory, within an uninhabited area of 280 acres.

'It was perfectly clear, from what we had experienced, that the OR energy field of the laboratory had been greatly extended and excited to a dangerous degree far outside the outer walls. Since there is no sharp borderline anywhere in OR energy functioning, the reaction seemed not only to persist all the time, *without any radium in the charger*; more, it seemed to extend rapidly. We began to worry about how far this spreading of the Oranur reaction would go and where it would halt. We began to feel responsible for what might happen to the village some four miles away. The closest inhabited building was at least one and a half miles away. We also wondered what could happen if we continued with the Oranur experiment: whether all hope of an anti-nuclear effect of OR had gone; whether an explosion was possible if a high concentration of OR would act upon some as-yet-unknown NR material; whether we would recover from the sickness we were suffering from, and whether it would leave any after-effects. Our eyes burned and the conjunctivae were heavily inflamed. . . . Common to all of us were: severe belching, nausea, pressure in the nasal bone structure, in the depth of the eyes, alternating cold and hot flushes, paraesthesias, feeling of disequilibrium, wandering pains in the legs, weakness in arms, especially in the ulnar region, dull headache, tension in the pharynx, severe headache. We had all fallen ill with Oranur sickness.'

Thus all their elaborate protective measures proved completely useless; as Reich remarks: 'at the height of the Oranur effects there were no means of protection for the personnel against an atmospheric energy running amuck, against the raging fury of the uncontrollable Oranur effects.' But it was observed that 'the originally strong organisms did not react severely, whereas organisms which had somehow been weakened *before* Oranur had started, developed strong reactions even if they lived away from Orgonon'. Similarly all their control experiments with the mice went by the board . . . DOR was ubiquitous, as they were to learn.

Three weeks later, i.e. on February 3rd, while they were endeavouring to sort themselves out, they sustained another shock – the New York Times reported high background counts roughly in a circle of 600 miles around Orgonon as an approximate centre.

The question was, had a chain reaction taken place? i.e. had the

Oranur effect travelled 600 or 700 miles in twenty-one days, an average speed of 30-50 miles a day or $\frac{1}{4}$ mile an hour? It seemed to Reich entirely within actual possibilities. They were in conse-, quence very worried. But worse was to come.

Elaborate and careful plans had been made in regard to the experiments with the mice, but, to quote Reich, 'as it turned out however, all these minute, elaborate details lost their significance with the tremendous impact of the Oranur experiment. It did not matter at all whether we had or had not treated mice prophy-lactically; neither did it matter whether or not we treated them afterwards with pure OR for half-an-hour or an hour. We soon had to realize that our former habits of careful timing of OR irradiation in terms of minutes had become meaningless, just as the elaborate health protection devices used in the atomic energy project had become meaningless. Our previous arrangements were to the Oranur action effects as would be the fiddling around with a small spark-producing induction coil to a lightning in the sky during a hurricane. The discrepancies between what we had been used to and what we now went through, were quite awe-some.'

On February 11th a mass death of mice occurred which was unprecedented and gave them a terrible shock, as deaths occurred in all the various groupings and at all distances from the labora-tory. After feverish investigations including P.M.s on each mouse no final answer was found to account for the disaster, but two conclusions were reached (and I quote):

'(i) Low bio-energy enhances Oranur death.

'(ii) Prophylactic high orgone charging of organisms will lessen the effects of Oranur much more effectively than applica-tion after the radiation illness strikes.'

Dr Reich's wife and son now fell ill with the Oranur sickness and had to be evacuated, as they both showed signs, as did all those with the sickness, of leukaemic changes in the blood.

'All through this period,' Dr Reich remarks, 'we felt, on the basis of our constant, steady contact with Oranur as well as with the workers in it, that something very crucial with respect to a future weapon of health had happened; we waited patiently for further developments.' They were not long in coming.

On February 19th occurred an incident that shocked them into 'a keen awareness of the ferocity of the force they were dealing with'. On that day one of his workers came into his library. 'She was,' to quote Reich, 'visibly in shock, frightened and in severe distress. She told me she had just cleaned out one metal-lined cabinet in the laboratory. In order to get things out she had had to reach deeply into the cabinet with her arms. She "smelt" something like Oranur and to make sure had put her head into the cabinet. Thereupon it had "hit her like a wall".'

For an hour and a half Reich fought for her life; at one point she stopped breathing, there was obvious involvement of the medulla oblongata and the thalamus. But finally at the end of two hours she began to recover and all danger was over, but it was a near call. This case taught Reich that Oranur attacks the weakest spot in a specific manner. Let me quote:

'What had actually happened was apparently this: when she had put her head into the unventilated metal-lined cabinet, DOR had hit her hard at her weakest spot in a specific manner; it affected the vagus and respiration centre in the medulla oblongata. This weak spot had been established for the first time in her life when some twenty-one years ago she had suffered from post-diphtherial affliction with a slight paralysis of her arms and legs, and slight impairment of her bulbar functioning. Thus, a syndrome of deadly symptoms had slumbered unnoticed for nearly two decades, only to be sought out, as it were, and reactivated by DOR in such a dangerous manner.'

Finally conditions became unbearable and it was decided to discontinue the experiment by completely dismantling all orgone accumulator devices of all sorts, the orgone metal-lined room was completely disassembled, all the sheet metal was torn from the walls, roof and floor and taken out to air, and everything was well washed down with water. The nuclear material was 'put half a mile away in a safe with heavy four-inch walls of steel and cement, not because the nuclear material was dangerous but because it excited orgone energy into oranur action'.

As a result of all these measures the background count of the laboratory came down to normal. However the walls of the

Orgone room still 'glowed' and it is apparently still unusable, but the laboratory, while still radiating, was usable again by August 1951. But it was found that directly any accumulator or similar device was reassembled, however small, the background count went up at once and remained so until the accumulator was removed.

The question as to how long the Oranur action will continue and whether it would disappear in time or go on indefinitely is still unanswered.

In regard to the workers it was found that they gradually returned to normal and looked and felt better in health than previously. The doctor who nearly died was better than ever before and was 'fully alive on a higher level of energy functioning. Another who had reacted severely became tanned and vigorous.' Reich's son returned 'to full and brilliant health', and Reich describes how he himself was more active and alive. 'I did not', he says, 'need much sleep, ideas and arrangements flowed freely and fully. I felt vigorous and imbued with great zest.'

To keep track of what was going on, blood tests were carried out every fortnight with every worker who had participated in the Oranur experiment. It was found that gradually the blood recovered from its leukaemic condition and returned to normal.

It should be observed at this point, and it is a matter of considerable practical importance, that other agents beside nuclear energy will produce the Oranur effect, e.g. X-ray. Reich had observed that orgone-treated cancer patients declined more rapidly if they also had X-ray treatment. This he discovered was because the orgone energy in the body reacted to X-ray with Oranur effects. He goes on to say: 'I should like to warn against using or living in high orgone energy concentration if any kind of X-ray, radium or similar radiation work is being done in the same building. This conclusion may well disturb the X-ray therapist.'

This appeared to be the end, for the time being, of the Oranur experiment, but it still had one more surprise and shock for them. You will remember that the radium and other nuclear materials had been put away in their lead shields in a safe half a mile away. On April 12th, 1951 Dr Reich and a medical colleague went down to it, the snow having melted, and were dumbfounded to find that at the safe wall the count was 20,000 c.p.m. and 700 feet away it was still 70 c.p.m. They had overlooked the fact that the safe itself had acted as an orgone accumulator. The Oranur experiment had actually been going on the whole time since February. They were afraid to open the safe, remembering what had happened to the doctor who had put her head in one, and were at a complete loss to know what to do – at one time they thought of sinking the whole safe, as it was, in the lake.

However, next day they put several mice of different types close to the safe and left them. They were all alive and well next day and the following day. The fact that after fifty-six hours the mice were still alive and healthy made them stop and think. In Reich's words: 'Were we here dealing with nuclear energy at all? Had orgone energy perhaps done its job of killing the nuclear energy completely? How otherwise could the good health status of the mice be explained? The thought that we had possibly reached our original goal of Oranur experimentation, went like an illumination through our minds. Perhaps . . . Possibly . . . If this would stand the most severe tests in the future, we were obviously dealing with several phases of the Oranur process.'

To summarize (quoting):

'Phase One. Nuclear energy affects orgone energy in a most damaging manner.

'Phase Two. Orgone energy after the first blow fights back ferociously. It runs mad, runs berserk – this is DOR producing radiation sickness.

'Phase Three. If orgone energy has the opportunity to keep fighting nuclear energy it will finally succeed in rendering nuclear energy harmless. It will replace the noxious secondary activity of the nuclear energy by penetration of the nuclear energy matter, and will put it at its service.'

Here at last appeared to be a firm basis for a belief in the possibility of immunization against atomic bomb effects.

Twelve days later the mice were still alive and healthy and so Dr Reich decided to open the safe himself, which he did, without mishap. Various tests were then carried out and important observations made which pointed the way to the control of DOR. They were as follows (I quote): 'Apparently when the nuclear energy material was within the heavy steel and concrete safe, the orgone energy, which can penetrate everything, could easily get *into* the safe, whereas the nuclear energy activity could *not* get *out* of the safe, so orgone energy was at an advantage. On the other hand, when nuclear energy material was not sufficiently shielded it had an even chance to irritate and to trigger orgone energy into DOR action. Therefore to reduce the DOR effect, one had to put the nuclear energy material into heavy shielding and thus confined, into the charger. Orgone energy would get at nuclear energy, but not vice versa.' If this reasoning is correct the Oranur effect could be secured without the DOR element.

There for the time being the Oranur experiment came to a pause. But its tremendous impact remained. As Dr Reich remarks: 'We all felt we had gone through some awful, deadly dangerous experience which we could not yet fully grasp, which had thrown us into some great depth, a hitherto well-hidden domain of cosmic functioning . . . nobody present during the experiment but had experienced a deep fear.'

When the bulk of the report was written in April 1950, the experiment was still exerting its frightening influence, and in the minds of both Dr Reich and his associates its very grave implications, especially those concerning national security, were uppermost. But as the months went by the pessimistic outlook gradually passed as new observations left 'no doubt as to the life-positive medical and biological results of Oranur'. These, it was stated would be published later in a separate report.

It is clear an immense amount of research work still remains to be done, but three main conclusions, of special interest to us as doctors, can already be deduced from this highly hazardous experiment.

(1) The true nature of radiation sickness has, according to Reich, been discovered beyond reasonable doubt.

When he started the Oranur experiment he accepted the current orthodox view that radiation sickness is due to *direct* damage of the tissues of a living organism by ionizing radiation either by gamma rays or neutrons; but it now seems clear that this is not the case, the sickness is an immediate expression of a severe reaction of the orgone energy of the body (what Reich calls the organismic energy) against the nuclear energy radiation. Radiation sickness thus becomes a problem of orgone energy functions and not of atomic radiation. Corroborative evidence is afforded by the fact that nuclear energy radiation is not the only cause of radiation sickness as Reich discovered. X-rays, for example, will produce the same symptoms in the presence of high concentration of orgone energy.

To us as doctors this interpretation may not be as surprising as it may be to the physicists, for, to take a very common medical example, suggested by Dr Reich, superficially an inflammation going on to abscess formation may appear to be the direct result of invasion by virulent bacteria, but we well know inflammation, high temperature, pus formation are the result of defensive reactions on the part of the organism against invading organisms. We also know that if the organism overdoes the defensive reaction it may become a true killer which would correspond to the DOR reaction in the Oranur experiment.

(2) Each person falling sick, to quote Reich, 'reacts according to his or her specific disease or disposition to disease. This effect is due to *selective* bio-energetic effects of orgone energy which attacks specifically the diseased part in the organism, at first driving the symptoms to higher acuity and then curing them if properly and conscientiously used. We can safely assume,' he goes on to say, 'that, with further detailed experimentation with Oranur, it will be possible to direct the healing power of orgone energy at any weak link in the totality of organismic functioning, with the orgone energy finding its way to the diseased organ or system. The dangerous nature of some of these reactions should not deter us. In applying chemotherapy or shock treatment, we endanger the life of the patient to a higher degree, just as we do with anaesthesia or major operations, *without* being able to direct the healing agent in the organism. *Now*, the specific autonomic, selective power of the orgone energy, combined with a well-worked, carefully applied dosage, would enable us to get at every spot in the organism therapeutically, and most likely, also in every

disease. It is clear that in Oranur we have one of the greatest healing powers mankind has ever possessed.'

At this point it is useful, I think, to compare the effects and results of high potency homoeopathic remedies when prescribed radiesthetically, which seem to do exactly what is described above. Is the mechanism the same? Here is a field of important research.

(3) Apart from these important medical uses, it would appear that it should be possible to produce immunization against the ionizing radiation of atomic bomb explosions, and thus obtain a powerful weapon against radiation sickness. This you will recall was the original purpose of the Oranur experiment, and to this extent the theoretical problem has been solved; it remains to carry it out in practice. Thus it might be possible to immunize the whole population by letting people use orgone energy accumulators excited to a known amount of Oranur.

From a more general scientific point of view the implications of the Oranur experiment are very far-reaching and would seem to require an entire reorientation in our method of approach to our mode of thinking of these fundamental problems. Let me quote Reich again on this crucial matter: 'Exactly at the point where the atomic theory dips into the pre-atomic functions of nature, into the realm of so-called "material waves" (a wrong, misleading expression), into the realm of the "wave particles" (again misleading), into the realm of electrons consisting of waves only, into the impossibility of determining at the same time position and momentum of an electron, the "law of merely statistical probability", etc. etc., the functional theory of orgonomy sets in. These primordial, pre-atomic problems are impregnable to methods of mechanistic or materialistic thinking. They divulge logical intelligibility only if approached functionally, i.e. orgonomically. The facts, observations and theoretical deductions have kept piling up for many years in a clear enough fashion to warrant the assumption that the whole electronic theory as far as it pertains to cosmic, *primordial* functions, will be replaced by a functional theory of the basic functions of the universe. These matters are naturally very serious and require intelligent, unprejudiced, open-minded, courageous efforts to clear the field of misconceptions, inertia in thinking, wrongly applied theories, etc. In addition, many reputations are at stake and personal feelings will be hurt.'

But beyond this even, it would seem we are rapidly approaching the point when the present water-tight divisions between Matter and Spirit, Science and Religion, Materialism and Mysticism, Physics and Psychology, Body and Mind, Objective and Subjective, are beginning to break down, and there is coming into view a vision of a basic unity founded on a true reconciliation of seeming opposites. Once again we shall have a Cosmology which is scientifically true and yet profoundly religious.

In subsequent correspondence with Dr Reich, when I asked for permission to quote so extensively from his 'Oranur Experiment', he wrote on March 17th, 1952, 'that we must be most careful in drawing final conclusions. The experiment is still running with *highly problematic* facts' (his italics). And he warned most emphatically against experimenting with Nuclear Energy sources in Orgone Energy accumulators.

To complete the story we must go back to 1947 to understand the sequence of the final events.

In 1947 – the year Reich announced his discovery of a motor force in cosmic orgone energy – the Federal Food and Drug Administration of the U.S.A. began an 'investigation' (was this a coincidence?) into orgone energy accumulators, instigated and kept going, according to Mr Wyvell, Director of the Publications of the Wilhelm Reich Foundation – 'as a conspiracy to kill orgonomy and to defame the discoverer of orgone energy . . . but the efforts to establish sexual defamation and to claim that the orgone energy accumulator was distributed for profit, completely failed, and the "conspiracy" died out in 1950.'

But in 1954 it was revived, and in March an injunction was obtained by the Food and Drug Administration and served on Dr Reich and the Reich Foundation, in which 'the defendants were enjoined from distribution of orgone energy accumulators . . . all accumulators to be disassembled, all printed matter regarding these or orgone energy to be destroyed, *on the ground that orgone energy does not exist*'!*

* Such a statement seems inexplicable, and that it should have been upheld legally is still a mystery.

Dr Reich, rightly or wrongly, did not enter the court as a defendent against the complaint or the injunction, as in his own words 'such action would, to my mind, imply the authority of this special branch of the government to pass judgement on primordial pre-atomic energy. . . . For, if painstaking, elaborated and published scientific findings over a period of 30 years could not convince the administration, or will not be able to convince any other social administration of the true nature of the discovery of the Life Energy, no litigation in any court anywhere will ever hope to do so.' He maintained that courts of justice cannot and must not judge scientific truth. To let them do so, according to Reich, was to make 'the government the final authority on matters of scientific research or religious belief, and such authority is the core of all dictatorship – it is dictatorship.' Dr Reich, in making this stand, according to Mr Wyvell, was 'not only protecting orgonomy, he is protecting our basic civil rights – at the risk of his own freedom'.

Reich and his co-workers, of course, appealed against this fantastic injunction, and the case dragged on throughout the rest of 1954 and 1955. Meanwhile, Reich had more important work to do.

As part of the research into the aftermath of the Oranur Experiment, Reich had invented and constructed what he called a 'cloud buster'. This was a device to break up and remove the ever-increasing DOR clouds in our atmosphere, so inimical to living things.

He found that deserts were largely the result of this DOR phenomenon. He therefore went to Arizona to work on this problem, as he considered that the world-wide increase in drought and desert development is *the* great problem facing humanity.

According to a report written in March 1955 the news was good. 'What is being accomplished by Reich and his assistants in Arizona in combating the desert with Cosmic Orgone Engineering equals and excels the most optimistic theoretical anticipation; that several long drawn out gentle rains – the kind that soak deep into the earth and keep it moist – have been achieved through the removal of DOR by artful use of the cloud buster; and that the laboratory findings at Orgonon concerning DOR and drought, have been confirmed in practice on a large scale.'

In the middle of this vital and important work for the future of humanity the blow fell. In May 1956 Wilhelm Reich and Michael Silvert, the Director of the Orgone Institute, were arrested for violation of the injunction and charged with contempt of court – a charge on which a jury could only find them guilty. The sentence of fantastic severity was announced a few days later – two years' imprisonment for Dr Reich, one year for Mr Silvert, and a fine of £10,000 for the Institute.

The appeal against this savage sentence failed, and so, not only did Dr Reich languish in prison, but the full rigour of the injunction was carried out, and, as far as it was possible, the whole of his work was destroyed. August 22nd, for example, saw the complete destruction, by burning in the Gansevoort incinerator, of all Reich's scientific books.

One could wish that this was the end of the sorry story and that it had a happy ending; but, alas, the tragedy was to be played out to the bitter end.

In November 1957 Wilhelm Reich died in prison of oranur sickness, 'a victim of the emotional plague he had fought so valiantly'.

It is difficult to believe that this attempt to suppress truth and destroy its discoverer is a contemporary event of the mid-twentieth century. We should like to believe it belonged to a far and distant past. But in fact the haters of truth are still as powerful, if not more so, than they ever were. Truth for them is too disturbing and upsetting, and so they turn and rend anyone who has the unenviable and thankless task of proclaiming it, especially if the truth is concerned with the Life Force itself.

Reich, for all his genius, was overwhelmed; but it is certain that what is sound and true in his work will survive in spite of everything, for Vis Medicatrix Naturae, in its essence, cannot be destroyed.

This, in the intervening years, has come about and there is now once again an American College of Orgonomy which publishes a semi-annual journal in May and November; also Orgonomic Publishers Inc. Box 565, Ansonia Station, New York, NY 10023, USA is republishing Reich and other authors, as well as new books. Orgone Energy is once more on the map.

CHAPTER SEVEN

Healing and Healers

After the somewhat horrific note of the last chapter it may be as well to return to more ordinary and mundane matters.

I have mentioned that I had found that I was unable to use a pendulum, and, as a result, if I wished to use radiesthetic technique, I had to get someone else to do the actual pendulum work. This I felt to be unsatisfactory, and I therefore looked around for something I could do which did not require reliance on the technical ability of other people.

Thus it was I came to healing by the laying on of hands. Here, it seemed to me, one had the whole concept of Vis Medicatrix in its simplest and best-known form, as in successful healing one must be using a healing force of some sort, and using it directly.

I was told I had this healing power. I do not know that I believed it, but it stimulated me to seek out those who had the power and were using it for healing, to study their methods and techniques and then try to apply what I had learnt.

My main mentor was that doyenne of healers, Mrs Kingsley Tarpey. I first came across her work in the *Journal of the British Society of Dowsers*. In the September number, 1942, there was an account of scientific investigation into the claims of a Mrs Kingsley Tarpey concerning alleged beneficial effects from looking at her pictures. One phrase in particular arrested my attention: 'I did not stay in the room, as some dowsers said they could perceive my radiation at a distance.' I remember wondering at the time what manner of healer this could be – evidently a very powerful one, if her radiations were so far-reaching. When I eventually met her some years later, I found she was, indeed, a healer of the first order.

She was at this time about eighty-five, but full of vigour both physically and mentally, and my first impressions of her were strengthened by increasing contact and investigation of her work both as a patient, a collaborator and an observer over a period of ten years until her death in 1957 at the age of ninety-six.

There was no doubt she was a healer of outstanding power and performance. An unusual feature was that the healing seemed independent of her own physical state and unaffected by her age; indeed, as she got older the power seemed to increase. Moreover, healing did not deplete her; if anything, she was more vigorous after the act than before. She was, as she expressed it, 'simply a "channel" for the power,' and did not use her own vitality as is done by 'magnetic' healers.

She was rare among healers for another quality – that of taking an objective and scientific attitude to her work. From the beginning she worked in the closest co-operation with scientists and doctors, and always gave every help and facility in the fullest investigation of her work. As a result her work had unusual scientific and medical value.

Her technique was as follows:

She first took the physical and 'psychic' thumb reading on her Bovis Biometer (see p. 18) as well as the reading of any particular part of the body which might be involved. Then, sitting in front of the patient, who lay back comfortably in a chair, she took his or her hands in hers, R to L, and L to R, and continued to hold them lightly for the duration of the treatment.

After a short while a throbbing started in the hands and the patient would feel a tingling which started in the hands and gradually spread up the arms and then would be felt in various parts of the body, usually those parts which were below par or diseased. Sometimes the tingling would be felt over the whole body, and, if treatment were continued after this, the patient would say he felt intoxicated. Patients varied very greatly in their reactions, some feeling nothing. I myself, when treated by Mrs Tarpey, felt very little. The throbbing, however, was almost always felt, and it usually rose to a climax and then died away. When it did, this usually meant the end of the treatment. At this point further Bovis readings would be taken, recording the rise which always took place both physically and psychically.

This general treatment was often followed by a local treatment of some particular area or internal organ which was diseased or out of order, e.g. head, lungs, heart, kidney. In this case the healing hands were placed on the front and back of the body, over and under the region or organ. Usually heat was felt, what Mrs Tarpey used to call 'human diathermy', though I think the sensation of heat was subjective, as there was no actual rise of temperature in the part. The idea was to concentrate the healing power in that part of the body most needing it.

Mrs Tarpey, as far as I remember, always placed her hands in actual physical contact with the patient, but other healers have found that better results are obtained by holding the hands four to six inches away from the part of the body to be treated.

The length of each treatment by Mrs Tarpey depended on the receptivity and sensitiveness of the patient and also on the degree of depletion. For the most part a general treatment would be from ten to fifteen minutes or a local treatment about five minutes. But Mrs Tarpey never timed her treatments; she seemed to know when the patient had had enough.

As will be seen, the whole procedure was very simple though most effective.

If further treatments were required and it was not possible for the patient to come to her she had a further procedure. She had found that her paintings, quite apart from their artistic and aesthetic value, appeared to be charged with her healing power.* If a patient sat in front of one of them for fifteen to twenty minutes the Bovis measurement would rise, not so high as with an actual live contact but sufficiently for it to be said that the patient had had a treatment.

She also found that she could charge up various substances, especially wool, silk and oil, with the power, so that she was able to give blankets, shawls or bandages, charged in this way, to absent patients to be used as and when required. In the case of the charged oil (castor oil), this was most effective treatment for any painful condition.

I have mentioned that Mrs Tarpey could increase the 'psychic' reading by her treatment, and it was due to this fact that she attempted to treat psychological cases, and in particular backward and difficult children, with whom, as the records show, she had considerable success. This is the more surprising as Dr Brunler, who first discovered that one could take these thumb readings,

* For a further discussion of this, see Chapter IX, p. 93.

always maintained that, while one could increase the 'physical,' the 'psychic' could not be altered – that was what one was born with.

But I am sure that Mrs Tarpey was capable of altering and increasing the 'psychic' reading, and restoring mental and emotional normality – whatever might be said to the contrary – an observation which should give hope to many sufferers who have given up all hope of improvement.

To readers who would know more of Mrs Tarpey and her healing I would recommend her little book *Healing by Radiesthesia*, published by the Omega Press in her ninety-fifth year. Here they will find a description and list of her more spectacular cases.

About this time too I came in contact with Mr L. E. Eeman, whose technique of healing was particularly interesting to me, as he appeared to have discovered and applied in a unique manner 'the laying on of hands'.

After an air crash in 1918 he was admitted to hospital a physical and nervous wreck. He was finally discharged in 1919 as permanently unfit for duty and with 100% disability pension.

Through his own discoveries, which he records in his book, *The Technique of Conscious Evolution*, he restored himself to complete health, and subsequently he developed them into a form of therapy which he practised with great success from 1922 to 1957 at his well-known consulting and treatment rooms at 24 Baker Street, London.

His main discoveries may be stated thus:

1. Any trauma, especially a psychological one, tends to set up a nervous muscular tension in some part of the body, which tension is unconscious, and a vicious circle tends to be set up. To resolve this it is necessary to make the tension conscious. As soon as this is done the tension goes and there is complete relaxation. Any tendency for the tension to return can be dispersed by conscious thought.

2. Removal of the neuro-muscular tensions tends to an emergence of the buried memories which first produced them, together with the emotional content, which consists of the psychic energy repressed with the memory.

3. This released energy is now available to the patient for his restoration, i.e. healing; or it can be added to the total available energy of the body.

4. This psychic energy has a polarity which can be used therapeutically.

Eeman's basic healing technique was based on these principles, and consisted in the first phase of practical instruction in the art and science of complete, conscious relaxation.

He would demonstrate on the patient that one must start at the feet and gradually work up the body, relaxing the various muscles in turn, paying particular attention to the chest and respiration, usually full of tensions, and finally ending up with the head and neck, in which last all the most refractory tensions seem to congregate.

One result of this muscular relaxation or 'Myognosis', as he called it, is 'emergence', by which Eeman meant a vivid and full reliving of the buried and unconscious original experience which had produced the tension and trauma. This, Eeman maintained, was real psycho-analysis, as in the course of teaching relaxation he would also enable the patient to gain relief from his hidden complexes. As he said: 'The fundamental soul, nerve and body healing factor in both confession and analysis is re-pentance, re-thinking, re-memorising and re-living.'

But he laid it down as axiomatic that this re-living can only be done thoroughly and cathartically if the patient is in a relaxation circuit and remains completely relaxed. It is of interest to note that Eeman used to accomplish in a comparatively few sessions what it might take an ordinary psycho-analyist years to uncover, if he managed it at all; and the result would be nothing like so good.

When Eeman was satisfied that the patient could at will relax every part of himself, and emergence had taken place to a lesser or greater degree, the patient went on to the second phase, which consisted of relaxation in circuit.

As I have said, Eeman rediscovered the body's polarity, viz. (a) that the right side of the body, including the right hand, is positive; (b) that the left side, including the left hand, is negative; (c) that the back of the head is positive, and the base of the spine negative. He found that if he joined up these poles a circuit was created. He did this by running a wire held in the right hand to a copper mesh mat placed under the sacrum, and similarly a wire in the left hand to a mat at the back of the head, and then joining the two mats together with a wire, so that he got positive to negative, negative to positive and positive to negative.

This 'set up' produced what Eeman called 'the relaxation circuit'. If the wires were reversed, so that it was negative to negative and positive to positive, then what Eeman called 'the tension circuit' was produced.

A single person could be put into his own relaxation or tension circuit, though it was found that it was more effective if others were also introduced into the same circuit.

Eeman experimented with all sorts of arrangements of the polarities and with various numbers of subjects in the circuit, and he finally came to the conclusion that a circuit which combined parallelism with serialism gave the best results, as this also enabled one or more subjects to depart without breaking the circuit. This was the beginning of his conception of co-operative healing, which it was his ambition to develop on a large scale.

But to go back to the patient who had been taught relaxation. The next phase of the treatment was to put him on a specially designed deck-chair in which he could completely relax as the polarities of the body were joined up for the relaxation circuit. Usually Mr Eeman and his assistant, Miss Cameron, joined in as well to reinforce the power. After a short while there was a feeling of increased relaxation, of warmth and of well-being, and then a drowsiness which usually ended in sleep, which might last thirty minutes, at the end of which all members in the circuit would wake at the same time 'with a greater sense of well-being than after a good night's rest and with a feeling that each had got more out of the pool than he had put into it'. In other words, the well could help the sick without detriment to themselves, which, however, was true only up to a point, as it is sad to think that Eeman's death at the comparatively early age of sixty-nine in 1958 was probably due to the fact that he took too many of his patients' illnesses on himself.

Eeman wondered, to start with, whether there was a difference of polarity between male and female, but, much to his surprise he found that the difference was not one of sex nor of incompatibility of temperament but of right and left handedness. To put a right-handed person in a relaxation circuit with a left-handed person, without reversing the wires, was to create a tension circuit, which was apparent at once in a tensing of muscles, a change in the rhythm of breathing, a coldness which might become intense, and an acute restlessness going on to an unbearable tension which could only be relieved by screaming. But immediately the wires, i.e. the polarities, were reversed, all was well.

As will have been noted, there is such a close analogy to electromagnetic polarity that at first Eeman thought he was dealing with this and formulated the hypothesis that 'conducted wireless radiations emitted by the human body can be used therapeutically provided polar opposites are linked by electrical conductors'.

But when I began to collaborate with him in his work it struck me that there was a much greater similarity to Reichenbach's positive and negative odylic force than to electricity or magnetism, and that it was far more likely we were dealing with an odylic phenomenon than an electro-magnetic one.

I suggested to Eeman that this could easily be tested by substituting silk pads for the copper-mesh mats and silk cords for the copper wires. If the force was odylic the circuit would still take place; if it was electro-magnetic, it would cease, as electricity is not conducted by silk.

Eeman agreed to experiment, and in the event he devised a much more elaborate and conclusive test which completely vindicated and endorsed my suggestion. Vis Medicatrix was not electrical, whatever else it might be.

For thirty years Eeman experimented ceaselessly and made discoveries of the greatest importance. For example, he found that drugs could be introduced into the circuit and could be identified by the person acting as the sensitive in the circuit by the effects produced and felt. It was discovered that this, in fact, was an excellent way to 'prove' a homoeopathic remedy. From this it was only a step to introducing drugs, either allopathic or homoeopathic, into the circuit for purposes of treatment, as it was found that better therapeutic results could be obtained in this way than by taking the remedies by mouth. The very effective auto-urine treatment was made aesthetically possible in this way.

He found, too, that subjects in circuit were much more open to suggestion, and he devised the experiment of getting one person to concentrate on some definite idea, and it was then found that all the rest in the circuit produced the same idea. He called this 'group telepathy'.

All these and many other things of considerable importance are discussed with a wealth of experimental data in his main book, *Co-operative Healing: the healing properties of human radiations.*

I hope I have been able to show how Eeman broke new ground in the exploration of this vast field of Vis Medicatrix Naturae, and that others may be stimulated to continue the work where he left off.

At the end of a paper on 'The effects of conducted radionic emissions from drugs and blood extracts in the co-operative healing circuit' Eeman quoted a letter which I had written him in support of his idea that in the co-operative healing circuit those convalescent from an illness, particularly if it was microbic or virus, could help those in the grip of the disease. I said:

'I thought you would be interested in the following quotation from van Helmont's famous treatise: *De magnetice vulnerum curatione*, as it seems to be a direct forecast of your discoveries about co-operative healing in infections, etc. This is what he says:

' "For he who hath once recovered from that disease hath not only obtained a pure balsamical blood, whereby for the future he is rendered free from any recidivation of the same evil, but also infallibly cures the same infection in his neighbour . . . and by the mysterious power of Magnetism transplants that balsam and conserving quality into the blood of another."

'It might be a description of your healing circuit!'

Eeman added in comment: 'And van Helmont had died before 1650! We had von Reichenbach a hundred years ago; Mesmer two hundred years ago; and now we have van Helmont three hundred years ago. What a humbling thought! And one, perhaps, which might lend some support to a suggestion that I have repeatedly advanced during the last twenty-three years; that is, that a radionic emission of drugs and blood extracts in the co-operative healing circuit should be investigated in the infection wards of one of our hospitals. After all, three hundred years is quite a long period of incubation, even for an idea!'

It is to be hoped that Eeman's work will not be overlooked or forgotten, as he has a very great contribution to make both in the physical and in the emotional and mental fields of therapeutics.

Personally I owe a great deal to Mrs Kingsley Tarpey and Mr Eeman, as they taught me most of what I know about the technique of modern healing by the laying on of hands.

But I also went further afield, and I was fortunate to make contact with the well-known spiritual healer, Harry Edwards. I satisfied myself that he was a genuine healer, i.e. a special source of the healing force – of Vis Medicatrix Naturae. And this in spite of the fact that he himself attributes his power to disincarnate spirits working through him. I would not deny that he may be right, but it seems to me to be unnecessary to invoke such an explanation when we know from our survey so far that there are other better ones, even if more mundane, to account for the healings. I could not help feeling that the spirits were there mainly as a most effective dramatization of the power and its work.

I was in fact instrumental in getting Harry Edwards to give a healing demonstration to the Medical Society for the Study of Radiesthesia, but unfortunately the cases were not followed up systematically, and so the demonstration had little scientific value.

Again I was fortunate to see and take part in the healings performed by Brother Mandus*; indeed, I presided at one of his healing sessions. Here we have the nearest approach in these times to what must have occurred in the early Christian healings, and I have no doubt myself that the vast testimony to the efficacy of divine healing through the instrumentality of Brother Mandus does represent a fact which we cannot and should not ignore.

As a result of all this I decided to see what I could do myself in the way of the laying on of hands.

Reflecting on the whole matter it seemed to me that the field of therapeutics could be divided into two main divisions, what may be called the Analytic and the Unitary.

* Founder and Head of the World Healing Crusade.

In the first falls most of modern medicine, as here the methods and techniques are essentially analytical – the whole endeavour is to arrive at an accurate analytical diagnosis, i.e. to ascertain exactly what part or parts of the organism are diseased, and the various factors, microbic, chemical, etc., which have produced the pathological condition, and then to treat the factors as well as the diseased organs or tissues.

The great disadvantage of the analytic method is that, as is illustrated so well by modern medicine, it makes for specialization and fragmentation. One tends to think in parts instead of wholes, and one does not deal with a person as such, but with a heart case or a liver case, a lung case, etc., and so on.

Though the second main division, the Unitary, is relatively obscure, it is of very ancient lineage, and is little used in modern times. Here the exact diagnosis is unimportant, except as a matter of interest and as a check on what is happening.

Dr Rebecca Beard, in her book on spiritual healing, entitled *Everyman's Search*, makes a point of this. She says: 'As time went on I found myself more and more reluctant, not only to make a definite prognosis of a patient's condition, but to make a diagnosis, because I realized that by saying to a person: "You have a serious disorder or a definite diseased organ" I was implanting into their subconscious mind a positive picture that it was going to be very difficult for them to forget or ignore.'

No attempt is made to pinpoint the trouble, except in general terms. One deals with a sick *person*, a person who is out of balance, out of harmony, physically, mentally, emotionally, spiritually – the object of therapy is to restore that person to a harmonious functioning as a whole. One uses for that purpose the Life Force itself, the Vis Medicatrix Naturae, under its many names, and relies on being able to generate a sufficient intensity and/or quality to produce automatic readjustment of any functional or organic disharmony. The therapeutic agent is general and not specific; it deals with the whole man and not his parts. Moreover, it is entirely beneficial, a most important and significant point, for, as McDonagh has pointed out, in modern medicine 'there is no remedy which is not an invader' and therefore detrimental to the body. He goes on to say that 'although the aims of treatment of disease are to prevent the change in the protein from being aberrant, yet its very nature makes treatment a possible aggravation of the damage already suffered by the protein'.

To the beneficial category of therapeutic agents belongs the laying on of hands by all the various techniques of the natural healer, Eeman's circuit, Reich's orgone accumulator, the Bach remedies, Homoeopathy in so far as it treats the whole man, some parts of Nature Cure, and, above all, real spiritual healing.

What I obviously wished to do at the time was to use some of the Unitary therapies. I found I had at my disposal the Bach remedies, the Eeman circuit in the form of the Autonormalizer, and my own healing powers. I worked out the following procedure:

After various preliminaries, including taking a full history, making a physical examination, 'baching' the patient, recording the Bovis measurements both before and after treatment, I would first teach the patient how to relax, using the Eeman technique. This would be followed by 'the laying on of hands', using the method Mrs Tarpey had taught me, which I have already described. Then a period of relaxation, for which I would use the Autonormalizer, a convenient piece of apparatus devised to give a self-contained Eeman circuit.

This apparatus had a device whereby one could introduce anything into the circuit that might be required, and, if Bach remedies were indicated, I would give them in this way.

Later on I would sometimes use Eeman's full co-operative circuit if there were two or three other persons who were willing to join in.

It may be asked why the patient was not put in the Eeman relaxation circuit to start with, but I found as a matter of experience that if I first raised the general physical vitality by the healing technique, as I was able to do, then the circuit when subsequently used was far more effective. Mr Eeman, indeed, used a very similar technique when he laid his hands on the patient after obtaining relaxation.

On the whole, this combined therapy gave good results, and to illustrate what was accomplished I will give two cases in outline:

The first was a married woman aged forty-five – a case of

ulcerative colitis – a notoriously difficult condition to deal with. She had been ill for nine months, and had both home and hospital treatment with no improvement, and she was finally told that her only hope was an operation. This she refused, and it was at this point that she came to me.

Treatment consisted of direct healing followed by a period in the circuit with the selected Bach remedies, plus psychological advice, for which last I enlisted the help of the husband. To put the whole position succinctly, she had in essence to be absolved to her own satisfaction (I emphasize this) from a state of mind she regarded as sinful – something much harder than curing the physical manifestation – the colitis. I did nothing directly about this latter, regarding it merely as a symptom of a much more profound disorder.

She remarked on this, saying that in hospital and at home it was the primary thing they were concerned with, whereas it seemed the last thing I bothered about. I might remark here that none of her medical attendants had gone into her psychological history.

I saw her in all twelve times, over a period of three months, frequently at the beginning and then lengthening out to a fortnight and finally a month. The last time she was not completely right but I assured her all would be well.

I did not see her again until a year later when I met her accidentally. She said she was perfectly well and had had no relapse. She was happy and leading a normal married life.

The second case was more difficult. I have partly chosen it as it is representative of that legion of neurotics who are the bane and despair of their relatives, their doctors and the hospitals.

She was a married woman aged thirty-nine. She was said to be a hopeless neurotic of thirty years standing for whom nothing more could be done, except continuous sedatives. The husband approached me in the first place as he said life was becoming impossible both for him and for her.

She was a pathetic object, thin, pale and fragile with a cowed look and attitude; she sort of crawled about holding on to things to avoid falling down. She was a veritable museum of symptoms.

Treatment, as in the first case, consisted of direct healing followed by a circuit with the Bach remedies, together with psychological treatment, including positive suggestions as opportunity offered, first at three-day intervals, then weekly, and finally monthly, over a period of six months.

Very gradually and with many setbacks the symptoms slowly cleared. She found she could eat anything and enjoy it. She started to put on weight.

She began to get out and do her shopping and to go out with her husband in the car and enjoy it without the penalty of a migraine. In other words, she started to enjoy life; something she had not done since early childhood. Her very aspect changed; she became more upright and began to walk with confidence, and her face lost its look of misery and apprehension. Her true personality began to emerge.

After six months of treatment I told her she could now manage on her own, and this she did most successfully for eight months. She then had a slight setback due to an emotional upset. One treatment quickly put this right, and she maintained her progress up to the last time I saw her, except for some return of the giddiness which had always been the most difficult symptom to deal with.

It may, of course, be said that, as these cases were psychosomatic ones, any treatment would have been effective. This may be very true, except that, as a matter of actual fact, no other treatment had.

I myself had had little hope of being able to do anything for them, and indeed no one was more surprised than I myself when I managed to make them functionally efficient for all practical purposes. In both cases no attempt was made to deal directly with any of the symptoms. Treatment all the time was directed to treating the patient as a functional whole, and in the course of this reintegration the symptoms, both physical and emotional, cleared up as well.

Eventually I gradually dropped this therapy, not because it was not eminently sound and certainly successful but because I thought I got even better results from the use of Radiesthesia. But if for any reason Radiesthesia was not available, or it needed reinforcing, I would most certainly use the technique again, as indeed I have on various occasions.

There was also another reason. I am inclined to think that in this scientific age and at this stage in the development of mankind spiritual healing, as it was carried out in the early days of Christianity, is not the appropriate form for divine healing. We should not in fact try to revive this sort of spiritual healing, as is being done by many and various religious bodies, but seek to find what is appropriate to these modern times. My own belief is that this will be found in the use of form, in therapeutic patterns. I will discuss this in the later chapters of this treatise.

CHAPTER EIGHT

Huna: the Secret Science

At this point one might well ask in the American phrase 'Where do we go from here?' Where indeed? For as the reader will be well aware, by this time a considerable field had been covered, in all of which glimpses had been caught of the one consistent clue – Vis Medicatrix Naturae – but the clue seemed to be increasingly difficult to define and pin down.

Was there in fact an ascertainable pattern, or was the whole field of phenomena just a disjointed collection of interesting but isolated facts, with various people working at their special pieces of a jigsaw puzzle which did not seem to fit together or to make much sense? The work of Dr Reich seemed to come nearest to what I was looking for, but even this lacked historical perspective, and, moreover, aroused an irrational antagonism which badly obscured the real issues.

This problem was answered for me at this time by a book which my friend Mrs Kingsley Tarpey lent me. It had the intriguing title of *The Secret Science behind Miracles* (Kosmon Press) and was by Max Freedom Long. Here to my astonishment and delight I found the sort of pattern which I had assumed might exist; for here, once again, was our clue, but this time in a systematic and coherent form.

The book opens with the following sentence: 'This report deals with the discovery of an ancient and secret system of workable magic, which, if we can learn to use it, as did the native magicians of Polynesia and North Africa, bids fair to change the world.'

In the rest of the book the story is told of how Mr Long, when he went to Hawaii as a young teacher in 1917, gradually uncovered and rediscovered, with infinite patience and perseverance, a hidden and proscribed tradition of magic which had been handed down until very recent times by the magicians, the Kahunas, the keepers of the secret, which, if true, challenged our accepted scientific conceptions fundamentally.

Traditionally, the Kahunas were able to do four impossible things, i.e. from the point of view of modern science.

1. They could at will walk barefoot, with complete immunity, over lava only just solidified enough to bear the weight of a man.

2. They could foretell the future with great accuracy and change that future if it appeared desirable to do so. Mr Long remarks that this formed a large part of their work, for they healed both body and purse, social and economic tangles.

3. They could perform instant healing or, in other words, work miracles. (Incidentally, I was interested to find that my conception of a miracle as a speeding up of, or an elimination of, the time element was also the Kahunas' conception.)

4. They could control the winds and the weather and man-eating sharks.

All these things except the sharks were demonstrated to the author, showing that the phenomena were controllable and repeatable as they are in an ordinary scientific experiment.

They were also able to do successfully ordinary healing which they called 'Lomi-lomi', which was a combination of massage, baths, manipulation, suggestion and the laying on of hands.

At mental healing they were adepts, and could deal successfully with insanity and other mental troubles.

They could demonstrate, and had a theory explaining, the whole of what we call Extra-sensory Phenomena.

Mr Long emphasizes that what makes this psycho-religious system of Huna outstanding and sets it apart from all modern systems, either of religion or psychology, is that it works. As he remarked: 'It worked for the Kahunas and it should work for us.' It was both practical and scientific.

Mr Long had an inquiring mind, and so he sought diligently to penetrate the barrier of silence surrounding the Kahunas' doings, but without success. He was inclined to regard the whole matter as superstition or as figments of the imagination, but he could not be quite sure. Finally, after four years of trying and getting nowhere he went to see the Curator of the Honolulu Museum, a Dr Brigham, then in his eightieth year, who, he understood, had spent most of his many years delving in things Hawaiian, hoping he would settle his problem and assure him it was all a lot of bunk and could be disregarded.

Imagine his astonishment and bewilderment when Dr Brigham replied: 'For forty years I have been studying the Kahunas to find the answer to the question you have asked. The Kahunas do use what you have called magic. They do heal. They do kill. They do look into the future and change it for their clients. Many are impostors but some are genuine.

'I have been able to prove that none of the popular explanations of Kahuna magic hold water. It is not suggestion nor anything yet known in psychology. They use something that we have still to discover, and this is something inestimably important. We simply must find it. It will revolutionize the world if we can find it. It will change the entire concept of science. It will bring order into conflicting religious beliefs.'

Long comments that 'it seems absurd to think that he (Dr Brigham) had been able to watch the Kahunas at work, had become their friend, had fire-walked (over lava) under their protection, and still had not been able to get the slightest inkling how they worked their magic'. And so it remained, for although Dr Brigham during the remaining four years of his life taught Long all he knew, and Long remained in Hawaii for another six years, he had to admit defeat and returned to California with the problem unsolved and indeed without a clue.

But in 1935, in the middle of the night he found the key which finally unravelled the whole thing. This proved to be an analysis of the root words making up an ordinary word; the roots, he discovered had a secret meaning. From this beginning he was eventually able to reconstruct the Huna system sufficiently to make it workable.

His first findings he published in 1936 under the title *Recovering the Ancient Magic*, and later, in 1948, a revised and greatly expanded work: *The Secret Science behind Miracles*. The publication of this stimulated great interest throughout the world, and for four years he acted as a central clearing house for reports from people who were experimenting with and trying out the Huna idea. During this time he published a bulletin. The result of all this experimental work was finally published in 1953 under the title *The Secret Science at Work* (Huna Research Publications).

In working it all out he was guided by a dictum of Dr Brigham's: 'Always keep watch for three things in the study of this magic. There must be some form of consciousness back of and directing the processes of magic; there must be some form of force used in exerting this control; and, last, there must be some form of substance, visible or invisible, through which the force can act. Watch always for these, and, if you find any one, it may lead to the others.' And in due course he found it to be a true guide to the nature of Huna – the Secret.

This may be summed up in what Long calls the ten elements of Kahuna psychology and philosophy.

Let me try to summarize them.

1. Man is first of all a triple trinity in a physical body. He is not one spirit, but three, showing an evolutionary progression.

(*a*) The low self or subconscious – the seat of the emotions and of memory.

(*b*) The middle self or conscious, which cannot remember but has full reasoning powers.

(*c*) The high self or superconscious – the Aumakua, which means older, parental and perfectly trustworthy spirit – the divine part of man.

These spirits form an evolutionary series from the purely animal to the divine.

2. There are three forms of the vital force or mana used by the three spirits:

(*a*) Low mana used by the low self, which can flow over threads of shadowy body substance – the aka threads. It can carry chemical substances or thought forms. It can be stored.

(*b*) Middle mana, used by the conscious mind spirit in all its thinking and willing activities. Used as Will it acts as an hypnotic force provided a thought form is introduced into the mind of the subject. It cannot travel over the aka threads.

(*c*) High mana used by the high self for various purposes, e.g. miracles.

3. There are three shadowy bodies in which the three spirits of man reside:

(*a*) The low shadowy body. This is of such a nature that it sticks to whatever we touch, and perhaps see and hear, and when removed from contact draws out a long invisible thread, making a semi-permanent union (the aka threads). It is an ideal conductor for the low mana and can be used as a storage place for it. When heavily charged with low mana it becomes rigid and firm enough to affect and move physical objects.

(b) The shadowy body of the conscious or middle self.

(c) The shadowy body of the high self.

4. The physical body which is used by the low and middle spirits during life, the high self being distantly connected, probably by aka threads from the low body.

It is, of course, a common belief that man is an incarnate spirit, a spirit which builds a physical body to manifest in the world of matter which is brought about through the formative forces. Long has an interesting commentary on this. He says: 'The Kahunas believed that all things and substance have corresponding aka bodies, which are duplicates of the things they represent, the aka body comes as the first part of creation, the physical as the second, and there is a definite amount of consciousness and mana tied up in all things, otherwise they would not exist or retain their shape.'

The secret of Huna was the interrelationship of the three selves and the way they interacted and used the various manas and the aka bodies and their substance. All this forms a fascinating study, especially when one leaves the magical field, either of healing or psychical research and enters the religious, and learns the true nature of prayer and how to make it effective, and the way to communion and union with the high self – the goal of religious experience and indeed the goal of our life here on earth.

Whatever we may think of this formulation, it must be remembered that the practice arising from these conceptions worked and worked to order, if the accounts are to be believed. They worked just as truly as Faraday's electro-magnetic formulations have worked in the electrical industry of today. Huna in the hands of the Kahunas worked, and the results could be repeated. It was not just theory or speculation, and when a theory works out in practice it can usually be assumed to be correct.

A good test too of the truth of a theory is whether it integrates, reduces to order, and explains a mass of hitherto unrelated theories and phenomena. This Huna undoubtedly does, for it reduces psychic phenomena in general to a unified and coherent whole, and gives a working theory of dowsing; of medical radiesthesia; of healing by contact, at a distance or miraculously; of psychic or extra-sensory phenomena, including telepathy, clairvoyance, psychometry, crystal gazing, materialization, apport, poltergeists, etc.; of hypnotism and mesmerism; of psychosomatic medicine; of analytical Jungian psychology; of various religious beliefs and conceptions, particularly the Christian. It is an interesting fact that after more than fifty years of psychical research no theory has been advanced which even covers the psychic phenomena, let alone the rest.

When we apply all this to our findings up to date, they would appear in the main to fit into the Huna concepts, especially in regard to the healing force. Indeed, I think it is clear that Mana is once again our old friend Vis Medicatrix Naturae.

It is important at this point to appreciate the distinction between ordinary healing – what the Kahunas called Lomi-lomi – and spiritual healing. In the first case one is using the low mana, and in the second, high mana; this explains the difference, particularly in time and quality, between the results. Some healers are capable of both, but in this case, when they wish to use the high mana, the healer, through the low self, concentrates the energies (low mana) on the high self, who accepts the mana and raises its vibratory speed to the spiritual frequency of high mana, after which it is returned and produces what we call miraculous results. Spiritual healing is the exclusive use of high mana.

I am not sure what Dr Reich would have made of it all, as he would have no truck with spirits of any sort. 'There is,' he says, 'no space full of spirits and phantoms which mysticism believes in but is not able to demonstrate,' and yet the Kahunas believed that the force was present in the atmosphere and had only to be collected, which is the essence of Reich's orgone accumulator.

Mr Eeman has, however, shown that the force has polarity, which the Kahunas did not appear to know, and has rediscovered what they did know, that when the vital force flows from one person to another it may carry various substances, hence the astonishing success of his series of drug experiments and the therapeutic effect of various drugs, crude or in potency, including the Bach remedies, which are put in the circuit or contained in the bodies of the people in the circuit in the form of acquired immunities, etc. Also the explanation of Eeman's telepathy experiments in circuit, as thought form, i.e. thoughts embodied in their tiny shadowy bodies, can also be carried in this way. This is the way, according to the Kahunas, in which suggestions operate. In Long's words, 'The art of suggestion consists in transferring to someone else some of your low mana or vital force and on the flow sending the thought form of the suggestion.'

This can be done at the same time as the laying on of hands, for once contact is made, to quote Long again, 'an aka thread thereafter connects the healer to the patient, and when a "willed" command is given to the low self of the healer to reach out along the thread and touch the patient, even at a distance, contact can be made and vital force and thought forms of suggestion sent . . . this is "absent treatment" or treatment by telepathic means'. Presumably the same mechanism is involved in the diagnosis of a blood spot by an operator at a distance using a pendulum or one of the diagnostic machines; as also the so-called 'broadcasting' of treatment.

Let me digress for a moment. It was found by American workers experimenting with a sensitive recording device that it would obey commands when a hand was extended towards it – but there was always a time lag of fifteen to twenty seconds. Long, commenting on this, suggests that this represents the time taken for the low self to project an aka finger or thread and the subsequent flow of mana along it to the object. He adds that we have possibly not given enough attention to this time lag (dealing as we usually do with the speed of light) and therefore get either no results or equivocal ones. He comments 'that the slow steps and recitals in the Mass must have been designed originally to build slowly the aka link with the collective High Selves – the aumakuas – and to send the force through it so that it might return to bless the worshippers'.

I do not know if English research workers have also noted this time lag. It would, for example, be interesting to know if there is a time lag in map dowsing, as presumably the same mechanism is involved in this as in other phenomena dealing with things at a distance.

The Kahunas further found that the suggestion was rendered more potent if some physical stimulus was used at the same time. The low self needs to be impressed by a material something or by some act. Hence the efficacy of the bottle of medicine. I remember once giving a patient a medicine which, pharmaceutically, should have benefited him, but he came back and said it had done him no good at all. I said, 'Ah, I know what you want; you want a very special medicine. What I am going to give you now will certainly cure you,' and I gave him exactly the same medicine, which I had coloured a brilliant green. He came back and said it was indeed wonderful medicine and had put him completely right. I used to keep a series of vegetable dyes, red, green, yellow and blue, for this purpose; and most efficacious they were.

Physical stimulus may be of any kind. This is presumably why any new remedy, however bizarre, has its cures, and why practitioners who use these remedies also use what appears to be a lot of showmanship and mumbo-jumbo. You remember what I said about Mesmer: 'His famous clinic with its lavish furnishing, costly carpets, its strains of music, its mirrors, and Mesmer, dressed in a silk robe, himself officiating with his wand, and, above all, the celebrated *baquet* . . . seemed the height of hocus-pocus – but was it? Might it not, on re-examination, make sense?'

The necessity for this sort of thing would apply particularly in those cases where the low self stubbornly holds on to fixed ideas – the obsession, mild or severe. We all know this condition. In such cases the low self refuses to co-operate because it has not been convinced. It requires something actual and tangible to impress it, something real behind the suggestion.

Such was the Kahuna's treatment of what we would call complexes. They found it was not necessary to search for the original trauma through psycho-analytic dream analysis or any other form of modern psychological technique; all that was necessary was to use the overpowering shock of a large charge of vital force, this charge being accompanied by a logical appeal to the patient's middle or conscious self and the offering of the appropriate suggestion to the low self. This charge was usually put in water. It was charged up by the healer and drunk by the patient. As far as I know, this therapy has not been tried in radiesthetic circles, but any competent psychologist who is also a healer could try it out in a suitable case.

This, presumably, is the rationale of the Electric Convulsion treatment, Insulin Treatment and possibly Leucotomy, and explains their comparative success, except that the force used is unsuitable and far too potent, being rather like using a steam hammer to crack a nut, with the result, as we know, that the low self is partially dissociated, as is shown by the loss of memory.

To sum up in Long's own words, 'the flowing vital force becomes almost human and intelligent in its response to the willed command of the middle self. It will go to the sick part of the patient's body and strengthen it. It will carry the thought forms of suggestion with it when suggestion is given silently. It will do the work better, however, if the suggestion is also given by voice and the low self of the patient made to understand what is being "willed" to happen by way of healing. If the vocal suggestion is made with the aid of physical stimulus, it will be most powerful, whether the stimulus be manipulation, massage, heat, bathing with some healing fluid, or giving some dosage.'

I do not wish to go into the more religious and philosophical aspects of Huna, but I will say a few words about the miracle or instant healing, and also the foretelling of the future.

The Kahunas believed and practised what they believed, that through prayer to the high self, which was conveyed along the aka thread from the low self, the high self would co-operate in instant healing. According to them it was done by the high self, using the high voltage of the vital force or mana dematerializing the injured or diseased parts and then rebuilding or materializing them into the normal. This latter is possible as the shadowy body of the low self is an exact duplication of the physical body, and still exists whether the physical body is there or not, and so forms a sort of mould for the materialization of the normal tissues. Note in this connection Mr Eeman's experiments with missing limbs (Chapter XXV of *Co-operative Healing*), which is a corroboration of the Kahunas contentions. A similar idea will be found in the novel by Beresford, *The Camberwell Miracle*.

There is, however, one essential proviso, viz., to quote Long: 'conditions must be right before healing is granted. There must be no complexed doubt or conviction of sin or guilt, particularly unconscious, that has not been cleared away. What has been called faith is a condition of freedom from any hindering complex or "thing eating inside", as the Kahunas call it.' So it may be necessary before miracle healing is possible to deal first with the complexes along the lines I have already discussed.

In regard to the future, the Kahunas held that the high self of each one of us formed the future, will-nilly, from the plans, desires and, alas, fears of the lower selves. Thus we literally form our future. But under certain conditions it is possible for the high self to remake the future if we are perfectly clear and definite about what we want, can generate sufficient mana and can embody it aright in prayer to the high self. This prayer need not necessarily be conscious or spoken if the middle and low selves are at one, though it helps very considerably if the correct ritual form is conscientiously and regularly carried out.

In this connection and in illustration let me end with the following personal experience which I feel is very relevant as well as thought provoking.

When our second son was about seven years old he developed a temperature which would not come down. I got my partner to attend him but he could find nothing adequate to account for it. When many days had gone past and it was still up he said he thought it would be well to have an ear, nose and throat specialist to see him, to be on the safe side. The specialist duly came down and found nothing, but suggested that it might be well to take the boy into hospital and have him under observation. This seemed a reasonable suggestion, so my wife and I agreed, and everything was arranged.

A little later we were both in the kitchen and my wife, while preparing a salad, was quietly going over the situation and assuring herself that in view of everything it was the right and sensible thing to do, when suddenly, without warning, she fell to the ground. I went to pick her up and asked her what on earth had happened. She said she had had one of her 'feelings', and that it had been so strong that it had thrown her down. I should remark that from time to time my wife had these true intuitions. I say 'true' because she can differentiate them from the false. When she does get one of them it always turns out to be correct. I ignore them at my peril. I asked her what the feeling had been and she said it was to the effect that, if our son went to hospital, and things were left, step by step to the ordinary course of events, he would never come out alive.

I was appalled, and did not know what to do, as all arrangements had been made, and to cancel all without any adequate and reasonable excuse seemed impossible. To say I wanted to call it off because my wife had had a 'feeling' the boy would die if he went to hospital would sound too feeble and crazy for words.

In this crisis I telephoned a friend of mine, a child psychiatrist, to whom I could explain the peculiar situation. He came down, and after an anxious review of the position his advice was that I should let the child go, as in his view we were not committing ourselves.

So my son duly went into hospital, and we tried to reassure ourselves that our fears were groundless and irrational.

Next morning I went up to see him, and I met the specialist, who said that unfortunately our son had now got middle ear trouble and he must puncture the drum. This was done. When I arrived home my wife said: 'There's no need to tell me; I know what's happened. He is worse – events have moved the first step – he will go on getting worse.' And that is exactly what happened.

Next day he was worse, though the Sister had not noticed it until her attention was drawn to it. The specialist was called and said the boy was developing a mastoid, and he would have to operate – the second step had started.

That evening my wife and I anxiously reviewed the whole position, and we came to the conclusion that the meaning of the warning was that, if things were left to take their ordinary course, which usually one would allow them to do (assuming competence on everyone's part) our son would die. Someone had to alter the ordinary course of events from outside the hospital, and I was the only person in a position to do it. I had in effect to pit myself against the whole vast machinery of a modern hospital, and, I may add, it was the hardest thing I have ever done in my life.

I considered what I should have done if I had had charge of the case, and I decided that I would have given a drug invented by McDonagh and called S.U.P.36. So, taking my courage in both hands, I went up to the hospital late at night, and, as Providence would have it, I met the specialist just leaving. I said I wanted the child given a dose. He said it would be quite useless, and showed very clearly he did not like my butting in and thought I was fussing. However, I insisted, and to humour me he gave instructions to have it given, saying he would operate in the morning. Incidentally, the house surgeon had never heard of the drug.

Next morning the boy was much better and our hopes soared. The specialist decided he had been mistaken; but next day the boy was worse again, and by evening he was so bad that he did not even know his mother. The specialist said it was essential to operate, and that right away. Things were again, step by step, taking their dire course, and we were in despair. Indeed, so convinced were we of the outcome that that evening we went through the pangs of bereavement. But I determined to make one last supreme effort. A mutual friend got in touch with McDonagh, told him about the case, and asked for advice. He said that the second dose of S.U.P.36 should have been given 24 hours after the first (as I indeed well knew), and added: 'But never mind. Give another dose tonight, and all will be well.'

Armed with this information I went up to the hospital for a final consultation, in which the specialist, my friend the child psychiatrist and I took part. My friend most skilfully managed to persuade the specialist to wait till morning. In agreeing to this course he said it probably meant signing the child's death warrant, and he would accept no responsibility for the delay. I said I would accept this, provided another dose of S.U.P.36 was given, and I added that, if the child was no better in the morning, he should have his way and operate.

You can imagine my feelings as I went up to the hospital next morning, for to us it was literally a matter of life or death. I was met by the staff nurse with a shining face, and she said: 'Your boy is perfectly all right, only very weak. It is indeed a feather in your cap.'

The specialist, who, I ought to say, was absolutely first class and famed for his diagnostic powers, especially where mastoids were concerned, could not believe it, and had an X-ray taken of the skull. It was completely negative. The child seemed well and normal in every way except for weakness. My only idea was to get him out of the hospital at the earliest possible moment, so I asked for his discharge right away. The specialist objected strongly and rightly from his point of view, seeing how ill the boy had been the night before. I insisted, and he in disgust said: 'Take your damned child away then,' which I thankfully did at once. His recovery was swift and sure.

Whether we were dealing with a miracle or not I do not know, but this dramatic incident taught me that the future can be altered provided that all of three conditions are observed:

1. That the knowledge of the future can be and is obtained.

2. That one believes in the knowledge thus obtained.

3. That one is prepared to act in the way the knowledge requires.

We observed all three conditions and thus altered the future, and, I am convinced, saved our son from death. In the light of Huna it would seem that the knowledge vouchsafed my wife came from her High Self in a flash of power – high mana – but it needed our co-operation for the High Self to remake our son's future from death to life.

CHAPTER NINE

Medical Dowsing in the Light of Huna: The Role of the Low Self in Dowsing

As a result of my study of Huna I felt that here at last might be a possible explanation of the phenomenon of dowsing, an explanation greatly needed. For, in spite of the long and intensive study of dowsing in the last fifty years, no theory has been advanced as to the 'how' of the phenomenon which would seem to cover satisfactorily all of the facts, and in particular to reconcile the two rival schools of thought – the physical and the psychic.

The Huna concepts seem to me to do this and throw a flood of light on the whole subject. The key lies firstly, I think, in the nature and activities of the low self, though the middle and, on rare occasions, the high self, have a vital contribution to make, depending on the conditions and what is required; and secondly in the properties of the mana and its manipulation by the three selves.

As I have already said, when I first came across the idea of Mana and its three forms, I was immediately intrigued, as it seemed to me that once again I had picked up the clue of Vis Medicatrix Naturae, of which mana in all its forms was just another name and aspect. I will not pursue this further, but concentrate on the nature and function of the low self, and see how it throws light on the whole phenomenon of Radiesthesia and in particular on the development of competent and reliable operators of the pendulum.

The low self in Huna, as already explained, is considered a separate and conscious spirit or entity, in the same way as the middle self or the high self though on a lower rung of the evolutionary ladder. It is, to quote Long, 'the servant of the other selves, and is attached to the middle self as a younger brother, and cleaves to it as though they were two parts of a thing which has been glued together'.

He goes on: 'the low self has control of all the various processes of the physical body and of everything except the voluntary

89

muscles. In its aka body it can slide into and out of the physical body. It is in the body as a pencil is in a case. It impregnates every cell and tissue of the body and brain, and its aka body is a mould of every cell and tissue or fluid.

'It and it alone is the seat of the emotions, and this is the reason why the major job of the middle self is to learn to control the low self and prevent it from running off with the man as it so frequently does.

'The low self manufactures all the vital force, or mana, for the use of all three selves. Normally it shares the mana with the middle self (mana-mana), who can use it as "will", but it has complete control of the low mana, or the basic vital force, and of any use of the aka substance of the shadowy body (as, for example, in the form of ectoplasm).

'The low self receives all the sensory impressions through the five senses and presents them to the middle self for explanation, the middle self being the reasoning self which knows what to make of the evidence presented and orders action if need be.'

To make practical use of all this the most important thing, according to Long, is to believe that there is a low self and that it is really there to contact, and then to establish friendly personal relationships with it. 'It is surprising,' he says, 'how rapidly one becomes aware in a strange inward way of the personality and "thereness" of the low self. A spirit of comradeship develops and a new awareness that was never there before.'

But the establishment of this relationship is not necessarily so easy to accomplish as it sounds, for the desire to secure co-operation may indeed fail at this point, either relatively or absolutely or, what may be worse, the low self may become perverse and 'play up' the middle self. But usually failure is due to three main causes:

1. A sense of guilt or sin on the part of the low self.
2. A fixation or complex or a whole group of them.
3. A lack of faith.

In Huna there is no sin other than the hurt of another human being, physically, emotionally or spiritually. You cannot sin against the high self, and so you cannot be forgiven in this way. Forgiveness can only come from the person wronged, and this may be a very hard thing to obtain.

Only the middle self can sin, i.e. know right and wrong, but the low self can acquire 'conscience' once it has received from the middle self a training in what is apparently right or wrong, and, once received, it holds on to this with tenacity whether it is in fact true or not; hence the complex or fixation.

A fixation can be defined as a memory plus a charge of mana in the unconscious, accessible to the low self but not to the middle self. A burden is a load of fixations,* at the heaviest a cross to bear. There are three degrees of fixation:

1. Slight; this may be resolved by oneself with the help of the high self.

2. Middle degree; such fixations require the assistance of another sympathetic person to unravel, as the condition is beyond help by oneself; hence the expression 'sharing one another's burdens'. This outside help takes various forms, e.g. psycho-analysis, dianetics, myognosis, etc., but all have for their aim three things: (a) to bring up and recover the memory from the un-conscious; (b) to rationalize it by (c) releasing the charge of mana attached to it; unless this last is done there is no release. The Kahunas called this 'the draining or drying out of mana from a memory-cluster-fixation'.

3. Severe degree; this may take the form of obsession, possession, insanity, etc. Here desperate measures are needed to rescue the patient. The Kahunas used shock treatment by conveying large charges of mana to the sick person, and it is possible that our modern E.C.T. and insulin treatment acts in the same way.

The question of the lack of faith involves the nature of faith. Let me quote Long: 'Belief on the part of the middle self is not enough. That alone is not faith. Only when the low self also believes is there genuine and workable faith. This is simply a different way of saying that if the low self has a fixation or even slightly complexed (stubbornly held) belief which is contrary to the one held at the moment by the middle self, the low self will refuse to co-operate.' This is what is meant by saying that a person

---

* Cf. Bunyan's opening description of Christian in *Pilgrim's Progress* – 'I saw a man . . . and a great burden on his back,' which he did not get rid of until he came to the Cross. 'So I saw in my dream that, just as Christian came up to the Cross, his burden loosed from his shoulders and fell from off his back . . . and a Shining One said to him': 'Thy sins are forgiven thee." ' See also p. 144.

may be intellectually free but emotionally bound – a very common condition. It also throws light on that well-known saying: 'Ye shall know the truth and the truth shall set you free.'

A true thing from the Huna point of view is one correctly and accurately thought of with the middle self reason. It is a memory fully rationalized. When a false conception is formed by the low self and made into a secret memory, it is the reverse of 'true', but, if the fixation memories can be dug up from the 'secret pit' of the low self and rationalized so that their correct meaning can be clearly seen, then one knows the truth and is set free of the bondage to the things of 'darkness' in the unconscious.

If one can surmount all these difficulties and become sufficiently rational and free and thereby secure friendly co-operation from the low self, one can proceed to the next step, which is to begin to train and educate the low self and in particular to train it to act on its own. This definitely requires training as in ordinary life. The low self is, to quote Long: 'completely responsive to the wishes of the middle self (unless there is a fixation or complex) and is only too anxious to serve the middle self in every way . . . it is endlessly faithful and eager,' and so without training in independence it will produce the answers that it thinks you want or, indeed, that you would like, to your great undoing.

Long found that the use of the pendulum* was the best method of training the low self in this independence, as we have, he says, 'in this method, owing to the fact that the involuntary muscles are used, a way of setting the low self free to make up its own mind about what its answer to a question will be, and then to make it known to the middle self by certain swings of the pendulum,' i.e. the convention of communication which must obviously be established and agreed before one can proceed further.

The next step is to instruct the low self in the sort of facts and data required, i.e. it must be correctly briefed. At this point the nature and character of the middle self is of great importance.

---

* 'The pendulum, because of its simplicity and because it can swing in various ways, has always been a favourite crutch to help the low self to tell his conscious mind what he has learnt when instructed to make a psychic investigation of something, be it underground water, minerals, or the condition of organs hidden in the body.'

For, given a trained, responsive and co-operative low self, to brief it correctly requires a middle self with intelligence, knowledge, imagination, experience, integrity, as only so can the right questions be asked and as a result the right answers obtained. This is probably the reason why a good radiesthetist does not like 'working blind'.

The low self is enabled to ascertain the information required by means of certain native faculties or abilities which are little understood at present but may be described as follows, and I quote Long abbreviated:

'1. The ability to sense "radiations" or emanations from things, objects and substances when these radiations are of such a nature that they are not registered by the usual organs of sense.

'2. The ability to fasten to a person or thing, with which contact has once been made, an invisible thread of aka or ectoplasmic substance of the shadowy body of the low self. Once such a contact has been made and an aka thread established, this thread is more or less permanent, and the low self has the faculty of reaching out a projection or finger of its aka body substance to follow the connecting thread and so make contact with whatever is at the end. Each time this is done the thread becomes stronger, more permanent and easier to follow.

'3. This aka finger can carry with it a portion of the aka duplications of the organs of sense and so can use all the senses to get impressions of the things contacted, and these sensory impressions, in the form more of memories, can be sent back and presented to the middle self for interpretation.' Or this process can be reversed and impressions sent the other way in the form of 'thought forms' – this, according to Long, is telepathy.

Let us now see what, according to Huna, happens when we dowse. We will assume a well trained co-operative low self and an experienced, intelligent and knowledgeable middle self, in other words, a good and reliable dowser or radiesthetist using some form of dowsing instrument or pendulum. In all cases, no matter what instrument is used, the idea is to furnish the low self with some mechanical means through which it can report its feelings to the middle self. Of course, for one who has sufficient psychic skill and training, it is possible to sense water under ground without the use of a rod or pendulum, but this is exceptional, and not the usual practice.

Let us take water divining first, the diviner using a divining rod. On taking the rod in one's hand with the intention of dowsing, immediately the combined aka substance and mana flow into the rod, and there under the direction of the mind of the low self exhibits its characteristic of acting as a living intelligent substance and force. Cameron, the great American dowser, spoke of this as 'throwing into it an auric charge'.

In this connection the article in *Radio-Perception* of June 1955 on 'Early Experiments with the Pendulum', as carried out by J. O. N. Rutter, makes interesting reading. The pendulum was suspended by a single thread of unspun silk from a horizontal arm of brass which was firmly attached to a rigid upright. When the upright was touched by the operator or other sensitive the pendulum gyrated. He made eighteen experiments in various ways on the different substances, and finally concluded his account with these words: 'Whether the motions of a pendulum, produced in the manner I have been describing, be truly and entirely electrical, or whether they be of a mixed character partly dependent on vitality and partly on electricity and which cannot be dissociated, is more than I will undertake to decide.' In the light of Huna he came very near the truth, and indeed it is difficult to understand how the pendulum, as he had arranged it, could move unless the effect of touching it was to activate it with aka substance and a mana charge.

Everything is now orientated towards what is being sought. In the case of water it is such a well-known substance that no sample is needed, but in other cases, presumably, the sample or witness is an objective method of briefing the low self.

The exact mechanism after this is not very clear; it may be that the emanation from the water is contacted and indicated by the movement of the rod, and once contact is made an aka finger can then reach the actual water and record depth, quantity, quality, etc., which information can again be passed back to the middle self by the agreed convention. Or direct contact is made with the water at once, as we know that the low self can penetrate coverings and investigate what is underneath.

In the case of the medical dowser the pendulum is activated in the same way, and then contact is made with the patient by means of a witness, usually a blood spot. It will be noted that a good radiesthetist will always swing his pendulum over the blood spot at the beginning of an analysis to make this contact.

Contact having been made, the low self is in effect asked a series of questions by means of the various witnesses, and from the answers a picture of the condition of the patient is gradually built up.

One can assume either that the blood spot contains all that is in the patient, that is to say, it is a sort of microcosm, which is the usual assumption, or, alternatively, that the blood spot is the end of an aka thread stretching back to the patient wherever he may be, and that the low self by means of an aka finger can project itself along the aka thread to the patient and thus collect information; in other words, it divines, and this includes the correct treatment as well as the diagnosis. The divination obviously depends on (a) the degree of co-operation of the low self, (b) the nature and extent of its training, (c) the nature of the briefing given it by the middle self, and (d) whether once briefed it is allowed to work entirely independently and on its own without interference from the conscious mind.

There remains the interpretation of the information obtained, and this obviously depends on the intellectual quality and integrity of the middle self. For false conclusions can be arrived at as easily by misinterpretation of the data, or an acceptance of them on their face value, as by wrong facts.

One tremendous advance in technique from mere communication was the introduction of measurement, so that an answer was not just yes or no or doubtful but an answer in figures as in the Bovis Biometer or, in its more advanced state, in degrees positively or negatively distant from a norm as in the techniques using the protractor.

This use of measurement opens up a new vast field of investigation. The late Dr Brunler, for example, increased the Bovis scale from 100 to 1000, and in this way he was able, using the pendulum and this revised convention, to measure the consciousness, the level of intelligence, the personality and the character. He went further and found that he could get readings from the great men of the past. To quote Long: 'Testing things they had left behind them, MSS, paintings, statues in marble and stone, he found that a signature on a letter, document or painting carried in some mysterious way the same radiation as its maker, living or long dead. This puzzling matter was never satisfactorily explained, except in terms of the aka thread, which allows the low self of the operator to "stick out a finger", follow the thread and make contact with the writer of the signature, be he alive or long dead and "in spirit"' (cf. Mrs Kingsley Tarpey's work on picture radiations).

Later on, Long, working with Cameron, who was using his aurameter, which is a pendulum acting horizontally instead of vertically, found that every signature had a definite aura 'which is as individual and unmistakable as a finger-print'. In Huna terminology 'the signature has an aka body which can only be accounted for by supposing that some of the abundant aka substance of the low self of the writer is fastened to the writing and remains there'.*

In regard to treatment, the determination of the appropriate treatment follows the same general lines as already laid down for ascertaining the diagnosis, i.e. the nature of the diseased condition, only in reverse; the one being as easy or as difficult as the other. In so-called 'broadcasting' it is probable that we have the same aka mechanism at work. If we suppose that the medicines have aka bodies, especially when in potentized form, the aka body material of the medicines will be carried on the mana flow over the aka threads from the blood spot to the body of the one being treated, the greater attracting the lesser, which is a general law of the pre-matter energies.

How are we to reconcile these conceptions with those so ably stated by Mr Maby in his preliminary report of ten years' research published in the June 1955 issue of *Radio-Perception* under the heading of 'Instrumental Recording of Radionic Fields'?

There can be no doubt, I think, that we must accept the fact that we have definite physical forces operating in dowsing. There have, of course, always been the two schools of thought on the subject; those who think it can all be explained by the ordinary

* See *Psychometric Analysis* by Max Freedom Long (Huna Research Publications).

laws of physics – the physical school, e.g. Madame Maury in her book *How to Dowse*, says, 'what interests us at present is the physical or, as one may say, the material form, and the possibility of putting it to real use and reducing it to a system' – and those who think it can only be explained mentally – the mental or psychic school. There have been abundant facts to support both sides, but the conclusion has been gaining ground of late that both may be right – but how? Huna, I think, may supply the answer, as it certainly deals with phenomena in both worlds. We must in fact assume that we are dealing with two different orders of energies, but which are in correspondence and operate in this way. Progress in understanding will come from an acceptance of this fact, and with research to disentangle the physical from the mental and indeed from the psychic and vice versa. In this way it will be possible to build up a science, as well as an art, of Dowsing and Radiesthesia from a basic understanding of the true nature of the facts and their inter relationship, particularly their correspondence.

The foregoing Huna material was written in 1954, and it seemed true at that time; but subsequent work has shown that there is one most important consideration to be taken into account when one is using ancient magical systems such as Huna. This is that, unless one takes into consideration the shift in the level of consciousness which has taken place in the last two thousand years as a result of the coming of Christianity, unless there is a 'renewal of the mind' in the Christian sense, systems such as Huna become atavistic, leading to various dangers, one of which is error in result.

That this is so, and is, indeed, such an insidious danger, may well appear strange, but I think all conscientious workers in this supersensory field of science would agree that such a consideration has to be taken into account if error is to be avoided. At the same time, if this is allowed for fully, then Huna is quite invaluable in radiesthetic research.

I shall have more to say about this in the chapter on 'The Radiesthetic Faculty'.

CHAPTER TEN

The Healing Miracles of Christ

From the first I had always felt that a study of the healing miracles of Christ in the light of our new knowledge would be most instructive and rewarding and enable us to get some idea of the modus operandi, as here we had the supreme example of the use of Vis Medicatrix Naturae by a Master Healer.

I decided therefore to study the miracles and see if there was any correspondence between our new knowledge and what is reputed to have happened.

As a result of this study I was able to give a preliminary talk on the subject. So fruitful was it to an understanding of much that had been obscure that I gave the talk again later in an expanded form. Here it is:

Probably more has been spoken on this and on kindred subjects in the last thousand years than almost anything else, and it would seem that everything that can be said has already been said ad nauseam. What then can I hope to add to the mass of exposition, assertion, bigotry and controversy? Surprisingly, quite a lot, even though most of it must be very tentative at this stage of our knowledge.

I found that the approach to the miracles has so far taken one of four forms:

1. The traditional theological. According to this view, the miracles are a manifestation of supernatural powers due to the divinity of Christ, and because of this they are unique, and it is sacrilege to question or investigate them. The miracle constitutes the chief claim of Christianity to be a supernatural religion. An unorthodox subsection are credulous spiritualists.

2. The traditional rationalistic. The miracles are now discussed as coincidences of naturally occurring events, or as fairy tales, which never happened; in fact, purely mythical embodiments of Christian doctrine: e.g. Hume maintained that no evidence, such as is available, can make a miracle credible.

Paulus dismisses the miracles as exaggerations and misapprehensions of quite ordinary events.

Harnack is of the unalterable conviction that what happens in space and time is subject to the universal laws of movement and that accordingly there cannot be any miracle in this sense, i.e. as interruptions of the continuity of nature.

Huxley was more cautious in that he recognized that we do not know the continuity of nature so thoroughly as to be able to declare that this or that event is necessarily an interruption of it.

A subsection of the rationalists maintain that the miracles were exaggeration of ordinary medical treatment; that Christ was a sort of medicine-man, having all the medical skill of the Essenes and that he used their remedies. Vinturini suggests the disciples carried around a portable medicine chest.

3. Faith healing. The contention here is that all the sick persons were cases of functional disorders occurring in neurotics and hysterics, and therefore open to cure by powerful suggestion, such as is conveyed by the words 'Thy faith hath made thee whole.' The result would necessarily be transitory.

4. The psychological approach is admirably voiced by Stanley Hall in the chapter on Miracles in his book *Jesus the Christ in the Light of Psychology*. He is willing to accept the miracles provided they are regarded as symbolic of higher truths. To regard them as literally veridical he considers evidence of an immature religious attitude, necessary maybe, but to be outgrown. For, in his view, genetic analytic psychology, while revealing the inner meaning and high value which the miracles enshrine, at the same time denies them any objective reality.

Maurice Nicoll takes a similar point of view in his book *The New Man*, as for him, too, the miracles are not actual objective healings, but symbolic dramas of the New Truth and Way of Life.

In other words, modern psychology sublimates the crude miracles right away! And yet I am sure that Stanley Hall sincerely thought psychology had said the last word.

But, as we now know, it had not. Even with our present knowledge I dare to assert that miracles have an objective, and not simply a symbolic, reality. We are living in an age when what seemed impossible to our ancestors and immediate predecessors has become possible. We are dealing with new concepts, new forms, new forces, as we are all becoming increasingly aware.

There should thus be a fifth attitude – the true scientific attitude – which is out to ascertain the *facts*, and, if possible, the modus operandi.

A book recently published (1957) is an excellent example of this scientific approach. It is entitled *Modern Miraculous Cures – a documented account of miracles and medicine in the twentieth century*. The authors are Dr François Leuret, who was for many years the President of the Medical Bureau and Scientific Studies of Lourdes, and Dr Henri Bon, the author of many medical works.

The full and detailed clinical data are not only impressive but convincing, for it was Pope Benedict XIV who laid it down that, unless a cure fulfilled *simultaneously* all seven of the following conditions, it was not to be considered a miracle (and here I quote):

1. The disease must be serious and impossible, or at least very difficult, to cure.

2. The disease must not have reached a stage at which it was liable to disappear shortly of its own accord.

3. No medical treatment must have been applied, or, if it were, it must certainly have been ineffectual.

4. The cure must be sudden, instantaneous.

5. The cure must be complete.

6. It must not be preceded by any crisis due to natural causes at the expected times; otherwise, the cure, far from being miraculous, must be considered either wholly or partially as natural.

7. Finally, there must be no relapse into the same disease after the cure.

'There can, of course, be true miracles which do not fulfil one or other of these conditions. But while the possibility of less complete miracles is not denied, it must be emphasized that they are not accepted officially, so insistent is the Church on signs which are exact, easily recognizable and leaving no loophole for error.'

Let us now come straight to the miracles, and see what we can make of them in the light of our new knowledge. It may be little enough, but it will be something.

The first thing that struck me was that, in general, the records must be authentic; they read like records of actual happenings, very remarkable and wonderful happenings, but the internal evidence makes them ring true, because in our very lesser ways we too have had experience of what is recorded. You will see what I mean as we go along.

In the second place, a new definition of a miracle is suggested as follows: A miracle in acute disease is the operation of the normal processes, restoring normality, speeded up until the time element is completely eliminated. In chronic or incurable disease it is the restarting of the normal processes of regeneration, restoring normality (this involves, certainly at present, unknown biological laws), speeded up until the time element is completely eliminated.

It follows from this definition that there is every gradation of healing from the ordinary to the miraculous, according to the acceleration in time. Or, to put it another way, the healing processes are speeded up to such a degree that, instead of happening in sequence, the whole thing becomes instantaneous.

Thirdly, it is clear that, lacking careful diagnostic data, we cannot claim that all the miracles are in fact miracles. The Faith-healing School may well be right that a large number were purely functional and not organic diseases, though functional diseases are not common among primitive people. But we need not be troubled about this, as the carefully attested records of Lourdes and other places show, as I have already pointed out, that true miracles do take place, and that, while a large number may be functional, a small but impressive number are not.

Before examining the miracles in detail I want to draw attention to a fact which is generally overlooked, viz. that the Gospels record healing done on a large and wholesale scale by Christ. The work was by no means done only on special or isolated occasions, as this passage from Matt. IV.23 and 24, clearly shows: 'And Jesus went about all Galilee teaching in their synagogues and preaching the gospel of the kingdom, and healing all manner of sickness and all manner of disease among the people.

'And his fame went throughout all Syria: and they brought unto him all sick people that were taken with divers diseases and torments, and those which were possessed with devils, and those which were lunatic, and those that had the palsy; and he healed them.'

It is interesting to note that most of the healing work was done during the earlier part of the ministry. After Christ left Galilee and went south there is very little healing or, at least, any record of it.

There are one or two comments I should like to make on the above passage and similar ones, recording mass healings.

Firstly, is there any connection between the manifestation of healing power and the huge crowds, so that Christ's already stupendous powers were raised to the nth degree so that he was able to heal anyone? Evidently there is some connection. The one religious body which includes healing in its ordinary services, the Elim Four Square Gospelers, employ the technique of working up the emotional tension of the congregation to a high level before the healing starts. One can say, of course, that all that is done is to employ mass suggestion. This, of course, is true up to a point, but there is something else, and this, I think, is shown clearly by Eeman's co-operative healing technique – the more people in the relaxation circuit, the easier and quicker the healing; in other words, there is more mana.

Also there is this observation which wants following up: My wife once took the physical and psychic measurement of a sensitive and healer before he went to speak to a large open-air meeting, and again on his return. The physical measurement was down half an inch but the psychic was up on the Bovis scale. This is most interesting, for it is quite possible that the healing measurement (Benham's No. 6)* would have been found to have increased if it had been taken.

Secondly, does the time of day make any difference?

The following passage is found in Matthew, Mark and Luke, and is a most meaningful narrative:

'At even, *when the sun did set*, they brought unto him all that were sick with divers diseases and many that were possessed of devils, and he cast out the spirits with his word and laid his hands upon them that were sick and healed them.' I am suggesting that

* See *Radiesthesia III*, p. 52.

the power is at the maximum at sunset, and, if also there was a large crowd, the healing power would then be at its most potent. The reason for this is an observation made by Reichenbach that the odylic activity of the human body has a periodic fluctuation, being at a maximum between 6–8 p.m., and at a minimum at dawn from 4–5 a.m. He also found that taking food, daylight and the active waking state also increased it. As far as I know, no one has ever followed up these most interesting observations.

Thirdly, are there any conditions which diminish or inhibit the power?

We are apt to think of Christ's healing power as being un-limited and unconditioned, as presumably it is, but listen to the following:

'And he went from hence and came unto his own country . . . and began to teach . . . and many hearing him were astonished saying . . . Is not this the carpenter, the son of Mary? . . . and they were offended at him. . . . And Jesus said unto them "A prophet is not without honour save in his own country." . . . And he could do there no mighty work, save that he laid his hands upon a few sick people and healed them.'

What a contrast!

This phenomenon is well known in psychic research. A hostile scepticism will diminish or render the manifestation of psychic power impossible, a state which the critics then claim as a de-monstration that there was nothing in the proceedings. I have no doubt that Christ's neighbours said that it was quite clearly demonstrated that he was an impostor, as he could in fact 'do no mighty work' – all his fame was a lot of ballyhoo.

I think this is the place to discuss briefly the question of faith which crops up continually in this question of healing. It is usually claimed that one must believe before a cure is possible. I will not say that it does not help, but I am sure it is not an indispensable condition of healing. Lack of *conscious* faith makes no difference to the healing taking place. As long as there is no actively hostile scepticism the power will work, faith or no faith. I am clear my-self that, in spite of phrases like 'Thy faith hath made thee whole,' the healing is not a pure faith cure; far from it. Indeed, I see that one eminent commentator suggested that the faith that was manifest in these cases was a *result* of the miracle and not the cause.

With this introduction, let us come to the miracles themselves.

I have classified them for my purpose in the following groupings:

Healing by 1. Touch only
2. Touch with physical accessories (saliva, clay and washing)
3. Touch and the word of command
4. The word of command
5. Casting out of 'unclean spirits'
6. Touching his garment
7. By direction
8. At a distance
9. Raising the dead
10. Power to others

1. *Touch only*

We have six instances of this; five are miracles and one is not.

a. Two blind men: 'Then he touched their eyes, saying: "According to your faith be it unto you." And their eyes were opened.'

b. Two blind men: 'He had compassion on them, and immediately their eyes received sight.'

c. Servant of the High Priest. 'One of them smote the servant of the high priest and cut off his ear, and He touched his ear and healed him.'

d. Man with dropsy. 'And He took him and healed him and let him go.'

e. Woman with spirit of infirmity (osteoarthritis case?). 'And behold there was a woman with a spirit of infirmity eighteen years and was bound together and could in no way lift herself up. Jesus said: "Woman, thou art loosed from thy infirmity," and he laid his hands on her and immediately she was made straight.'

f. Children, presumably normal, fit and well. 'Then they brought him little children that he should put his hands upon them and pray, and he laid his hands upon them.'

Here we are on fairly familiar ground – the ground of the 'Healing Hand'. All down through the ages it has been known that healing could come by 'the laying on of hands', and, indeed, the Church with its 'Sacrament of Unction' has made it an integral part of its ritual. It is here combined with anointing with oil – a most significant combination. For we know that various substances can be charged with the healing force, e.g. cotton, silk, wood, and, above all, oil, which is the reason, presumably, why oil 'has ever been regarded as the aptest symbol and vehicle of the holy and illuminating spirit'. The formula for preparation and consecration of the oil was as follows: Holding the vessel containing the oil between the two hands, the following prayer is made: 'Send forth, O Lord, we beseech thee, thy Holy Spirit, the Advocate, from heaven into this fatness of oil, which thou has deigned to bring forth out of the green wood for the refreshing of mind and spirit; and through thy holy benediction may it be for all who anoint with it, taste it, touch it, a safeguard of mind and body, of soul and spirit, for the expulsion of all pains, of every infirmity, of every sickness of mind and body.' Note Mark VI.13: 'And they (the disciples) anointed with oil many that were sick and healed them.'

But in course of time two curious things have happened: the rite is now only used for the dying – Extreme Unction, and it is thought that the power is only spiritual, the use of oil and the laying on of hands being simply a symbolic act. Thus it is believed that only the ordained clergy can perform it and make it work.

This restricted belief still holds, even though a great revival of interest has arisen in recent years in what is called 'Spiritual Healing', though the various organizations which employ it are not quite sure what they mean by 'spiritual healing'. For example, the spiritualistic Spirit Healers think the healing is done by spirits, the Christian Scientists by complete and absolute faith in the healing power of God.

But there are a few who are aware that 'the laying on of hands' is not simply a symbolic act but that actual power does in fact pass from healer to patient. This fact may well account for the difference between a good nurse and a bad nurse, and why some masseurs are so much better than others with greater technical skill; and the same applies to osteopaths. There is also the observation that a healer by holding a piece of meat or fish between his hands can mummify it so that it is immune to putrifaction, and remains so.

2. Touch with physical accessories

This is a very interesting group, for in Huna terms the accessories might well be claimed as being a means of impressing the Low Self.

a. Blind man. Christ took him by the hand and led him out of the town, spat on his eyes and put his hands upon them and then asked him whether he saw ought – 'Men walking as trees.' After that he put his hands again upon his eyes and made him look up: 'and he was restored and saw every man clearly.'

The interesting points here are (1) the use of saliva, which is one of the three fluids of the body which contain all the forces of the body; the other two being the blood and the urine; (2) the fact that the cure was not instantaneous – there is a definite time element.

b. Man blind from birth. Christ spat on the ground and made clay with the spittle and anointed the eyes of the man with the clay. 'Go wash in the pool of Siloam'. 'He went his way and washed and came seeing.'

Here again we have the use of saliva but this time combined with clay, which as we know radiesthetically, corrects faults in the external field of the Etheric body. Also, there is again this time element, but a longer delay than in the previous miracle. Note, too, the washing. It is well known in occult circles that washing will get rid of the disease-laden auric forces. Hence the washing of one's hands after a treatment.

The sequel of this miracle, as narrated in John IX, is worth reading in full as giving the typical reaction of sceptics who could not or would not admit any supersensible event; equally applicable today.

c. Deaf and dumb man. Here again we have the use of saliva: 'He put his fingers in his ears, and He spit and touched his tongue. And looking up to heaven he sighed (the only other time this is recorded is in the raising of Lazarus) and said: "Be opened!"

And straightway his ears were opened and the string of his tongue was loosened and he spake plain.' It is possible that sighing here meant deep breathing, in order to accumulate mana.

3. Touch and the word of command

a. The leper. ' "Lord, if thou wilt thou canst make me clean," and Jesus put forth his hand and touched him, saying: "Be thou clean," and immediately his leprosy was cleansed.'

b. Peter's mother-in-law – sick of a fever. 'And he stood over her and rebuked the fever, and took her by the hand and lifted her up, and immediately the fever left her.'

c. The nobleman's daughter ⎫ See classification No. 9.
d. The widow's son ⎭

4. The Word of Command

Here the healing appears to be done simply by the word of command, with no physical contact or laying on of hands.

a. Man sick of a palsy. This is recorded in Luke v. 18–20, and should be read in full, as it raises a very important question – no less than: what is the nature of this healing? I might add that the question arises in the modern miracles as recorded in Dr Leuret's book *Modern Miraculous Cures* (Peter Davies).

It is clear from several passages that Christ was quite clear about it, viz. that it was a manifestation of the power of God; the healings were to the glory of God; and that this power not only healed physically but healed on *all planes*. Hence the meaning of the query: "Whether it is easier to say "Thy sins be forgiven thee" (i.e. the fixations and complexes are resolved), or to say: "Arise, take up thy bed and walk." '

It is very evident that with this power we are dealing with something which heals the *whole* man, with a healer of the complete personality, and by healing at a fundamental level the physical healing also takes place. This is where the religious people are right in invoking spiritual healing; they are right in what they assert, and wrong in what they deny.

This fundamental healing was known to all the great physicians, as, for example, Paracelsus. He was well acquainted with the pattern of illness, the occult development of a sin (that is, a weakness of the Ego) and the line it pursues until it materializes in a material or physical expression, whether an acute infection or a chronic disease. This will not appear to us as so strange as it did to our predecessors, as psychosomatic medicine has shown quite clearly that certain illnesses are associated with definite character make-ups.

I will not say more here on these deep matters but just add this: that, according to Paracelsus, this fundamental healing cannot take place unless it is what he calls the Hour-in-Time. 'God hath created the medicines for prevailing over sickness, likewise hath he created Leeches for the same, yet doth he withhold these from the sick man until it be the Hour-in-Time: then do Nature and Art go their ways, but, mind ye! not before it be that the time hath come.'

Evidently with the man sick of a palsy it was the Hour-in-Time.

Wolfram in his book *The Occult Causes of Disease* in a commentary on this says: 'When and where can disease pass over into health? The answer is this: Only when the Ego has acquired those capabilities, the want of which was evinced in the disease, and then is the Hour of Time!'

Failure to acquire those capabilities is probably the fundamental reason why some patients, in spite of all treatments, never get well.

b. Man with a withered hand: ' "Stretch forth thy hand." And he stretched it forth and it was restored whole like the other.'

c. Man with infirmity thirty-five years. Could not get in the pool. ' "Wilt thou be made whole?" . . . "Rise take up thy bed and walk," and immediately the man was made whole,' and later: 'Behold thou art made whole, sin no more, lest a worse thing come to thee.'

5. *Casting out of unclean spirits by the word of command*

This is something outside our modern experience as it is no longer scientific, thanks to modern psychology, to believe in either evil spirits or spirit possession. But I wonder, with the shocking, wanton 'inhuman' murders of recent times, whether we are as wise as we like to think we are.

Chapter XVI in *The Secret Science behind Miracles*, entitled

'How the Kahunas fought the horrid things of darkness', will repay careful reading and studying in this connection; the Kahuna method of shock treatment by the use of large quantities of mana transferred to the possessed or insane person together with the appropriate suggestion might well be used in modern therapeutics, given a sufficiently powerful healer.

There are only five of the miracles, and the usual explanation is that they were all on epileptics.

a. The man with the legion of spirits
b. The demoniac child
c. Man with unclean spirit
d. The dumb demoniac
e. Blind and dumb demoniac

Of the last two all we know is that the devils were cast out and the sufferers were healed. With the others the main point is that the evil spirit or spirits immediately recognized Christ as the Son of God – the one with supersensible knowledge and authority. Christ's reaction to this was to rebuke them and command them to come out. In the first case the command was: 'Come out of the man thou unclean spirits' ('My name is Legion; for we are many') and they went out – and into the swine. In the second: ' "Thou dumb and deaf spirit I charge thee come out of him," and the spirit cried out and rent him sore, and came out of him, and he was as one dead.' And the third: ' "Hold thy peace and come out of him." And when the unclean spirit had torn him and cried out with a loud voice he came out of him.'

There is a point in the case of the demoniac child which needs comment. You will remember that the disciples had tried and failed, and after Christ had succeeded they asked him why they could not do it. And he said: 'Because of your unbelief. If ye had faith as a grain of mustard seed, nothing shall be impossible to you.' It would appear from this that the healer must have implicit faith in his power. If he doubts, the power fails. I think this may be made a little clearer by a great saying of Paracelsus: 'Resolute imagination can accomplish all things,' which means that if it is possible to hold absolutely steady and clear-cut in the imagination whatever is desired, then, imagination being actively creative, the thing will come to pass. So that, if a sick person were imagined in this way as hale and whole, then he would become hale and whole.*

6. *Touching his garment*

Here we come to miracles which are especially interesting radiesthetically, as we know that fabrics can be charged or impregnated with the power, and, once impregnated, the power remains, apparently undiminished. Mrs Kingsley Tarpey, the healer, used regularly to charge bandages, wool and silk, which she would hand or send to patients so that they could have treatments independently of her bodily presence.

And, if this can be done by ordinary healers, how much more must the garments of a supremely powerful healer such as Christ have been saturated with His power, so that the following passages are quite explicable.

'And the whole multitude sought to touch him for

power went forth from him
there went virtue out of him } and healed them all.

'And whithersoever he entered into villages, or cities or country, they laid the sick in the streets and besought Him that they might touch if it were only the hem of his garment; and as many as touched it were made perfectly whole.'

One miracle of this sort is recorded in detail, viz. the woman with an issue of blood for twelve years, Mark v.25-34; and the account rings true, as I have had experience of just such minor miracles.

7. *By direction*

a. Ten lepers. 'Jesus, Master have mercy on us.' – ' "Go show yourselves unto the priests." And it came to pass that, as they went, they were cleansed.' Only one, it will be remembered, came back to thank Jesus.

b. Blind man. 'Go wash in the pool of Siloam.' Again the healing by washing.

* Compare Dr Hector Munro's technique described in *Radiesthesia IV*, p. 41.

8. *Healing at a distance*

 a. Centurian's servant sick of a palsy. The faith of the master.
 b. The Syrophoenician's daughter, vexed with a devil.
 c. The Nobleman's son, sick unto death.

In each case he did not see or go near the sick person, but simply said it was all right. These miracles are explicable on the Huna theory of telementation, a healing method used by modern healers.

In the case of (*a*) it was: ' "Go thy way, and as thou hast believed, so be it done unto thee." And his servant was healed in that self same hour.' With (*b*): ' "O woman great is thy faith, be it unto thee even as thou wilt." And her daughter was made whole from that very hour.' And with (*c*): 'Go thy way, thy son liveth.' On inquiry as to when the son had begun to mend: ' "Yesterday at the seventh hour the fever left him," so the father knew it was at the same hour in which Jesus said: "Thy son liveth." '

9. *Raising from the Dead*

 a. Jairus's daughter. *Luke* VIII, 41–56. *Matthew* IX, 18–26
 b. The Widow of Nain's son. *Luke* VII, 12–16
 c. Lazarus. *John* XI, 1–46.

In previous editions of this book I said that with our present knowledge, these miracles are too difficult for us to understand; but as later, I have come in contact with the spiritual science of Rudolph Steiner, this difficulty has been overcome, as it is evident we are here dealing with the special factors of Karma, Initiation and Reincarnation, an increasing knowledge of which throws a flood of light on these supreme miracles of Jesus Christ, as the Lord of Karma.*

All we could say with our existing knowledge was that according to Huna, as long as the Aka thread was intact, joining the etheric body to the physical, the etheric (or life body) the astral (soul) and the ego bodies could depart from the physical body, in which case the physical body would appear to have no life, but the other subtle bodies could return at any time. But if the Aka thread was broken,

*Karma is the sum of a person's actions in one of his states of successive existence, viewed as deciding his fate in the next. In other words we ourselves make our future Karma, for good or ill.

it would require an act of the High Self to restore it – in other words, a miracle. Max Freedom Long gives an example of a drowned youth brought back to life after being 'dead' for eight hours (Chapter XII of *The Secret Science*).

a. Let us take first the miracle of the Raising of Jairus's Daughter. It is suggested we are only dealing here with a state of trance which, according to Stanley Hall, is quite common with the onset of puberty: 'Modern literature abounds with death-like trances and swoons at this epoch and all that Christ did was to bring her out of it.' But according to the narrative the people around her did not think so, for when Christ said "The damsel is not dead, but sleepeth" they laughed him to scorn, knowing she was dead.

For the true explanation of all the occult factors involved, I would refer my readers to that given in Emil Brock's book *The Three Years* p 151 – 152, because the woman with the issue of blood which she had had, in spite of all treatment, for twelve years – but was now healed by touching the hem of the robe of Christ on his way to Jairus's daughter – is also involved. Brock explains how her unsolved Karma had a vital relationship to the twelve year old girl. The woman's healing, physically and karmically, now made possible the girl's miracle of healing from initiation death in a former life. The actual technique used by Christ, as recorded in the gospels, is very interesting.

b. Similarly, the widow of Nain's son's case is usually explained as a case of cataleptic trance. Here again we are dealing with a mystic death in the course of an initiation in a former life, repeated again in his adolescence in his present life, from which he was released by Christ, moved by compassion at this repetition of a former karmic death. The technique was again simple, Christ came and touched the bier but not, apparently, the dead youth, and when the bearers had come to a stop there was heard the hierophantic command, (the 'initiation command') – "Young man I say unto thee arise" and he that was dead sat up and began to speak. (See Emil Brock's *The Three Years* for a full explanation of this miracle, pages 5 and 6).

c. Lazarus. This is the most profound and remarkable of these miracles of raising from the dead and the account in *St. John's Gospel* should be read very carefully and thoughtfully as every word is important and significant. See *St. John's Gospel*, Chapter XI 1 – 46.

Here again are the three factors of Karma, Initiation and Reincarnation; for a full spiritual comment and explanation of the miracle see *The Gospel of St. John,* Chap VIII pages 112–13, *Christianity as a Mystical Tract* Chap VIII, both books by Rudolf Steiner; also *The Three Years* by Emil Brock pages 156, 7, 8 and 9; and *The Raising of Lazarus* by John Cornish. For a general account of Steiner's life and work, see *A Scientist of the Invisible* by Canon Shepherd.

Christ's delay in going to the rescue of his friend, a delay that is so puzzling, is now seen to have been so that the initiation sleep of three days could be completed. Nevertheless, Christ as the hierophant was deeply affected as he twice groaned in spirit and wept; but coming to the tomb, acting as the hierophant, he cried in a loud voice "Lazarus, come forth" and he that was dead came forth, bound hand and foot with grave cloths and his face bound about with a napkin. Jesus said unto them "Loose him and let him go." This clearly shows that it was an actual resurrection of the physical body of Lazarus.

10. *Power to his disciples.*

'Gave his disciples power and authority over devils and to heal all manner of sickness and all manner of disease. And as ye go preach saying "The Kingdom of Heaven is at hand" – heal the sick, cleanse the lepers, raise the dead and cast out devils.'

I hope I have shown that we know something, even if only a little, about the modus operandi of a miracle. I am convinced that, as the century goes on, our understanding of these things will become much greater, for with the increase in scientific super-sensible knowledge we shall know more and be able to do more. It will become clear, too, that this power is not simply a sign and prerogative of divinity but that it is also a token of our very humanity – in so far as we are sons of God – for, as Christ said: 'He that believeth on me, the works that I do shall he do also; and greater works than these shall he do.'

CHAPTER ELEVEN

McDonagh's Unitary Theory of Disease

During all this time, and while exploring all these other aspects, I was steadily pursuing my investigations into medical Radiesthesia, and I became increasingly impressed with the great possibilities that it seemed to offer.

In the autumn of 1953 I gathered together all my clinical material into a paper entitled 'The Contribution of Radiesthesia to the New Medicine', which I read to the Medical Society for the Study of Radiesthesia in November of that year. This I followed up in January 1954 with a clinical supplement entitled 'Towards Radiesthetic Reliability – further Clinical Examples'.

I do not propose to include any of the clinical details here, but I think it is important to discuss one or two important considerations upon which those clinical results were based.

The title of the second paper gives a clue to one of them, viz. radiesthetic reliability. It had long been clear to me, as it had been at the beginning of my wanderings, that, unless it was possible to rely on the accuracy of the radiesthetic findings, there was little future for medical Radiesthesia; in fact, it might well become a menace instead of a blessing, for, as things are, any Tom, Dick or Harry, or their female equivalents, who finds that he has the least aptitude in swinging a pendulum, can set himself up as competent to diagnose and treat any and every complaint! Verily a perfect example of fools rushing in; how true it is that a little knowledge is a dangerous thing.

The truth is that the more one knows about medical dowsing, the more one is aware of the pitfalls and the extreme difficulty of arriving at a true diagnosis and treatment. I think the general public is sensible of this, as, while it feels, quite rightly, that there is something in Radiesthesia, it is at the same time sceptical.

In view of the importance of finding an answer to the whole problem I had devoted much time to it, and had made some headway. Part of the answer we have already discussed in Chapter IX in considering the light which Huna throws on the mechanism of dowsing, and how the low self can be trained and disciplined.

But I found that more than this was needed. I found indeed that anyone taking up the work had to begin to think in a different way and to approach the whole subject from an entirely different viewpoint from that usually assumed.

This may very well explain the slow progress that has been made by Radiesthesia, as this reorientation of thinking is very difficult, inasmuch as scientific thought has been dominated for the past three hundred years by the philosophic concepts of Descartes, concepts which, while they are correct, for the investigation of material phenomena, are not appropriate for Radiesthesia and other allied pre-matter phenomena.

Moreover, there is an added complication for doctors in that their training is based fundamentally on pathology; indeed, it is almost a truism that it is pathology which has made modern medicine and rescued it from its medieval stagnation. But pathology deals only with the gross final results of the disease process; it can tell us nothing of the causes which operated before the first pathological changes began to be manifest – which is presumably the sphere of Radiesthesia.

But the matter goes deeper than this, for, as Dr Wilhelm Reich has said, 'these primordial pre-atomic problems are impregnable to methods of mechanistic and materialistic thinking. They can become intelligible only if they are approached functionally.' We have thus got to develop *functional* thinking. The results, says Reich, 'are of quite decisive significance for our further natural research, particularly for the investigation of living nature, into the general natural processes, and for the fundamental comprehension of non-living nature.'

It is not possible here to do more than mention this deep subject, but for anyone wishing to pursue the subject I recommend Dr Reich's essays on 'Orgonomic Functionalism' in the *Orgone Energy Bulletin*.* Its special bearing on our present discussion is that it lends support to McDonagh's 'Unitary Theory of Disease', and also gives us, to quote Reich again: 'A new criterion for the judgement of biological health and disease. The undisturbed totality of organismic functions in both the somatic and the

* Vol. II, No. 1, 2 and 3; Vol. IV, No. 1 and 4.

psychic realms establishes health or normality in the bio-energetic sense. Every disturbance in this totality or unity, be it in the somatic or psychic realm, will be the basis for disease to a greater or lesser extent.'

This, put in radiesthetic terms, would mean that health and disease can fundamentally only be defined in terms of energy patterns. A balanced, harmonious behaviour of energy patterns constitutes health; any loss of balance and disharmony, however slight, constitutes ill- or sub-health; gross and chronic disharmony is disease.

Unfortunately, most radiethetists have not grasped the necessity of thinking differently. The majority still think in the same old way, and particularly in terms of pathology instead of function, of disease instead of health, of matter instead of energy, hence the diagnoses are in the main only a more refined and accurate account of pathological changes in the body, and the vital information which we want, and Radiesthesia can give us, is not forthcoming.

Given this fundamental way of thinking, it should now be possible to break new ground, and to recover in a new and modern form an integrating philosophy of medicine which will bring order and simplification into the ever increasing complexity, fragmentation and specialization of modern medical science, which, unless we can find some medical 'Newtonian' theory, threatens to overwhelm us completely with a plethora of unrelated detail.

I am going to suggest that in McDonagh's 'Unitary Theory of Disease' we may well have the integrating theory for which Medicine has long been waiting; and for which it would appear to be content to go on waiting. Although McDonagh has published at various intervals reports on the Nature of Disease, the significance of his fundamental thesis seems, like that of Dr Reich, to have been entirely overlooked or ignored by the medical profession.

He himself has propounded his theory, its implications and results in a series of publications, especially the 'Nature of Disease' series, published by Heinemann, covering the years 1924 to 1959. But the difficulty for most readers is that there is such a mass of data covering such a wide scientific field that it is very difficult to see the wood for the trees. McDonagh, I think, has realized this, as he has himself summarized his theory, firstly in the opening chapter of *A Further Study in the Nature of Disease*, and, secondly, in his latest work, *A Final Study of the Nature of Disease*, in the last chapter, 'Evolution of the Protein in the Blood'.

Attempting a summary here is fraught with great difficulty, as there is a distinct danger of over-simplification and distortion. However, I think it is worth making the attempt in view of the importance of the theory and the many implications it has.

McDonagh postulates a primordial 'Activity'* from which matter is formed in an evolutionary spiral series. Such matter exhibits pulsation and three fundamental functions – storage, radiation and attraction.

The cycle starts with the subatomic particles, of which the proton and the neutron are the most typical.

In the second cycle the atomic elements appear, 92 in all, of which 76 are metals and exhibit predominantly the function of radiation, 10 non-metals which exhibit attraction, and 6 inert gases which exhibit storage. But of these only 14 plus 6 trace elements are required for future evolutionary progress.

The third cycle comprises the crystalline products, of which carbon and its compounds are uniquely important, as it is around carbon that the organic world was built. These three comprise the pre-colloidal half of the spiral.

This is followed by the fourth cycle, in which we find the colloids, the class to which protein belongs. The hall-mark of the colloidal state is, to quote McDonagh, 'independence, which enables all three functions to be exhibited simultaneously instead of one at a time, which is all a crystalline product, a molecule or an element can do'.

And this leads to the fifth where the colloid – protein – is differentiated into the various structures of the vegetable world which now exhibit the beginning of interdependence. To quote

---

* 'Activity' is, to my mind, yet another name for Vis Medicatrix Naturae, the primordial pre-matter energy which I have discussed in Chapter IV under so many names.

McDonagh, ' "Life" and "interdependence" are synonymous terms. Both imply the harmonious working of the three portions of the protein as a single unit.'

And finally the sixth cycle – the animal products – in which the protein becomes the matrix of the tissues and organs, of which Man is the final product, exhibiting complete interdependence.

At this point let me quote McDonagh: 'Health and disease are the equivalent in the vegetable and animal products of progress and regress in the atomic, crystalline and colloid products. Indeed, these two changes are two of the most fundamental ones every product is capable of undergoing, as "activity" describes its pulsatory cycles in them. "Activity" is enabled to describe these cycles by a form of it which I call "Climate" (by which McDonagh appeared to mean 'Activity' which manifests itself chiefly in the form of varying high energy rays) continually penetrating every product to very varying depths and releasing "activity".

'As a result, products pulsate, alternately expanding and contracting, and in the process they exhibit the three functions of activity in the order: radiation, attraction and storing. To the exhibition of these three functions not only can be reduced the behaviour of every product, but also every product can be divided into its radiating, attracting and storing portions, be the product the hydrogen atom or Man, which were the first and the last products to have been generated.' (*An Up-to-date Correlative View of the Nature of Disease* p. 2.)

Protein is no exception; it pulsates rhythmically, as "activity" describes a double cycle through each of its three parts.*

As long as all functions normally and rhythmically we have a condition of health, but, if any part ceases to do so, we have a condition of disease. Thus, in this sense, there is only one disease,† as all diseases are merely aspects, in various ways and forms, of unbalance or aberration of the protein, and no disease can be cured unless the balance is restored.

But, although there is only one disease, it is, according to McDonagh, 'divisible into manifestations of which there are several; into stages of which there are three – acute, subacute and

---

* Compare the basic pulsation of Reich's Cosmic Orgone Energy.
† Compare Paracelsus; see p. 31.

chronic; and into morbid conditions of which there are two – inflammation and cancer'. (*A Further Study in the Nature of Disease* p. 1.)

As regards manifestations, the part of the body affected and the symptoms produced depend on which particular one of the three portions of the blood protein has been thrown out of balance.

For from the Storer-functioning portion (mesoblast) originated the ovaries with the musculo-skeletal system; the testes with the cardio-vascular system; the cortex of the suprarenal gland with the urogenital system.

From the Radiator-functioning portion (hypoblast) the parathyroid gland and the blood; the thymus with the respiratory system; the islets of Langerhans with the portal system; and the thyroid.

From the Attractor-functioning portion (epiblast) the adrenal medulla with the skin and eyes; the posterior pituitary with the nervous system; and the anterior pituitary gland and the pineal gland.

Abberrations or imbalances may obviously arise from a variety of reasons in one or all three parts and manifest in the corresponding tissue or organ as disease.

The main abberration is an over-expansion or over-contraction of the protein as a whole or of any of its parts. 'In the process of over-expanding,' says McDonagh, 'further "activity" is liberated, together with various constituents of the protein. In the event of the liberated "activity" ionizing, fever is produced. In the process of over-contracting still more "activity" is lost to the protein through successive radiation. Over-contraction also results in the clotting tissue of the protein being shortened; in the separation of over-contracted parts from the junction between the storing and radiating portions (the first bridge), to produce what are called "viruses", which are thus the products of disease and not causes of its manifestation.' (*A Further Study in the Nature of Disease* p. 3.) A statement of the greatest significance.

Let me sum up in McDonagh's own words: 'It may be stated (1) that there is only one disease; (2) that disease is fundamentally the same in plants, animals and Man; (3) that there are several manifestations of disease; (4) that these manifestations of disease are caused through the damage suffered by the protein in the blood, in the case of animals and Man; (5) that the manifestations occur in the tissue and organs which originated from the damaged regions of the protein; and (6) that the factors responsible for the damage are (*a*) "climate", (*b*) faultily grown food and (*c*) pathogenic activity of the developmental forms of the cocco-bacillus which reside in the intestinal tract,* and, (*d*) the unnatural conditions under which animals are forced to live . . . as well as the measures adopted to make an animal yield more produce than Nature ever intended it should.' (Third Annual Report Nature of Disease Institute p. 39.)

'Far and away the most important of these factors is the *quality* of the food upon which plants, animals and Man are made to subsist, because it is inferior-quality food which is apt to render excessive the amount of "activity" which "climate" releases from the protein in which it is stored. . . . Food upon which plants live is derived from the soil, and the quality of this food depends upon the quantity and quality of the life in the form of bacteria, fungi and protozoa in the soil, which forms its so-called "heart".' (Third Annual Report, Nature of Disease Institute, p. 35.)

If this quality falls below normal for long periods of time, which is the case today, then the protein becomes inferior (in an energy sense), and the vicious circle of disease, so ubiquitous in these times, becomes the order of the day; a vicious circle which can only be broken on the physical level by a restoration of quality protein obtained by a right attitude, intention and action to soil, plant, animal and man.

This briefest of outlines does less than justice to McDonagh's general theory, but I hope that I have brought out the central concept.

One man was quick to see the profound significance of this theory, and, taking it at its face value, he proceeded to find out

---

* The cocco-bacillus are responsible both for the infections from within, as well as the development of pathological forms which are able to live outside the body and give rise to the infections from without – the true infections. But it should be noted that the appropriate homoeopathic treatment, instead of eliminating the micro organisms may first have the effect of producing *mutations* of them before they revert to the original form – the cocco-bacillus (which McDonagh says is the common parent) – and then finally disappearing.

whether it worked out in practice, and whether a therapy could be based upon it actually to deal with disease in a basic and fundamental way. This man was Dr George Laurence.

He was qualified to do this as he had had a lifetime of wide and varied experience, as surgeon and special and general practitioner, and had all his life been an earnest seeker after medical truth, particularly basic causes. But it was not till he came to Radiesthesia that he found what he was looking for. He became in due course a skilled radiesthetist and developed a high degree of competence in the field of medical dowsing.

He found that using a special but essentially simple radiesthetic technique he could detect these aberrations or imbalances of the protein, and could thus diagnose disease, i.e. a departure from health, at a fundamental level – the level of the basic protein in its energy aspect.

Possibly what was even more important was that he found he could also determine the exact remedies (mainly homoeopathic) which would rectify these imbalances and thus restore the protein to its normal state of rhythmic pulsation.

Dr Laurence published a brief account of these fundamental discoveries of his in *Radiesthesia IV* (1952) in an article entitled 'The Unitary Conception of Disease in relation to Radiesthesia and Homoeopathy'.

I have been privileged to work with Dr Laurence for several years now, and to explore with him this new and fascinating aspect of medical science.

As a consequence I am convinced that in combining McDonagh's theory with the radiesthetic technique as developed by Dr Laurence we have a unique instrument for diagnosing in a fundamental way; and, what is more important, of curing chronic conditions which hitherto have resisted all forms of therapy.

To any worker in the radiesthetic field the contrast with the situation presented by modern 'scientific' medicine is, to say the least, startling.

In spite of all the brilliant medical research work, in spite of new 'wonder' drugs, there is an almost complete failure to deal with chronic disease and certainly to prevent it. The reason is plain. A true diagnosis is seldom made in the sense that the fundamental or basic cause is ascertained; and, as the real cause is not known, the treatment must of necessity be empirical and largely guess work.

Modern medicine has thus become largely a question of giving a name to a complaint, and then of treating its signs and symptoms. This is neither intelligent nor scientific and certainly no matter for complacency and, still less, for ignoring any theory, such as McDonagh's, which might lead to the truth.

In the last six years Dr Laurence and I have learnt much, and, the further we go into matters, the more promising the prospects, which include, among other things, a new insight into and understanding of Hahnemann's Miasmic Theory of Chronic Diseases (which I do not think has really been understood since Hahnemann first propounded it a hundred and fifty years ago),* together with a new homoeopathic therapy to deal with such chronic diseases – a therapy it was not possible to develop in Hahnemann's day, as the essential knowledge was not then in existence.

But all this must be left for description and discussion in another place. I would only add that I am satisfied that in all this I have at last found (to quote myself) 'a more exact and subtle method of finding out precisely what was the matter and of applying early remedies', which so bothered me in my early days.

Let me end this chapter with an observation of Dr Laurence's: 'As far as I am concerned, Radiesthesia has proved McDonagh's theory to me, and McDonagh's theory has enabled me to use Radiesthesia much more systematically and efficiently.'

* For a further discussion of this see p. 145.

CHAPTER TWELVE

The Search for the Pattern of Health

In 1954 my search took a new and unexpected direction, as in that year I met a very remarkable man in the person of Mr W. O. Wood. I was introduced to him by the late Dr Winter Gonin (well known as a research worker in these fields of medicine), who told me that Mr Wood was greatly interested in Radiesthesia and allied phenomena. This surprised me greatly, as at the time I met him he was engaged in considerable overseas business ventures, and his background was the Indian Police Force, which he had made his career, and the Intelligence Service in the Middle East during the Second World War. All of this did not appear to have much relationship with medical dowsing.

However, I found that he had in fact a most extensive knowledge of the whole subject, had met all the leading exponents, and had intensively studied all aspects since 1951. He was determined, if it was at all possible, to unravel some of the mysteries of this most baffling of subjects.

At this time there was great talk about and search for the automatic radiesthetic detector to eliminate what was felt to be a source of great weakness in radiesthetic work – the unreliability of the human operator. Personally, I was very sceptical about even the possibility of such a device, as I felt that the human operator was a vital part of the detection, and to try to eliminate him was in essence to try to play Hamlet without the Prince of Denmark.

This problem, it will be remembered, was the same problem as originally confronted Dr Abrams, and he found no instrumental solution other than the human sensitive.

Mr Wood threw himself into the search with his usual thoroughness and enthusiasm, and one device in particular seemed to be most promising, but it all ended in failure, and no automatic detector was forthcoming.

The search for it, however, had one good result in that it tended to clarify the nature of the problem we were up against.

In the first place there was the curious fact that during the past thirty years Radiesthesia had made no major advance in technique, application or results, although in the same period in almost every other scientific field the advances had been spectacular. Mr Wood in his lecture to the B.S.D. in 1955 had emphasized this point. He said:

'To the observer, the dowsing field presents a scene of curious contrasts – contrast between the vigour of advance in scientific knowledge and achievement, and the absence of anything fresh in the British dowsing world . . . there is, indeed, little to add to the Congress of Radionics and Radiesthesia in 1950 (itself largely barren, save for the disputed field of Radionics). The dowsers would seem to have been living in great measure on inherited capital, and to have increased little in stature. This gives one all the more to think because of the public awakening to the implications of sensitivity.'

Why was this, and why this curious stagnation?

Wood's answer was that possibly we had been regarding Radiesthesia from a wrong point of view.

Was it, in fact, right to regard Radiesthesia as just a physical phenomenon, explainable in terms of modern physics? Mr J. Cecil Maby, who has devoted his life to a study of the whole subject, leaves no doubt from his researches* that dowsing on a physical level is a reality and is governed by the forces well known to science. But is that all?

In no sphere is it truer than in this that progress depends on one's fundamental beliefs. If one believes that Radiesthesia can be wholly or mainly explained in terms of modern physics, then one will undoubtedly miss the incredibly wider field which cannot be included or explained in terms of a purely materialistic science. Columbus believed in his land beyond the western ocean in spite of the combined wisdom and expert knowledge of the State Council called together by Queen Phillipa, which proved conclusively that such an idea was impossible. By sailing Columbus proved them wrong, and any radiesthetist by transcending physical Radiesthesia can demonstrate that the present concep-

* See his two papers, 'Instrumental Recording of Radionic Fields' and 'Some Physiological and Psychological Aspects of Dowsing'.

tions of modern science cannot explain Radiesthesia in its fulness.

Signore Pereti, a great practitioner and exponent of Radiesthesia, was asked: 'How would you define Radiesthesia, and what are its limits?' He replied: 'Radiesthesia is a means of knowledge and of action which is exercised outside the ambit of the five physiological and traditional senses; there are no limits to our art, save those personal to each operator.'

Mr Wood was very clear that, if we were ever going to solve the mystery of Radiesthesia, we should have to enlarge and re-orientate our ideas and concepts in a very vital and fundamental way. The physical and materialistic outlook is not enough. It is valid as far as it goes, as we have seen, but beyond that limit there is a vast world which is at once scientific and religious, and can be understood only in the light of 'spiritual science', to use a Rudolf Steiner term, a term which expresses exactly what is required for a true understanding of the universe, and expressed most cogently by the Rev. J. A. C. Murray in the following quotation. (From his paper, 'Science and Religion Open a New Chapter in the Evolution of Man'.)

After recounting the blow which science has lately received to its supposed fundamental concepts by various nuclear discoveries, he goes on: 'From the maelstrom of change, which is still going on, many things have emerged. Science has, of course, had to build afresh from the very foundations, its house of knowledge; and scientists have learned to be very careful indeed in formulating their laws. They have become, in the process of being dynamited, much more open-minded in regard to certain realms of experience which previously they had ignored; they know that reality is a bigger thing than the facts which they have gathered about it. And – what is relevant to our present purpose, one department of science, experimenting with the new forces inherent in matter, and with certain powers of radiation which seem to function in a new dimension, independent of space and time, has evolved a healing method so revolutionary in its premises as to threaten all the established ways of medicine, and so etherial in its command of vibration and radiation as to knock at the gates of the spiritual. I refer, of course to radiesthesia, which seems to me to be the nearest thing yet discovered by merely human means, to the intimations of eternity themselves. Coupled with the new concepts of matter already referred to, radiesthesia reveals most clearly the fact that there is no hard and fast frontier between matter and spirit. The artificial divisions created by centuries of materialism taken as a matter of course until very recently, have been abolished. In their place, we begin dimly to see a continuum of vibration, of radiation, extending unbroken from the heart of so-called "dead" matter, right up through the octaves of the rays of flesh and blood and the etheric processes of the mind, to a region beyond the human spectrum in which powers from another dimension begin to be apparent. It is therefore more than possible that just here the long battles between science and religion will find their truce at last, and that the radiations found and plotted out by man's intellect, will coalesce with and intermingle with those discerned by the spirit. We shall discover something of the unity of creation, a unity which is of the essence of its Creator, a unity which must be reflected in His works. We seem to be presented once again with that strange pattern of the ascending spiral which leads without a break from the heart of the stone to the heart of immortality.'

Finely and truly said. But what did it mean in the actual practice of Radiesthesia?

To discover this Mr Wood and I formed a small group for study and research. The membership varied over the period it was in existence, but to start with it consisted of a nucleus of four: Wood, Major C. L. Cooper-Hunt (a retired clergyman) and his wife, who acted as a sensitive, and myself. Later, Major Cooper-Hunt and his wife dropped out and were replaced by Major Blythe Praeger, with my wife as the sensitive, and the work i deeply indebted to these two most excellent and reliable lady operators.

In order to try explaining the facts we started with the assumption that the dowser or radiesthetist operates on various levels.

The first, the physical, has in fact been extensively explored by very many workers, whose findings go far to settle the reality of physical Radiesthesia. The human dowser is, on this level, only a very sensitive instrument for picking up and recording the 'radiations' sent out by various substances, especially water, oil and minerals. The physical dowser is indeed a sort of sonic walkie-talkie with his twelve senses* as the tuning controls. But on this level it must be recognized that, in so far as the dowser is responding to actual physical radiations, he may well be ousted by the invention of mechanical instruments which will be even better than the human one and without the disadvantage of the emotional factor; and this is indeed happening.

On the next level the dowser uses his senses and/or his E.S.P. faculties, consequently his range is wider and not limited by orientation in the earth's magnetic field, as, for example, in the well-known phenomena of map dowsing. Maby (to whom I have already referred) would prefer to call it 'divination', rather than Radiesthesia. But this psychic dowsing is basically still the same as physical dowsing. All that has happened is that the dowser has brought into play other aspects of the faculty to deal with the new range of vibrations, and uses his nervous system for recording instead of his glands as in physical dowsing.

It is possible with an operator who can function efficiently on this level to use his sensitivity to ascertain knowledge by the technique known as Question and Answer (Q & A), but, if this legitimate method is used, it is necessary to observe the following conditions:

1. Everyone taking part must be single-minded in his desire for the truth, and there must be no ulterior motive in the search.

2. The whole procedure must be carried on in full consciousness and awareness. There must be no trance condition, or mediumship in the ordinary sense, or spiritism.

3. All should have, as far as possible, and particularly the question-master, a real knowledge and intellectual grasp of the subject on which further light or confirmation is sought.

4. If possible the problems should first have been discussed with other co-workers, and answers arrived at by ordinary intellectual means. Q & A should be used only when it is impossible, by taking thought, to arrive at an answer.

* According to Steiner, we have not only the five traditional senses but seven extra ones, in groups of three: awareness of personality, balance, and awareness of thought; sight, perception of the pattern of light, and temperature; touch, perception of the pattern of movement, and hearing; smell, perception of the pattern of sound, and taste.

5. Failing this, the nature and scope of the information required should have been most carefully thought out and the relevant questions formulated.

6. Questions must be clear and positive. Muddled, confused and ambiguous ones must be avoided, as also cross-thinking and lack of concentration on what is being asked.

7. Answers received must be submitted to the scrutiny of common sense (the divine gift of wisdom), and must make sense. Wrong answers can usually be traced to lack of clear thinking, lack of proper formulation, or lack of concentration.

8. In general, the whole investigation should proceed by a combined use of intellect, sensitivity, and healthy, down-to-earth common sense.

In the early months of 1956, during the intensely cold spell, Mr Wood and I used to join Major Cooper-Hunt and his wife and hold sessions in which we employed the technique of Q & A, Mr Wood making an ideal question-master.

His skill at this was quite remarkable, as he had an exceptional flair for framing the precise and correct wording of the question, and following it with exactly the right supplementaries. He had a quick and agile mind, yet at the same time it was balanced and was usually completely under the control of his highly informed reason. An ideal combination.

The sensitive in the early sessions used a de la Warr 'stick box', but later when my wife took over, a pendulum was used with a simple Yes and No chart.

As the work went forward a curious thing happened. It was found that, in the case of the sensitive especially, and in the other members of the group to a somewhat lesser degree, the level of consciousness began to rise, as measured on the Brunler scale.*
What had started off as an ordinary functioning of the dowsing faculty on the second level, already described, ceased after a while to be radiesthetic sensibility and became instead rather a receptivity of understanding, i.e. it ceased to be either physical dowsing

---

* According to Brunler, this could not happen, as one is born with a 'brain radiation' rate which does not change throughout life. It will be remembered that Mrs Kingsley Tarpey challenged this view, as she had often changed it in her healing work with a patient. But such cases are exceptions, and for the vast majority Brunler's brain radiation rate does remain the same.

or divination. When the Brunler reading reached 508, the sensitive arrived at a third and new level, but now appeared to be on a mental level of full consciousness and became independent of the limitations of both time and space, in the sense that it was possible to recover the past, and neither witnesses nor actual remedies were required, and orientation was unnecessary. This state has been described as the eighth level of consciousness.

There also appeared to be still higher levels, of Clairvoyance and Clairaudience, but not in the ordinary psychic sense, as the vision and the speech were inward and not outward. It is the inner vision and the still, small voice which is apprehended in full consciousness, and not the apparition or the trumpet of the seance room under trance conditions.

We found that the technique of Q & A, already described, was particularly appropriate to this third level of receptivity, as a whole new world of knowledge and understanding appeared to be available without the limitations of the lower levels of consciousness, and this technique was in fact used to elucidate various problems.

Let me summarize what has been said so far. The ordinary radiesthetist or dowser uses psychosomatic faculties in obtaining his results, which may be purely physical, purely psychic, or a combination of both. But the pendulist working on the higher levels requires receptivity rather than sensitivity and is conditioned by a conscious understanding of the implications of truth. What has emerged is thus a combination of receptivity, knowledge, discrimination, reason, imagination, and, not least, common sense. It has, moreover, given access to those higher levels of consciousness which we learnt in all reverence to recognize as the threshold of contact with the mind of the Christ. It became increasingly clear to us that the truth needed for these times can only be obtained and be forthcoming from this Source.

Let us now consider the nature of the ground covered in this way and the findings which were arrived at, partly by intellectual reasoning, partly by direct revelation or intuition (with which Wood seemed particularly blessed) and partly by Q and A. This latter was used when it was impossible to arrive at the truth by any other means, and, in doing so, we relied on the promise 'For where two or three are gathered together in my name, there am I (the Truth) in the midst of them.' On such occasions the pendulist operating on the high level of consciousness tuned herself mentally to contact the truth, opened herself to receive it, and recorded it with the 'stick' or the pendulum.

We addressed ourselves first of all to the subject of Radionics which, as has already been explained, is an instrumental development of Radiesthesia.

It is clear to anyone who has used and had experience of any form of radionic apparatus, whether Abrams's, Drown's, de la Warr or any other, that the instruments do work, in that they produce results, usually good, but sometimes equivocal to the patients treated with them. But why did they work? What were the forces and influences involved, and how did they work?

Not being satisfied with the usual explanations, particularly of the so-called 'broadcasting', it occurred to us that possibly the solution lay in the *pattern* itself of the instruments.

Although the conception of pattern or form as that which makes a thing what it is, is an old idea, it is an idea the development of which belongs essentially to the twentieth century. For instance, Whyte in his book *Accent on Form* (Routledge, Kegan Paul) regards pattern as the dynamic idea of the science of the future, just as number, space, time, atom, energy, organism, mind, unconscious mind, historical process and statistics have each in turn been the dynamic ideas of the past, serving, as he says, 'directly as instruments for understanding the universe'.

'To understand anything,' says Whyte, 'one must penetrate sufficiently deeply towards the ultimate pattern . . . only a new scientific doctrine of structure and form, i.e. pattern, can suggest the crucial experiments which can lead to the solution of those master problems of matter, life and mind.' These problems he defines as 'the theory of fundamental particles, the theory of the pulsating structure of organisms, and the theory of the pulsating structure of the brain'. He goes on to say: 'Many of the special sciences of today require a way of making complex systems appear simple, so that a single observation can reveal something about a system as a whole. When such a method appears, it may be possible to apply it at once to a system of particles, to the internal arrangement of an organism, and to the working of the brain.'

In view of Whyte's use of the word brain in conjunction with mind, it is very important at this point, in order to avoid confusion, to distinguish clearly between intellect and mind. Intellect belongs to the physical level of man's make-up and is a function of the physical brain. That is why it is becoming possible to invent machines which are already carrying out, even better than the human brain, a great number of intellectual activities. Thinking is largely a mechanical activity.

The activities of the mind, on the other hand, are very different and cannot be mechanized inasmuch as they consist of awareness, discrimination and imagination, all attributes of wisdom and understanding. Steiner, you will remember, said that man consisted of four levels: the physical with intellect; the emotional with inspiration; the mental with imagination; the spiritual with intuition. In addition, just as the emotional plane is the scene of the struggle for balance, so the mental plane is the scene of the struggle for freedom, the reality of which has been brought home so terrifyingly by the recently published book *Battle for Mind* (Heinemann) by William Sargent.

But to come back to the main theme: Pattern, it would seem, is of supreme importance, especially if one remembers that the ultimate pattern is twofold; it is both a resultant and a force in its own right.

From all this it seemed to us that possibly the radionic instruments functioned by virtue of their pattern, and failed in so far as this pattern was incorrect or incomplete.

Experiment proved this to be the case, at any rate, in part, and thus we were led to try and find the right patterns which not only worked but provided the clues to the nature of the forces involved and showed indeed that the patterns provided the necessary focus for the unknown cosmic forces to manifest.

It was clear that, if we were dealing with patterns of healing, and especially of spiritual healing, the pattern must include all aspects of man, and that there must be a causal chain running throughout from the spiritual to the physical and vice versa.

We are all aware that there must be a relationship between our bodies, with their physical functions, and our senses, feelings and emotions, our mental states, and our spiritual conditions; but very little appears to be known of these relationships, or of the causal sequences which must connect them.

If such knowledge were available then we should begin to understand the true nature of man, the true nature of health, and the real inwardness of spiritual healing. It would be possible, moreover, to detect the blockages on the various levels, which impede the free flow of forces, blockages which manifest to us as disease or disorder. It should also be possible to measure the amount and quality of the flow, and whether excessive or deficient.

That these ideas may appear strange is only because we are largely unaware of the existence of the chain, of the nature of the relationships, and the causal sequences which do exist; nor can they be determined, as the necessary pattern of interpretation is lacking.

Early on in our work this pattern of interpretation was forth-coming and proved to be the master pattern, governing, as well as interpreting, all subsequent work.

The emergence of this master pattern constituted the first phase of our work and occupied most of the winter and spring of 1956.

Thereafter, the work became centred on my estate on the border of the New Forest, as Mr Wood came to live there and I was able to place a caravan (a masterpiece of gypsy van-building, at least one hundred and twenty years old) at his disposal. Whether this remarkable old van made any difference to our work I do not, of course, know, but during the twelve months that he lived there he produced material which could only have been forth-coming intuitionally, in an almost embarrassing quantity.

A series of derivative patterns from the basic master pattern began to emerge. First of all there was the 'Diamond', but scarcely had we begun to assimilate this than the second appeared – what we called 'The Celtic Cross', and not so long after that still a third one, known as 'The Star of Bethlehem'. This series of three constituted what we came to know as the 'Static Patterns'.

At the time I thought this was the full range, but I was wrong;

for in due course there appeared a dynamic pattern for every one of the three statics. Thus there was first 'The Dynamic Diamond', then 'The Dynamic Celtic Cross', and after that 'The Dynamic Star of Bethlehem', again a series of three. Then finally, and most unexpectedly, to crown the whole series and make seven in all, a composite pattern which was a combination of both the static and the dynamic patterns, which had no name. The fundamental difference between the static and dynamic patterns was apparently one of ratio, the static being 1-3 and the dynamic 2-5.

It was difficult enough to obtain the patterns and to understand them, but it was even more difficult to learn their use, and all this occupied a great deal of our ordinary study time, and of the special Q & A sessions.

It appeared that the purpose of these derivative patterns was to help in the understanding of the master pattern, although they also proved to be healing patterns in their own right – the right of the particular pattern.

Of the three static instruments, the static Diamond appeared to be a stabilizer and an energizer; the static Celtic Cross dealt with functional disorder, and the static Star of Bethlehem with pathological conditions.

The static patterns, we found, required the addition of actual substances to the patterns, whether they were Bach remedies, biochemics, nosodes, elements or various 'poisons' in homoeopathic potency, all these having their exact positions on the different patterns. The dynamic appeared to work without the actual substance; only the names in the right positions were required.

Again, in the case of the static the mode of action of the 'forces' appeared to be from within outwards; therefore they 'radiated', and precautions had to be taken when operating them, as we found out to our cost.* In the case of the dynamic the 'forces' seemed to work in the reverse way (from without inwards), so that they did not radiate, and no precautions had to be taken.

It occurred to us that, instead of having them just in two-dimensional drawings, it would be interesting to construct the

---

* So much was this the case with the static Star of Bethlehem that it was made in detachable parts and could be dismantled at the end of a treatment.

patterns in three dimensions. Accordingly we made the three static patterns and the first dynamic one (the Diamond) in plywood.*
We found that, made in wood, four levels were obtained represented by three concentric rings and a base. These levels, we understood, represented symbolically the four states or levels of man, as formulated by Steiner: the physical, the soul-emotional, the mental-formative, and the spiritual, i.e. body, soul, mind and spirit.

These instruments, as we now called them, we started to use therapeutically. The remedies which were required to be placed in addition on the instrument in any given case had to be determined by ordinary radiesthetic means. Both the static Diamond and Celtic Cross used exclusively the twelve biochemics and the forty Bach remedies, i.e. the thirty-eight plus the Rescue remedy and the Radiation remedy.

But in the last of the static (the Star of Bethlehem) we found a most remarkable and unexpected state of affairs, viz. that the automatic element had entered in quite a different way to what we had imagined or indeed sought for originally.

We found when using this instrument for healing that it was not necessary to determine before treatment what remedies were required for the patient (as in the other two static ones). All we had to do was to place the patient's specimen (blood spot) in the centre of the pattern with all forty of the remedies in position, and then leave the specimen for the indicated treatment time.

All dynamic instruments were also indicated as working in the same way (i.e. they were automatic); but with the exception of the dynamic Diamond we did not in fact test them to see if this was so.

Readers will doubtless be as astonished as we were at this totally new conception of healing, wherein one pattern with its remedies seemed to cover all types of disease, and it is the patient (or animal) himself who selects what he needs, and not the operator or doctor.

Eventually it was found possible, in addition to the derivative instruments, to get a series of patterns of the various levels – the

* It should be noted that the cost of these therapeutic instruments is infinitesimal compared with modern orthodox therapeutic apparatus.

spiritual, the mental-formative, the soul-emotional and the physical, which, as the same master-pattern ran throughout, gave quite clearly a series of comparable relationships, and the causal chain connecting them. This series of connected patterns of the various levels we called just simply 'Man'.

From such a complete set of patterns it is possible to make a fundamental analysis, finding out on what levels, and whereabout on any level, blockages are present, and tracing the effects of such blockages both up and down. The linkage we found was *colour* manifesting on all planes, each colour manifesting in the same position and in the same relationship on the patterns, thus making it possible to compare one level with another and effect a true correlation.

In this correlation, and indeed with the whole research in general, we were greatly helped by the existing work of three outstanding figures of this century: Dr Edward Bach, Dr Rudolf Steiner and Dr Bullinger. Indeed, without this contribution, it would have been quite impossible to have made intelligent progress.

Dr Bach's contribution we have already considered in Chapter II. As readers will remember, he originally discovered twelve remedies, followed by a further seven, and eventually by a final nineteen, making thirty-eight in all. These thirty-eight, we found, could be divided into three groups, each dealing with a different level. The original twelve dealt with the soul-emotional level, the next seven, plus seven more from the last nineteen, fourteen in all, with the mental-formative, and the remaining twelve with the spiritual level. To this level must also be added the famous Rescue Remedy, and the one discovered by our group, the Radiation Remedy, a composite remedy which Dr Bach did not discover in his day, as nuclear radiation was still in the future.* The

---

* The actual list of the three groups of remedies is as follows, in their pattern order, going clockwise:

Soul-emotional (Second or middle circle)	Mental-formative (Third or inner circle)	Spiritual (First or outer circle)
Scleranthus	Red chestnut	Sweet chestnut
Vervain	Vine	Walnut
Impatiens	Heather	Elm
Gentian	Star of Bethlehem	Radiation Remedy

[continued overleaf

physical level was dealt with indirectly by the Bach remedies and directly by the Biochemic salts.

In regard to Dr Rudolf Steiner, my own personal experience as the work went on, was that I found his teaching on many things, especially the fundamental make-up of Man and the formative forces controlling this, was absolutely essential for an understanding of our work. Accordingly I read everything I could of his that appeared to bear on our problems, and in every case his views were astonishingly fruitful and illuminating. All his concepts which gave meaning and cohesion to our work were obviously a part of what he called 'Spiritual Science', and made our work on pattern fall into the proper place in reference to material science. In particular, I felt that at last I had the clue to the real nature of Vis Medicatrix Naturae in Steiner's 'formative ethers'.

It is a curious thing that one does not grasp the significance of a person or an idea until one is ready to receive what there is to be given. In the case of Steiner I had contacted the Anthroposophical Society, of which he was the inspirer and founder, round about 1928, and had found nothing that appealed to me; rather the reverse. It was not until after thirty years of the research work I have been describing that I came to realize that Steiner stood for everything I had striven and worked for, particularly in his concept of a spiritual science, which was the complement and antidote of the overgrown and overbearing materialistic science of this century. I can now say without any hesitation that Steiner is the most outstanding and significant figure of this age, and his influence must steadily increase, because he has the answers to the horrific problems of these times.

That being so, the reader will find frequent references to

Soul-emotional	Mental-formative	Spiritual
Chickory	Wild Rose	Hornbeam
Cerato	Rock Water	Holly
Clematis	White Chestnut	Larch
Agrimony	Olive	Aspen
Mimulus	Chestnut Bud	Willow
Rock Rose	Oak	Pine
Century	Mustard	Rescue Remedy
Water Violet	Honeysuckle	Beech
	Gorse	Cherry Plum
	Wild Oat	Crab Apple

Steiner's ideas in these pages, and, if he finds them puzzling, as having reference to unfamiliar concepts, I would suggest the reading of three books (out of the hundreds which have been written by Steiner himself or his disciples), which will make what I have been talking about in these pages much clearer, viz. *A Scientist of the Invisible* (Hodder and Stoughton) by Canon Shepherd, *The Etheric Formative Forces* (Anthroposophical Publishing Co.) by Dr Wachsmuth; and *Man or Matter* (Faber and Faber) by Ernst Lehr, 2nd Edition.

The work went on with intervals throughout the summer, autumn, winter and spring of 1956-7. In the early part we were still exploring and working out the patterns and finding out their therapeutic possibilities. In the late winter and spring of 1957 the emphasis changed over on to other work, probably of an even more important nature, but which is not relevant to our present theme.

In the summer of 1957 Mr Wood left Godshill and went to London to work with the Hon. Mrs Shuttleworth on the astronomical implications of the work. I must confess that by this time the subject had got too advanced and deep even for the other members of the group to follow, and its undoubted significance has still to be explored and understood.

Throughout the winter, spring and summer Mr Wood had worked under a sense of great urgency, which he had conveyed very forcibly to the whole group; hence the work was at some times hectic. We thought at the time that the urgency had reference to the deteriorating international situation, as a good deal of his later work had an indirect bearing on it, but, when in the autumn of 1957 he died suddenly and peacefully in his sleep, the sense of urgency was largely explained.

His death came as a great shock to all who had taken part in the work, but on reflection it was clear that, owing to the tremendous drive of his latter days, he had largely accomplished what he had set out to do, even though it was in a totally different form to what he had envisaged in the beginning.

His work has indeed opened up new vistas and great possibilities, due in large measure to the fact that he was obedient to the call to devote himself, come what might, to the promptings of his Inner Voice. From the worldly point of view only it looked as though he had sacrificed everything for nothing.

After Wood's death Major Blythe Praeger joined me in a determined attempt to explore more intensively the further therapeutic possibilities of the instruments.

Major Blythe Praeger's qualifications as a radiesthetist particularly qualified him for the work, as he had already done a great deal of original research especially with the Lesourd Rule, as well as original work of his own along these lines, and in the event this was the best possible preparation for our research, the results of which I shall recount in the next chapter.

Subsequently the late Malcolm Rae carried on the pattern work but in a different form; at first it was to see if any better and more powerful therapeutic patterns could be resolved. His main finding was that the original patterns of Wood did not contain the golden mean, a most important ingredient, but nevertheless they still worked effectively in their own right as we had originally found to be the case, duly recorded.

Later he carried on the work in another way and found that it was possible by using the Q and A radiesthetic technique to ascertain the pattern of anything, so he discovered a large number of archetypal patterns of homoeopathic and Bach remedies.

This pattern is first expressed in numerical terms, what he called co-ordinates, which can then be drawn as a diagram or pattern from the figures. From these he found could be prepared for medical use any homoeopathic remedy and in the required potency, using a special simple magnetic instrument he devised; of great use practically, especially when a remedy is urgently required.

These remedies were all carefully tested clinically and found, if anything, to work better than those prepared by the usual traditional homoeopathic technique. A most remarkable and unexpected achievement.

A large number of these pattern cards were drawn and are available. For further information and a supply of cards write to:
Mr and Mrs M. Belsham, 45 Downhill Road, Catford, SE6 ISX

CHAPTER THIRTEEN

Spiritual Healing: New Style

In the Chapter on Healing and Healers, it will be remembered, I said that I thought spiritual healing by the laying on of hands was not the most appropriate method for these modern times. But before we examine what may be appropriate let us consider in more detail the gulf which undoubtedly exists between modern scientific medicine and Healing as it was understood in the Ministry of Healing by the early Christian Church, and the reason for it. We shall then be in a position to know better the requirements of the modern age and the form which spiritual healing might now take.

It is clear from the records that in this Ministry there was not only healing by the word of command, by the laying on of hands and simply by prayer, but also the power to perform genuine miracles. One might say that in those days preaching the Gospel was almost synonymous with healing the sick. Indeed, it is clear from James v.14 and 15, that this was considered all that was necessary: 'Is there any sick among you? Let him call for the elders of the church; and let them pray over him, anointing him with oil in the name of the Lord. And the prayer of faith shall save the sick, and the Lord shall raise him up; and if he hath committed sins they shall be forgiven him.'

But as the centuries went on, this power gradually faded away, apart from the case of exceptional individuals, and the Ministry of Healing can be said to have been lost by the Church.

In recent times, however, there has been renewed interest and an endeavour to recover the lost power. This is more especially evident in all those numerous Christian bodies which, at the present time, endeavour with more or less success once again to heal the sick by the prayer of faith and the laying on of hands.

The well-authenicated miraculous healings at Lourdes, to which I have already referred, and of which the Roman Catholic Church has recognized fifteen between 1939 and 1949, have stimulated great interest in this obscure aspect of healing, even though modern medical science has at present no explanation of what are undoubted facts. Nor will it have until there is a totally different outlook. As Dr Leuret, joint author of *Modern Miraculous Cures*, says: 'The doctor has to widen his horizon if he wishes to grasp the total cause of the cure. . . . The study of miracles demands we raise and broaden our view beyond the present anthropomorphic limits and rise above the level of the sort of law laid down dogmatically by nineteenth-century scientists which is now quite out of date . . . for when we look closer into the intimate nature of miraculous activity, we realize that there is no question of arbitrary, irrational action, upsetting the order of things, but instead, the action of an overwhelming power.'

But so far all attempts to recover this lost power have come up against certain definite snags: 1. There would appear to be a randomness about the healings which is disconcerting. 2. When they do happen they do not appear to conform to any particular pattern. 3. Results are unpredictable and uncertain. 4. Faith seems to be demanded without understanding. Compared with the actual and predictable results of modern science, healings are essentially unreliable and non-repeatable, the key to which may be Paracelsus' concept of 'the Hour-in-Time' (see p. 108).

The fact is that any attempt to recover and revive the Ministry of Healing in its old form is largely impossible, and this for a reason which is not appreciated by all those sincere and earnest souls who seek to use this form of healing.

Let me explain. On looking back into the past we tend to attribute to men and women of past ages the same intellectual, emotional and mental outlook as we have today. This is a profound mistake and leads to comparisons which are completely fallacious.

In those earlier times the relationships of the various (subtle) bodies of Man were different. Let me quote Steiner from his *The Gospel of St. Luke*: 'People have quite a false idea of human evolution when they imagine humanity was always so constituted as it is today, Man has changed ever and again and human nature has undergone great transformations. If we compare a body of the ancient Indian civilization with one of today, we can say that in the case of the former the etheric body was still comparatively

free and the soul could unfold forces which worked into the physical body; the etheric body absorbed the forces of the soul, being then less closely bound to the physical body; moreover, it had greater dominion over the physical body and the result was that the influences brought to bear on the soul were transmitted to the physical body and had a tremendous effect on it. .... Because of this, it was possible to work on the soul of another by means of a word teeming with the right impulses of will. ....
Given some idea of the desired effect to be achieved in the other soul, it was possible in cases of disease to exercise the right effects upon the soul, in the way indicated, and thereby upon the body – the result being a restoration to health.'

Thus it was eminently possible to do direct spiritual healing in those ancient days. This was still possible in Graeco-Roman times when there was a condition of relative equilibrium between the physical and the psycho-spiritual; hence the direct spiritual healing we read of in the early Christian Church.

But since then, to quote Steiner again, 'the physical has gained predominance, and dominates the psycho-spiritual; so much so that the psycho-spiritual has become impotent in certain respects and can be entertained only in its more theoretical aspect'.

From the point of view of evolution of Man this was inevitable, as it was essential for Man to develop inwardly and with increasing self-consciousness. This necessitated an even greater descent and immersion into physical matter, with an almost complete loss of awareness of the spiritual worlds, i.e. as far as direct experience is concerned. This reached its climax roughly about the middle of last century when the materialistic conception of the universe was at its height. I may remark here as an aside, that its supreme expression, Dialectic Materialism, is thus a hundred years out of date, but does not make its deadliness any the less.

Since then, however, there has been a change, and mankind is again on the upward path and once again the psycho-spiritual will be able to dominate the physical increasingly, but this time from the other side in full consciousness and directed by a mind aware, alert and informed by the intellect.

It is because of this change that interest in spiritual healing is reviving and its possibilities are being perceived. But, as I have said, the approach must be different; indeed, it must be in the idiom of these times, viz. by the inductive method of science reaching out into a new spiritual science.

While all this was undoubtedly true, the question still remained – What did this mean in practice; what, in fact, was the modern approach, and what was its form?

I think I should make it quite clear at this point that I do not rule out the possibility of spiritual healing in the old biblical sense even on a mass scale in these times, such as, for example, is claimed by T. L. Osborn in a booklet called *Java Harvest*, describing mass miracles in Java.*

That among simple and primitive peoples the psychic conditions are still such as to make this possible, I can well believe. But this is not the issue.

Our problem, and a very real one, is the form spiritual healing is likely to take in the scientific civilization of the West, which is now rapidly becoming world-wide.

Medicine as it has developed in these modern times is engaged in an ever-increasing elucidation of all the material factors which contribute to healing on the physical plane. This now embraces a wide range of sciences and specialities, and there is no denying that great advances have been made by the application of science and the scientific method to the physical aspect of medicine.

Lately, of course, it has been recognized that emotional factors also play a very definite part in the cause and cure of disease, and thus psychology has been added, somewhat reluctantly, to the material sciences dealing with medicine, and a linkage made in the form of the now fashionable psychosomatic approach. But this is as far as any causal chain has got.

It is recognized, of course, that in some vague and undefined way cures occasionally take place by means of spiritual healing, but, if it happens, it is usually put down to suggestion, coincidence, or something which cannot be explained. The Church, as already mentioned, has lost the Ministry of Healing and cannot, as yet, find out how it can be recovered; and, even if it did, the gulf would still remain between it and the psychosomatic outpost of modern medical science. Here then is the existing position.

* Reported in the *Weekly Religious Review*, January 27th 1961.

The question we asked ourselves at this point was: did our work described in the foregoing chapter, throw any light on the problem, and might it begin to bridge the gulf?

Our answer was 'Yes', as further study of the patterns and their therapeutic use showed quite clearly that we were dealing with a new form of healing – of spiritual healing.

It soon became clear to us that we appeared to have discovered what can only be described as the Master Pattern of Health. This, if true, was important, for, whereas in material medicine we have disease patterns from which we endeavour to approach health, in spiritual healing there is a health pattern, departures from which constitute disease. So for the first time it is really possible, in McDonagh's phrase, 'to approach disease through the gateway of health'.

The really essential point appeared to be this: in this age and time, the scientific age, it would seem that spiritual healing requires a physical and material *focus*; it requires an actual concrete pattern (of health) for the manifestation of the cosmic forces.

According to Steiner there are seven non-material, spiritual forces which are constantly impinging on the phenomenal world maintaining it in a constant state of equilibrium between creation and disintegration. Three of these are concerned with the higher states of Man, and the remaining four, called the formative ethers, with the various states of matter. The first, the warmth ether, giving rise to the state of heat; the second, the light ether, is primarily concerned with the gaseous and electro-magnetic state of matter; the third, the chemical or sound ether, with liquids and magnetism; and the fourth, the life ether, with solids.*

The free flow and harmonious and balanced interaction of all these forces constitutes what we have called the state of health or wholeness. But, if for any reason there is an interference with the free and unimpeded flow with a consequent damming back, cutting off, alteration and distortion, then certain conditions of deficiency,

---

* 'The mutual relation between the etheric forces is such that the later ether, more highly worked, always contains in itself the attributes of the earlier, yet always develops, as a new entity, an activity clearly distinguishable from that of the other. Thus the life ether contains in itself the warmth ether, light ether and chemical ether; the chemical ether contains light ether and warmth ether; and so on.' Wachsmuth – *The Etheric Formative Forces.*

imbalance, overgrowth, etc., arise, and we call them disease.

This conception of disease as an interference or blockage is interestingly enough one of the central teachings of Huna, where it is called 'Blocking of the Path', and it may occur on any plane.

My close study of Huna has clarified the whole conception very much for me personally, but modern psychology, particularly Freudian and the scientology of Hubbard, has made all of us familiar with the idea, on the psychological plane, of blockages in the form of fixations or complexes which have to be resolved or removed before psychological health is possible.

Similarly, in the religious sphere, the conception of sin as a blockage cutting us off from contact with the Divine is familar to us all; this again must be removed before we can have spiritual health. The same as in the lower realms of the etheric and physical, as stated above.

There is in fact no essential difference between what is called 'sin' and what is called 'disease', each being a blockage. It is merely a question of the level on which the blockage occurs and the particular force concerned. Hence the reason why Christ said to the disapproving Scribes: 'Why reason ye these things in your hearts – whether it is easier to say to the sick of the palsy "Thy sins are forgiven thee," or to say "Arise, take up thy bed and walk"?' For him removal of the blockages on the spiritual level was to heal the palsied man in the physical sense.

It stands to reason, therefore, that our task is enormously simplified if some means is found to remove blockages wherever they occur on each of the four planes, as it should then be theoretically possible to effect fundamental and lasting cures. One would be restoring a person to what should be his normal state, a state of health and wholeness which is, as we have seen by definition, a state of free, unimpeded flow of all the forces involved in the creative maintenance of a human being.

Bearing all this in mind, experimentation with patterns as healing instruments showed that healing appeared to involve three main factors:

Firstly, the location and removal of blockages wherever and upon whatever plane they occur.

These blockages may be either racial, i.e. hereditary, or acquired by the individual. For example, if we take the three racial miasms* which are the curse of humanity, these manifest on the physical plane in a variety of ways, of which the ultimate pathological forms or conditions are tuberculosis in all its forms, venereal disease in all its forms, and cancer in all its forms. But they also manifest on the other planes as well. This may be very difficult to understand, but our work showed that Sycosis, Syphilis and Psora (Hahnemann's names for the miasms) have spiritual counterpart which produce blockages on the spiritual plane; and, similarly, on the other levels.

In truth the matter is even more complicated, and it explains why miasms are so difficult to deal with. It can be demonstrated radiesthetically that these miasms are present in the soil, in the plants grown on that soil, in the animals and humans fed on the plants so grown, and, finally, in the excreta of the animals and humans which goes back to the soil, so that the pathological cycle remains complete and continuous. Hence the need to cleanse and heal the soil if we are finally to eliminate these curses of humanity, and obtain a healthy soil and healthy food, full of vital energy.

Secondly, when the blockages have been removed the flow of forces remains to be restored. Long-continued disuse may have produced disfunction or disorientation of the forces which can only be restored by placing the patient, via his blood spot, in the full healing pattern, in which the forces are all flowing normally and freely.

The failure to recognize this factor may be the reason why so often, when in the course of treatment all the blockages have apparently been removed, the patient is still not well, and, indeed may oftentimes relapse.

This brings me to the third factor – the necessity for a rise in the level of consciousness. For a lasting, permanent and complete cure it is essential to raise the permanent level of consciousness,

* The term 'miasm' was first used by Hahnemann, the founder of Homoeopathy, to denote an entity which appears to be non-physical, which has the power to produce ill-health by the aberration or imbalance of the protein of the body. Miasms might be described as the 'etheric counterparts' of the original causal organism whether microbic or virus, and as such are the main cause of chronic disease. During the course of our work we came across a fourth miasm which we called the 'Andromeda miasm'. This seemed to have a close affinity to nuclear fall-out, except that it came from a 'natural' stellar source.

as only so can the patient acquire the necessary insight and understanding which will make him of his own free will obey the law –
the spiritual law of health.

Let me quote you a passage from Diogenes' weekly article
'The Search for Meaning'.* He has been discussing the lack of
correspondence between virtue and experience and Christ's comment that we must 'not expect in this world to find that there is
any necessary connection between wickedness and disaster, or
between virtue and reward. Deliverance from the "law of accident" comes from repentance.' He goes on: 'Now it is a great
misfortune for the understanding of many of the most pregnant
things that Jesus said, that for us the word "repentance" has come
to possess an emotional, breast-beating, tearful, remorseful significance. We associate it with revival meetings and penitential
forms, with confessions of a guilty past and promises of better
conduct in the future. But the Greek word translated for us as
"repentance" does not possess these connotations. The word is
"metanoia" and it signifies a "change of consciousness". If we
want to avoid "perishing" in the amoral, chaotic, accident-ridden
world we have to undergo an internal change of mind. We have
to cease to seek the answers we need outside ourselves, and seek
them within ourselves in a change of mind, an alteration of
consciousness.'

Such an alteration in this present age and time means the raising
of consciousness on to the mental plane – the Christ plane of
inward understanding, of imagination, of discrimination, of
pattern. It is, I think, significant that one of the Bach remedies
which deals with blockages on this level, viz. Cherry Plum, is used
in cases where there is the fear of the mind losing control. This
fear can be very real, for, if control should be lost over a fair
period of time, then not only is understanding lost, but pattern
as well, which means that the formative force is no longer under
control, and so may manifest uninhibited on the physical plane as
a cancer, for example.

It is of interest that the raising of the level of consciousness
appears to be an automatic effect of using the right, i.e. the
appropriate, pattern required by the patient.

* *Time and Tide*, June 22nd 1957.

Almost all the healing work was done by so-called 'broadcasting'. This is, incidentally, a complete misnomer, in that the impression is given that radiations are broadcast to the patient. What in fact happens is something quite different. The patient, in the form of his blood spot, spittle or urine specimen, is placed on the appropriate instrument, i.e. the correct pattern required, and, inasmuch as this pattern is a pattern of health, the bloodspot is subjected to forces tending to restore the patient's health pattern by the removal of blockages, restoration of flows, and a rise of consciousness. This is mystery enough, but the main mystery is the nature of the relationship of the blood spot to the patient, as for all practical purposes the blood spot and the actual patient can be regarded as identical.

The question which naturally rises is whether in fact these patterns are effective; do they do their work; do they represent therapeutic fields of force?

Perhaps the following two examples will help to elucidate this point:

1. My wife and two of my grown-up children were very anxious to be on top of their form as there was a particularly busy time immediately ahead, and so I suggested that they should have a treatment on the pattern called 'the Celtic Cross'. Treatment was given and it was followed by the usual stabilization for twenty-four hours on the 'Static Diamond'. But next day, to my consternation, instead of feeling fine, all three felt quite ill and very much below par – the exact reverse of what I and they had expected. This was puzzling and disconcerting, but most fortunately one of the sensitives of the group came that day and suggested we should give another treatment, but take continuous radiesthetic readings as to what was happening as the treatment proceeded. It was found in all three cases that after the initial rise in vitality, which always occurs to start with, it quickly fell to normal (which indicates the end of the treatment) when only half the supposed time of the treatment had elapsed; carried on after this the vitality would have continued to fall, i.e. there would have been over-treatment. So what had happened the previous day was that we had got the length of the treatment wrong, twice what it should have been, producing a lowering of vitality, and

they had then been held or stabilized at this low level by the twenty-four hours on the stabilizer. So no wonder they felt bad. As soon as this was realized, the three were given the correct length of treatment and next day they were feeling fine.

This was a clear, though inadvertent, indication that the patterns worked in their own right, and that the results were due to forces in the pattern, and not due to suggestion, which can in fact be ruled out.

2. Before coming to the next example I must explain a little more about the colour therapy which I mentioned earlier on.

One of the main snags about giving colour treatment has been the difficulty in obtaining pure filters or screens of the exact colour requirement. The late Madame de Chrapowicki, who was one of the leading experts on this form of therapy, told me that it was almost impossible to obtain anything really satisfactory, and it was therefore tending to be in abeyance.

But with the coming of the patterns and the Static Diamond in particular Major Blythe Praeger and I found, to our great surprise, that apparently we had a perfect instrument for giving colour treatment without having to worry about actual colour at all.

This was possible, as each colour had a definite position on the pattern. It was only a question of placing the blood spot of the patient in position, and colour treatment could be given on any of the four planes, using the full range of the twelve-colour spectrum of Steiner, viz. Peach, Infra-red, Red, Orange, Yellow, Yellow-green, Green, Blue-green, Blue, Indigo, Violet, Ultra-violet, and back to Peach.

The positions of the colours on the pattern already being known, it only remained to find out radiesthetically what colour was required for the treatment, on which plane or level, and the timing.

With this explanation let me give the second example. A patient who had had a skin irritation for six weeks said it was becoming intolerable and asked me to treat her. Colour therapy was indicated on Violet.

On testing her radiesthetically we found green to be her dominant colour, while both Indigo and Infra-red were contraindicated, i.e. for some reason she was having an excess of both colours, which presumably was responsible for the irritation.

Treatment for seven and a half minutes was then given on Violet. After treatment there was no reading on Indigo, and later in the afternoon it was found that Violet was now her dominant, i.e. she had jumped from Green to Violet.

During the evening a telephone message was received from her to say she was feeling on top of the world, very well indeed, and for the first time for six weeks the irritation had completely gone – to her intense surprise. Suggestion can be ruled out completely, as she had no knowledge of what we had done or indeed if any treatment was being carried out. Subsequent investigation showed that the cessation of irritation coincided with the time of treatment. No further treatment was required at that time.

We had many other cases which, when treated in this way with colour, gave excellent results. Colour therapy, if indicated, usually was most effective, and certainly easy to give.

The most impressive evidence, however, of the effectiveness of the patterns is provided by a series of 370 cases treated on the Celtic Cross by Major Cooper-Hunt. He has used the pattern and the technique as originally worked out over a period of three years and he informs me that he has had complete success with 95% of the cases treated. The remaining 5% represents patients who had already got to the point of no return, but even in these cases great help was given.

The therapeutic results, which in varying ways and degrees were obtained with all the healing patterns experimented with, can, I think, best be expressed in this way – and I should make it clear that it was not what I had expected as an ordinary medical man. Given the full co-operation of the patient, the general effect of therapy is to give release to the soul, to give a sense of independence, so that those patients who may have been seeking health for years and have depended on other people, suddenly say that they feel they can now be responsible for themselves and can tackle their own problems with occasional help and assistance. Whether physical improvement takes place appears to be of less importance; it is rather one of those things which is added to those who seek first the Kingdom of Heaven.

In illustration let me quote the following case, which I shall recount in detail as in many ways it is very remarkable and significant.

Mrs X, aged sixty-four, was admitted to hospital on November 22nd in a moribund condition for an exploratory laparotomy for ascites and vomiting. Her peritoneum was found to be riddled with cancerous metastatic deposits and nine pints of fluid were drawn off. Her condition was considered hopeless, so she was sewn up again and her relatives told that, for her sake, it was hoped she would not survive long, and three weeks were given as the utmost limit.

At this point I was asked whether anything could be done. I said that, if her relatives were agreeable, I would try the theoretical possibilities of the instrumental patterns. As the case was considered completely hopeless I felt I was ethically justified in trying the new treatment even though no one knew what its effects would be. Consent was given and the necessary co-operation of the patient obtained in that she was asked if she would care to have a form of spiritual healing evoked on her behalf.

The instrument used for treatment was what we call 'The Star of Bethlehem'. The technique is to place the blood spot on the central star and leave it for the indicated time, which in this case was eighteen hours.

Treatment was started at 8.30 p.m. on December 3rd, and finished at 2.30 p.m. on December 4th. The blood spot was then transferred to the 'Static Diamond' for stabilization with the indicated Biochemics for twenty-four hours.

At the start of the treatment the patient was very dopey and confused, a state she had been in since the operation, but when she was seen on the evening of the 4th she said she felt better and was talkative.

For the next week she was given daily follow-up treatment on the 'Celtic Cross', and her son reported she improved steadily day by day.

I will now give his daily reports as passed on to me:

December 11th

His mother got up today (just over a fortnight after the operation) and he was frankly amazed at her improvement; it was better than he ever expected – she was even thinking of having a hair-do. She is bright and cheerful and is eating well. The hospital says she is too well for a nursing home. The son said he felt the whole situation was fantastic.

December 12th

The improvement is frankly amazing. There has been more progress in the last two days than in the previous seven. She feels better; better than she ever thought she would feel. Before she was stricken down her eyesight had been getting progressively worse; she had 'bad heads' and suffered from stiffness in the joints, particularly of the fingers. All this had cleared up, eyesight is perfect, head clear, and no stiffness.

She is bright and smiling and more communicative. Eating well and enjoying her food.

The sister said it is obviously absolute nonsense that she has only three weeks to live. Asked what she thought about her recovery, she said it was due to Mrs X's willpower and her will to live, but her son says his mother has never had a strong will.

One symptom which worried the doctors was a sort of trance she went into. She now described these to her son. She said she had had five in all, and these were the worst part of the recovery. She thought the earlier ones had not been noticed, or, if they had, it was thought she was asleep. She says that she is fully conscious and knows everything which is going on, but she feels as though she were frozen and is completely rigid and paralysed. A trance lasts about an hour, after which she is perfectly fit and well.

December 13th and 14th

Improvement continued. She is very well indeed and has had a bath. She has nothing wrong except a slight swelling of the feet.

She is in no pain or discomfort. She looks remarkably well and is bright and cheerful and at peace. Her voice is strong and her wound has completely healed.

The surgeon who has been seeing her every day says that she has done far better than he thought possible and he could not understand it.

On this day she told her son about a remarkable experience she had had; why she had not mentioned it before is unexplained.

She said that some time after her operation, when she was

feeling very ill, coinciding, her son thinks, with the treatment on December 3rd and 4th, she had a vision.

Two angels were conversing together, and then one turned to her and said, 'We are looking after you – you are going to be all right,' and after a pause: 'Be yourself; you have a right to your own personality. You have a mind of your own and you have got to use it and not be dominated and directed by others.'

The son ended his report this day by saying that he could only describe his mother's condition as a complete transformation.

On December 17th she went to a nursing home for convalescence, and I visited there on December 22nd; this was the first and only time I had seen her. I was much struck by her appearance, as she gave an impression of well-being which was quite at variance with her medical history. She looked well nourished. There was no sign of cachexia, and, indeed, she had been putting on weight.

She told me that she had made a wonderful recovery and felt better and younger than she had done for years. She was convinced that something remarkable had happened, something real, and that a definitely change of personality had taken place in her.

About the vision she told me that it was still as vivid and real as when it took place. She said the angelic advice was very much to the point, as she had always been inclined to submit to other people and have no mind of her own.

She said her eyesight was now excellent – in fact, apart from weakness, she felt completely well.

Examination of the abdomen showed the operation wound had healed perfectly by first intention. The cancerous masses could still be plainly felt through the abdo wall, but there was no trace of any fluid, although it was now more than four weeks since the operation.

In further conversation she said she was feeling very happy and contented and had never lost faith; indeed, it had been enhanced, and she found that the Bible and the Prayer Book, to which she had now turned, had more meaning for her than ever before.

She continued to improve up to about January 2nd, but then, two days before going home on January 4th, she started to slip back physically to some extent, and the abdo fluid began to return. On January 16th she had another tapping, i.e. the first since the operation on November 22nd, but there was not so much fluid, and the surgeon remarked that she was much better than he had expected. Her son reported at this time that in spite of the return of the ascites she seemed to keep at the same fairly good level of general health. Emotionally and mentally she remained in good shape until January 30th when she suddenly rapidly declined and died peacefully on February 3rd.

At no time since the original treatment on December 3rd and 4th did she have any pain, and she complained of nothing to the end except the discomfort of the abdominal fluid, and repeatedly told her visitors that she felt no pain.

I am well aware that one swallow does not make a Summer, and that this case will be completely unacceptable from a purely physical point of view. But I think I would claim that it provides a striking commentary on the truth of the general thesis, especially when one considers the vision, the trances, the various healings, the cessation of pain, the change of personality, increased understanding and the regaining of something of the bloom of youthful vigour.

All those who saw this patient were agreed that the 'recovery' was due to a profound mental change. Indeed, the son said that it was the first time he had seen his mother as she really was in her true individuality; previously she had been so retiring and unapproachable that they had had little in common. This would accord with the interpretation that Spiritual Healing is a renewing of the mind and a process of understanding by a rise in the level of consciousness from which physical transformation may, but not necessarily must, result.

The cure of the actual cancer was never completed; it was only arrested for the time being. Indeed, the knowledge which might have completed it was not ours. When all is said and done, we are still profoundly ignorant as to what constitutes a cure in the fundamental sense. We are too prone to judge everything by a physical cure, and overlook the true needs of the soul.

In the new age which is coming, we shall have to recognize these needs and reorientate our ideas to allow for them, and this can only come about if we are prepared to put first things first.

For, as Steiner says, 'the time has come when we must realize with full and clear consciousness that supersensible knowledge has now to arise out of the grave of the materialistic outlook'.

Thus ended for the time being a most stimulating and illuminating experience – an excursion into modern alchemy; for most unfortunately, apart from the work with the Celtic Cross by Major Cooper-Hunt (already referred to) it has not been possible to follow up this promising and indeed unique piece of research. It remains for the future to realize the full extent of the healing power – the Vis Medicatrix Naturae – which was revealed to us in this new form of spiritual healing.

CHAPTER FOURTEEN
The Radiesthetic Faculty

It will be remembered that in Chapter III on Medical Dowsing I was troubled by various problems which at that time seemed to have no satisfactory answer. But our journeyings since then should have enabled us to review the whole subject of Radiesthesia with much more discernment, and to provide acceptable solutions to most of the problems.

Let us therefore in the light of our new knowledge re-examine the situation and seek to determine the proper function and scope of Radiesthesia and of its instrument the Radiesthetic Faculty, the peculiar key to these new realms.

I can well remember at a meeting of the Medical Society for the Study of Radiesthesia, after Dr Guyon Richards had read a paper on 'The Occult Forces behind Divining', a doctor getting up and asking, apparently with every justification, what on earth Dr Richards' paper had to do with the investigations of the Society. If I remember rightly, most other members agreed with him. Dr Richards' reply was simply 'Everything,' and in saying this he was prophetic, though at the time it seemed largely nonsense. But, as I now know, Dr Richards was perfectly right. Radiesthesia cannot be understood nor even begin to be explained simply in terms of materialistic science, because it belongs at the same time to the sphere of spiritual science.

It is time that this was understood, so that Radiesthesia may assume its proper place – a place, I believe, which is of the greatest significance for these modern times, and particularly for science and scientific thought, if only we can begin to think about it in the right way and in the right terms.

Mr Wood puts this point very clearly when he says: 'The important point is the dowser's apparent unwillingness to tackle the full scope of the gift of sensitivity, and his tendency to restrict his thoughts to what has been described as the hewing of wood and the drawing of water. The thinking public are now well aware that the range of sensitivity cannot thus be circumscribed. The problems facing mankind are greater than the locating of wells and the matching of remedies – plumbing and plastering, so to speak – and we have to come to grips with the issue of our times and face realities as they are. It is necessary that the sights of the dowsers be raised in line with those in science and philosophy in the forefront of the battle for knowledge.'

The truly spectacular advance of materialistic science on all fronts is common knowledge to all. Never in the history of the world has man known so much about the material universe and the nature of matter. Never has he had such knowledge of the physical laws which govern it, and as a result, mastery over its manipulation, so that he is able to create and destroy on a scale which fifty years ago would have been deemed impossible.

But this unprecedented advance in the knowledge and manipulation of matter is making for a lopsidedness which it is of the greatest urgency to rectify by a corresponding scientific exploration of the immaterial or spiritual aspects of the universe. Traditionally this has been the role of religion and metaphysics, but this scientific age is unwilling to accept the findings of the mystics or the metaphysicians unless they can be proved scientifically.

There is some confusion of thought as to what is meant by this, if, as is usually assumed, the findings must be explained in terms of materialistic science, then one is asking the impossible and nothing but error results; but if we mean the application of the scientific method, i.e. the investigation of directly-perceived facts by clear rational judgement, even though these facts are supersensible, then true progress can be made and truth results.

But this seems to lead to an impasse. Direct perception would seem to be limited to what our ordinary senses can tell us, the information we can obtain by physical sight, hearing, touch, taste and smell, and the deductions which reason can derive from such data. Obviously our physical senses cannot give us information about what we cannot sense.

But supposing we could obtain direct perception of these immaterial worlds. It would then be possible to apply the same thought, reason and critical study as is given to the ordinary sense data of materialistic science, and in this way satisfy the perfectly

correct desire of modern man to subject supersensible sense data
to scientific scrutiny and assessment.

The crux of the situation would thus seem to be whether this
direct perception of the supersensible can be obtained. To this the
answer of the spiritual scientists is a very definite and emphatic
'Yes.'

They assert that all men have undeveloped non-material sense
organs which can, with appropriate training techniques, be
developed, and that such developed senses will give us information
and knowledge of these immaterial realms, in the same way as our
ordinary physical senses give us information and knowledge of the
material world.

In his book, *Knowledge of the Higher Worlds*, Steiner has given
us such a practical manual for the development of these higher
sense organs; but those who have been students of this esoteric
training know how difficult it is and what demands, quite rightly,
it makes on one's patience, perseverance and wholehearted devotion. Nevertheless he who is prepared 'to shun no exertion, fear
no obstacle and count no time' can obtain entrance into the
mysteries and gain direct experience and first-hand knowledge of
the realities of the higher worlds. But in its very nature this, at
present, is for the few and therefore the vast majority of mankind
must be content with the everyday world of physical sense data.

Yet, as I have said, direct experience and knowledge of the
spiritual worlds is absolutely essential at this time to give balance
to an over-materialistic science which bids fair to destroy us.

One solution adopted by very many is to hark back to the past
and to try and revive the ancient magics in their *old* forms which,
while perfectly sound and legitimate to the times in which they
arose, have little or no relevance to modern times, and any revival
is retrograde and atavistic and lays one open to evil forces.

What then is the solution?

In pondering upon this very pertinent problem it occurred to
me that possibly in Dowsing and its wider form of Radiesthesia
we might have a key to our problem for these times in which we
live.

Water Divining or Dowsing as such, has an ancient ancestry,
but I think it is true to say that it has risen to prominence only in

the last thirty years, in other words, Radiesthesia is a *modern* phenomenon. It has reached its present degree of development largely through the painstaking work of certain French priests – a fact which I believe to be of significance, as I shall hope to show later.

It seems to me that in Radiesthesia in its modern form, we may very well have a remarkable faculty or instrument for exploring the supersensible worlds, particularly the Etheric. It is, if you like, a sort of halfway house between our ordinary physical senses and our developed occult senses – the difference lying in that, while both these are apprehensive of phenomena in full consciousness, in the case of dowsing it is a sense which does not yet function on the plane of ordinary consciousness. Indeed, in Chapter IX of this treatise I suggested that the faculty was one of the properties of the Low Self which by definition is a subconscious Self.

I know it is generally assumed that the pendulum or rod, via the dowser, picks up radiations of one sort or another. Archdale, in his little book *Elementary Radiesthesia and the Use of the Pendulum* stated it like this: 'I want you to accept from me as a fact, that all objects, both animate and inanimate, give off radiations, which, if the objects are sufficiently close to you, you can pick up.' And Franklin, in his most excellent book *Radiations* – a summary of modern teaching on the subject, and published by the B.S.D. – assumes that this is the key to the dowsing phenomenon, though he admits in the concluding chapter 'that something unknown is operating we don't know how'. This belief that modern physics holds the key is still, in the main, the accepted view. But, I am coming to think that we have been badly misled in Dowsing by analogies with the physical world. Matter certainly radiates, a fact which has made possible our modern technological civilization, particularly the whole world of communication; but I doubt very much whether it is the reason for the radiesthetic phenomena.

Let me put it like this. Map Dowsing is usually regarded as an awkward exception to the rule, as it is difficult to see how the explanation of physical radiations can possibly come into it. But suppose the difficulty is one of our own making, made by a wrong assumption, viz. that the radiation theory explains Dowsing. Suppose instead that Map Dowsing is the normal and natural functioning of the radiesthetic faculty, which has nothing to do primarily with picking up physical radiations as such, but is a supersensible sense which makes direct contact with the etheric world – the world of the formative forces, and under special conditions with higher realms as well.

Objection may be made to this in so far as it is obvious that physical dowsing can detect physical substances such as water, oil, gold and other minerals. It may be, as is usually assumed, that the detection is by picking up the physical radiations, but equally, even in the case of actual physical substances, it may be direct apprehension of the etheric counterpart.

I am not however going to deny that actual physical radiations can be picked up, but this is only incidental to the main function of the radiesthetic faculty. In any case I do not regard physical dowsing of first importance, because I am convinced, as I have already said, that instruments will be devised which will be able to pick up physical radiations (and I emphasize physical) with greater accuracy and constancy than the average dowser, though the human dowser will always have one great advantage – the ability to map dowse.

But at this point we must be clear in distinguishing between the faculty and its mechanism of expression. If my surmise is correct that the faculty is a supersensible sense, its expression is a physical one, viz. a nerve and muscle reaction, causing the swing of the pendulum or the movement of the rod. Again you see a sort of halfway house between the spiritual and the physical.

I have been led to this view of the radiesthetic faculty by a very curious phenomenon which all practising medical radies-thetists must have come across and which has caused great con-fusion and many doubts.

Time and again in cases suffering from some incurable disease and which are in fact dying as, e.g., a chronic cancer case in the last stages, it has been found that the radiesthetic readings do not reflect the actual physical state, very often the readings show an improvement; whereas in fact the patient may be at the point of death. This is most disconcerting, and a favourable prognosis, based on the readings, such as I used to give before I knew better, and which turns out to be utterly wrong, by the patient dying, has brought discredit on radiesthesia in general, and grave misgivings to the practitioner as to the accuracy of his readings.

Let me at this point repeat the case I reported in chapter III. It was a case of cancer in the last stages. Between reports on her condition and progress the patient died – a fact known to me but not to the operator. You can imagine my amazement when I received the following report: 'There is an improvement in the patient's condition.' I made the following comments in a letter asking for further light on what to me was an extraordinary situation: (1) How was it possible to get readings at all if the patient was dead, much less to get readings showing an improvement; (2) If readings were obtained, as they were, it would appear they have no basis in fact, the patient being dead; (3) If this is so, how can one know that one's readings, while the patient is alive, have any basis in fact?; (4) The only conclusions one can legitimately draw are either (a) that the readings are unreliable, as they may be accurate, but there is no means of knowing when they are, or (b) that they are not readings of physical states at all.

But if the last conclusion, i.e. that they are non-physical, is correct, as I believe it is, this only makes the whole business more mysterious as, if the readings are etheric readings, how does one get physical ones as one certainly appears to do?

Curiously enough I have recently had a similar case to the above in which, in spite of all my experience, I was again caught out in the same way. This was a case of chronic kidney and heart disease in the last stages, i.e. it had got to the point of no return, but the latest radiesthetic readings showed definite improvement. On the strength of these I wrote the patient accordingly – but before my encouraging letter reached her, the patient died. The readings clearly did not reflect in any way the physical state of the patient. I should perhaps add that it was not possible for me to check up clinically on this case.

I believe the explanation of this seeming paradox is as follows: It is true that all radiesthetic readings are etheric readings, but at the present time in the evolution of mankind, the etheric body has sunk so deeply into the physical body and is so firmly attached that for all practical purposes they are identical, and this state of affairs maintains under all ordinary conditions of life and health.

Readings of the etheric are thus readings of the physical. But in those cases with pending dissolution by death, the etheric body is gradually drawing apart from the physical and so the radiesthetic readings, while they give a true picture of the state of the etheric body, give little or no clue to the physical, which may indeed be at the point of death.

Similarly, remedies which appear to balance the condition, do in fact act favourably on the etheric, but by so doing accelerate the separation. I am now convinced that in all cases which have passed the point of no return, especially cancer cases, treatment which improves the etheric, actually hastens the physical death of the patient. The operative words are 'the point of no return'; this can only be ascertained by a very close watch on the correlation between the radiesthetic readings and the clinical state of the patient, and emphasizes the necessity for accurate clinical observation, instead of the usual remote control.

I was interested in discussing this with a doctor of a homoeopathic hospital to find that the same conclusions had been reached by observation of the effects of homoeopathic treatment on patients in the last stages of chronic disease.

If I am correct in all this, we have been quite right in assuming that radiesthetic readings do give a true picture of the physical condition under ordinary and normal conditions, but for a very different reason from that ordinarily assumed from current theories.

There are four consequences which follow from this view of things which are of some importance.

Firstly, one of the claims of medical Radiesthesia is that it gives us the ability to detect the oncoming of a diseased condition *before* it manifests in the physical or even before it has produced any symptoms. This is particularly true of cancer – pre-cancer states can be detected long before there is any physical manifestation. The reason for this is obviously that the state pending manifests first in the etheric, and only after a lapse of time, which may be considerable, passes over into the physical in the form of a tumour.

Let me illustrate this. In a review of Julian Huxley's new book, *Biological Aspects of Cancer*, the reviewer says: 'A malignant tumour occurs as a complex process of development towards autonomy.' Huxley recognizes two main stages in this process. In the first, 'during a period of initiation or promotion, a train of events is set in motion which may be preventable, but is not treatable, since physical changes are not yet manifest and the cancer is latent'. From an orthodox medical point of view this statement is absolutely correct, but from a radiesthetic one it is emphatically not, for (1) cancer can be diagnosed in this pre-cancer stage, and (2) in this form it is eminently treatable and curable in the real sense, as this latent state can be completely eliminated. Obviously we have here the basis of true preventive medicine, but the proving of this scientifically is another matter, as, apart from letting the process go on to the material manifestation as a malignant tumour, there is no means at present of proving this pre-cancer diagnosis – and that is no consolation to the patient for whom everything would now probably be too late.

The following case is of interest in this connection and presents some unusual features. The patient had developed gastric and other worrying symptoms which did not yield to treatment. A radiesthetic investigation was done and revealed a definite pre-cancer condition of the stomach, but the patient was not told of this. The appropriate indicated treatment was given, and the pre-cancer condition cleared up, but the patient did not improve as she should have done; in fact, she gradually slipped back, though the pre-cancer condition did not return. Finally, after four months it was clear that some anxiety element was present, but careful inquiry failed to reveal its nature.

However, quite casually she mentioned that twenty-five years before she and a friend had visited a gypsy fortune-teller who had told the future of them both. In the case of the friend everything had turned out as foretold, and so now the patient had begun to worry about herself as the prophecy in her case was that she would die in her fiftieth year. I asked her whether she was about to enter her fiftieth year, and she replied that she was. So then I told her that although this was so she now had nothing to fear. The gypsy had been quite correct in her prophecy: she would have died in her fiftieth year, if no other factor had entered in, but one had, viz. she had consulted me, and through Radiesthesia I had picked up what was going to happen, a cancer of the stomach, and I had been able to deal with it at the stage when it could be dealt with. I had altered the future, and the prophecy no longer held true. From that time on – nearly four years ago now, she has never looked back, and is at present in excellent health.

Let me give you another short example of pre-clinical diagnosis. In the course of a routine radiesthetic check-up the report came back that my wife had a very heavy reading on Micrococcus Catarrhalis and theoretically should have been suffering from acute naso-pharyngeal and respiratory symptoms. She was, however, feeling well, without even the suspicion of a cold. I, on the other hand, had had a persistent sore throat and cough. Had the blood-spot witnesses been mixed up, or was the diagnosis right off the rails? Thirty-six hours later, however, my wife proceeded to develop all the symptoms one would have expected with the infection. The treatment originally indicated, and which if taken then would probably have prevented the attack altogether was now taken and quickly resolved the acute condition.

This picking-up of the pre-state is also the probable explanation of another difficulty of radiesthetic practice, in which the radiesthetic readings indicate a serious and alarming condition, but the clinical condition gives no indication of anything untoward physically. An example of this was a case which had readings which would lead one to suppose there was a serious and critical cerebral condition, but most careful clinical investigation revealed nothing. Confronted with this, one's first inclination is to imagine that the readings must be wrong, but from what I have already said I think one may take this as additional evidence that one is dealing with etheric readings, which indicate what is going to happen physically if the etheric state is not rectified.

Secondly, for the first time in history there is now the possibility of dealing with the racial miasms, which, ever since the Fall of Man have dogged and plagued mankind in the form of chronic disease of all sorts – as these miasms are in fact the fundamental cause of all chronic disease.*

These miasms are hereditary, and it has been impossible to deal

* See Chapter XIII, p. 145.

with them, as the heredity has been etheric and not physical, though in each individual the etheric miasm manifests physically in aberrations of the protein. This is the reason why McDonagh's Unitary Theory of Disease has given such remarkable results, both diagnostically and therapeutically when directed and controlled radiesthetically.

Radiesthesia has now made it possible to detect these etheric miasms and to treat and eliminate them from their physical manifestation in the protein, provided always the pathological state is not irreversible.

It is difficult to overemphasize the importance of this to the human race if it could be done on any considerable scale, as theoretically it should be possible, in a child, to detect and treat miasms at a fundamental level and in a fundamental way, and so to eliminate them completely – thus breaking the etheric chain of disease and making possible a disease-free humanity as far as heredity is concerned.

Thirdly, it will be obvious that these concepts can be applied in other ways than the medical, and indeed I know they have been applied to historical research. A sensitive working in conjunction with an historian, using the Q and A technique, investigated an obscure period of French history, with apparently astonishing results, if the very favourable reception by those most competent to judge is any criterion.

To explain this sort of thing one must perforce assume that the occult tradition is correct in postulating what is called 'The Akashic Record' – a sort of imperishable spiritual tape recording of all past events of the world's history. The tradition moreover is that this record is in the etheric and therefore accessible under proper conditions to the radiesthetic faculty.

It may be noted in passing that as this record was available to initiates in the past, material records were unnecessary; it is only since men became too sunk in matter to be clairvoyant in this way that written records have become necessary – the so-called historic period of mankind.

I would point out that this method or technique has unlimited possibilities (provided the essential conditions are observed) in many other fields of research, e.g. agriculture, which have hitherto been neglected so that, to quote W. O. Wood, 'the result is a paradox. The principles the dowsers seek are known to others, who seek in turn the means of proving them; the dowsers have the means of proving them, but appear these days to be blind to the principles.'

Fourthly, it may now be possible to get some idea of what is apprehended by the radiesthetic faculty. If, as I have said, it is not physical radiations nor even psychic radiations – whatever they are, what is it? I venture to suggest that it is the etheric patterns of the formative forces discussed in the last two chapters. But if we find some difficulty in adjusting ourselves to this conception, then I think television can help us, with what I think may well be a true analogy. For as we well know the television picture or pattern is obtained by a process of scanning, as is also the creation of the image in the electronic microscope. In a similar way I suggest that the radiesthetic findings (i.e. the picture or pattern) are obtained by a sort of psychic scanning. This pattern may be in the form of a figure sequence as in the Drown and the de la Warr 'rates'; as departures from a norm stated either lineally or in degrees – the usual form of expression of most pendulists; or as actual patterns which appear to symbolize the state of wholeness or health of the human being.

If we find this in turn difficult to appreciate as being so utterly different from the anatomical or physiological representation of a human being, I suggest that some of the schools of modern art such as Cubism or Surrealism may give us a clue. Indeed it may well be that a surrealist picture of a human being may in fact be a poor attempt to depict the etheric pattern of the formative forces lying behind the physical body. The formulae of modern chemistry and especially the pictorial symbols of the chemical composition of various substances should also help us, though the equating of H_2O and Water is now so familiar that it no longer appears the strange thing it is.

I throw this idea out as worthy of some consideration, particularly, as I have already suggested, because the science of radiesthesia has got held up by attempting to explain it in terms of modern physics. I believe these numerous attempts to do so have in fact obscured what may possibly be the true explanation, and have indeed led us up an entirely false trail and created little else than confusion. This, I feel, is especially true on the radionic front, including the Unitary Field Theory advocates, where a sustained attempt has been made to explain all radiesthetic phenomena in terms of modern physics – but with very little success.

Let us come back to the radiesthetic faculty and its functioning. It will be clear from what has been said so far, that if the faculty is the instrument for the exploration of the supersensible realms which I have claimed, then we must be able to rely on its efficiency and reliability, i.e. on the truth of its findings. What then are the conditions or factors which make this possible?

But first the faculty itself.

I regard the faculty as a gift of God, like any other gift, whether in sport, music or art. It is possessed by the many in some degree, but only the few are real masters; but whether average or superlative the natural gift can be trained and developed, either by direct training and demonstration from an expert, or by studying the various text books which describe and explain the various techniques. Having thus acquired some degree of proficiency further development of reliability depends, in my view, on three main factors:

(1) It is essential that the radiesthetist operates in full consciousness. It is fatal, at this stage of world development, to go into any sort of trance or semi-consciousness: one must remain fully awake and fully aware. This rules out any sort of Spiritism or trance mediumship, which is disastrous if one's real aim is Truth; for to let consciousness abdicate is at once to lay oneself open to spirit possession to a greater or lesser extent, or to invite error and falsehood. The operator thus, even though the faculty operates subconsciously, *must* retain full conscious control all the time.

(2) One must ask the right questions. This is of paramount importance, as all radiesthetic work, including water divining, is in essence the asking of questions. If we are to get the right answers we must ask the right questions, which may be unformulated and unspoken as in most water dowsing, or they may be specific and spoken aloud as in the technique of Q and A.

To be able to ask the right questions one must first of all have

166

actual knowledge and information on the subject being investigated. Thus if it is water divining then a knowledge of geology, mineralogy and hydrology is very necessary. If it is agriculture, then a sound knowledge of the theory and particularly the practice of farming is required, together with the ancillaries such as ecology, animal and crop husbandry and the science of soil, etc. If it is healing, then a thorough knowledge of medicine, such as is given in the training of a doctor is invaluable. Indeed, I regard this as the reason why, other things being equal (which includes open-mindedness and spiritual awareness) a qualified doctor gets better results than a lay practitioner.

This is the correct use of intellectual knowledge; it should provide a reservoir of facts and information from which the intellect can gather material to formulate the right question. But beyond this one must have the ability to reflect, to give proper time, thought and consideration to thinking out in detail any given problem and formulating it precisely. The possession of the faculty is no excuse for poverty of facts or intellectual laziness.

In passing I may say that I believe that this is the explanation as to why it is so difficult for different radiesthetists to get the same answer to a specific problem. In so far as no two people think exactly alike they in fact ask different questions and so receive different answers. If they could only ask the same question, they would get the same answer.

All this is the reflective side of thought, but two thousand three hundred years ago Aristotle defined the working of thought in the human organism as primarily creative and only secondarily reflective. This creative aspect is something which we have almost completely forgotten in these modern times and yet it is of considerable importance to the matter under discussion.

Let me quote Canon Shepherd from his book *A Scientist of the Invisible*. Talking about Steiner's influence on thinking, he says, 'He himself (i.e. Steiner) in direct experience found in thought the doorway into the perception of the spirit world. He had discovered, in the evolution of sense-free thinking, the one means whereby he could understand and relate together his experience of different levels of supersensible knowledge and apply to it, at every level, *conscious rational judgement*. Moreover, in discovering the new powers and possibilities of thinking as an instrument of knowledge, he had also discovered in it functions of which man had lost all knowledge. He had discovered that it operated in creative formative forces in the life of man, both in the spiritual and physical worlds, a creative function which in its own way was more primary to it than its function as the instrument of human knowledge.'

I do not propose to pursue this matter further as it is too vast a subject to do more than mention, but it makes the task for the future quite clear – the raising of the powers of thinking from the bondage to sense impressions – materialistic science – into direct perception of supersensible reality – spiritual science. This is what Steiner means by 'the redemption of thinking'.*

Let me quote Canon Shepherd again: 'Two thousand years ago, Christ initiated human feeling and devotion into faith in the spirit world and in the reality of man's spirit destiny, and so made possible the evolution of his ego-consciousness and the development of his powers of thought. To-day He would make possible for him the recovery in clear knowledge and understanding of his true spirit-heritage, by initiating his thinking into direct spirit-experience. The redemption of human thinking is the completion of the spirit-initiation of mankind in Christ.'

(3) This brings me to my last point – how can we seek to avoid the inevitable error in all human thinking? – the reason why the redemption of thinking is so necessary.

Let me say quite simply that I believe such a redemption is only possible through Christ and his redemptive powers, as revealed to us in the profound mystery of Golgotha.

It may seem strange at the end of a treatise which has endeavoured to be scientific to introduce such a note. But you will remember that earlier on I said that Radiesthesia in its modern form was very largely the work of the French priests. I do not regard that fact as accidental, indeed I regard it as of the greatest significance. They had two very positive assets – they strove to be Christ-centred and they had the time and leisure for creative thinking – the result was Radiesthesia, which points a moral for us today.

* *The Redemption of Thinking* by Rudolf Steiner (Hodder and Stoughton).

All human thinking, since the Fall of Man, is liable to error and untruth, only through the Spirit of Truth can we be preserved in this materialistic age from falsehood and destructive thinking. I believe it is literally true, in so far as science is the search for truth, that Christ – the Way, the Truth and the Life – is a scientific necessity, and this applies equally, strange as it may seem, to such a humble science as Radiesthesia.

'God hath chosen the foolish things of this world to confound the wise and God hath chosen the weak things of the world to confound the things that are mighty;

'And base things of the world, and things which are despised, hath God chosen, yea, and things which are not, to bring to naught things that are.' 1st Epistle Corinthians, Chapter I vv 27 & 28.

In the eyes of the world Radiesthesia is a thing of no account compared with, say, nuclear or astro-physics or atomic research, and yet, as I have tried to show, it can, when properly understood, open to us the mysteries both in this world and the world invisible. It can reveal to us the Truth in so far as our finite minds can comprehend it, so that, to quote, 'Once again a corner of the Veil has been lifted.'

The following quotation is from Steiner's book *True and False Paths in Spiritual Investigation*, written in 1924.

'We live now in an age which despises the spiritual much in the same way as men of a far-off time despised the material world, because the spiritual world was accepted as a matter of course.

'We must try to enter again into the understanding of those times so that we shall once more be able to accept, and place side by side with the teachings of the astronomers and astro-physicists, of zoologists and biologists, what the spiritual knowledge of the divine inner content of being reveals. The time for this has come. We must be ready to meet it if we are ever to solve our problems; if we are ever again to discover religious art, and the gifts of healing and so forth.

'Just as in ancient times mankind was spiritually enlightened so that the material world was despised and as at a later time material knowledge grew so strong that it extinguished the spiritual, so now an age must come when men must rise from their marvellous and all-inclusive knowledge of the external world to a renewed mystery reality – to a new art of healing, a deepened artistic life and penetrating spiritual knowledge in humanity.'

I believe profoundly that it is the privilege of Radiesthesia, through the radiesthetic faculty, to make its very special and, in some ways, unique contribution to the reintegration of material science and spiritual science, and to that restoration of wholeness of vision and outlook, of feeling and thinking, which is the task of this age.

Note

For further information see booklet entitled "The Radiesthetic (or Dowsing) Faculty" which consists of two lectures, both given to the B.S.D., mine in 1972 called "The Role and Scope of the Radiesthetic Faculty in the Modern World" and the other by Malcolm Rae in 1973 called "The Scope and Limitation of Radiesthetic Investigation."

CHAPTER FIFTEEN
The New Medicine

Readers of Bunyan's great spiritual allegory, *Pilgrim's Progress*, will recall that Christian arrived, after much difficulty and many vicissitudes, at the House of the Interpreter, where he had time to consider his pilgrimage thus far and have many things made clear to him which had been obscure during his journeyings thither.

I feel that we too have arrived at such a point in our search together. It is not the end by any means; indeed, in many ways it is only a beginning. But this concluding chapter is a good place to ponder on the ground we have covered, to assess its significance, and to see what has been given to us in increased knowledge, awareness of, and insight into those supersensory realms of being where in Lehrs' pertinent phrase we come to the 'country in which Man is not a stranger'.

Let us review the situation.

Under the impulse of ever-increasing scientific advance modern medicine has made spectacular advances on all fronts. The latest researches, for example, in organic chemistry have made possible a galaxy of new and powerful drugs able to influence almost any and every diseased condition, even the treatment of mental and emotional diseases of the personality. New techniques in medical diagnosis, including radioactive isotopes, have made possible the exploration of almost every part of the human body, and the latest discoveries in nuclear physics have been utilized to bring the forces of nuclear fission to bear on the treatment of disease. In surgery there is now practically no part of the human body which is not accessible to surgical technique, and operations are successfully performed which even ten years ago would have been completely impossible.

And yet – in what has been called 'this Golden Age of Medicine' – there is a horrid suspicion that all is not well. We seem to be faced with a bewildering paradox: the more we seek health, the less we find it. We talk health but get disease. So much is this the case that when we use the word 'health' we actually mean disease, as for example, in the phrase 'The National Health Service'.

Disease appears, almost frighteningly, to be hydra-headed. We get rid of one disease only for others to appear in its place, and the new ones are usually more intractable.

Thus we have in the main eliminated the infectious fevers, only to be confronted with diseases which attack the central nervous system, e.g. poliomyelitis; with systemic diseases, so that more than five and a half million people in this country suffer from some sort of severe rheumatism or arthritis, i.e. 14% of the entire population.

We lower the infantile mortality rate, but are faced instead with cardio-vascular disorders of middle age, in particular, the killing coronary disease. As a medical expert recently put it: 'It is a great pity for a person to reach his prime and to be at the very height of his activity and usefulness only to be struck down by a heart attack or stroke.'

We materially reduce the incidence of tuberculosis, only to be confronted with an increase in cancer, particularly in its most distressing form, cancer of the lung.

We employ psychiatric treatment as never before, but are faced with an ever-increasing volume of mental and emotional disorders, which affect one in twenty of the people of this country.

We master the acute microbic diseases, only to be beaten by new and intractable complaints due to virus infections.

We are obsessed with clean food campaigns, but overlook the fact that our food, probably the primary factor in degenerative disease, was never so processed, sophisticated, adulterated, demineralized, devitalized, or, in the expressive vernacular, so 'mucked about' as it is at present. It would, indeed, be pertinent to inquire whether there is a direct connection between modern civilized diet and the enormous increase in the crime and the moral degeneration of these days; a connection which Weston Price* suggests is directly due to bad and wrong nutrition during embryonic life, but which can be remedied by right feeding.

Never before did we know so much about disease and pathological conditions – and so little about health and wholeness.

* See his monumental field-work study *Nutrition and Physical Degeneration*.

Modern medicine is indeed in a vicious circle, and there is no escape so long as we continue to think in purely materialistic terms.

To escape from the impasse it is essential to begin to recognize that there are in fact forces which lie behind the manifestations of matter. These forces under the general name of Vis Medicatrix Naturae we have traced here and there down through the centuries to modern times, in various forms and under various names until we found its nature elucidated by Steiner in his concept of the Formative Forces, etheric, astral and spiritual.

We have seen how the great difficulty of modern man, and especially the scientist, is the acceptance of the existence of these supersensory forces, as to do so means thinking in a different way, in a new mode, which Reich called 'functional thinking'; and even if he does manage to do this he still has no physical sense with which to apprehend them, and therefore assumes that they do not exist.

In this very real difficulty we have seen how the radiesthetic faculty has come to our rescue and opened up entirely new realms of thought and action.

It has made possible the essentially simple concept of Health as a balanced pattern of forces between the forces of matter and the cosmic (supersenory) forces, and disease as an imbalance brought about by an excess, deficiency (due to blockage) or distortion of the forces involved, Moreover, these imbalances can be measured as deviations, either plus or minus, from the norm which is health.

This is the new science and art of Medical Radiesthesia.

Here for the first time we have the possibility of a true preventive medicine, as we can now detect these deviations from the norm before they have manifested physically, at which early stage they are eminently treatable, or become set in the pattern which we know as pathological disease, when they are not. The result of this would be in practice to maintain a state of relatively harmonious and normal balance of the body as a whole on all planes, which is designated in my book *Health Abounding* as the Perfective Aspect of Medicine.

While this is the true and proper sphere of Radiesthesia, it can in this day and age be of inestimable use and value in ascertaining the basic cause or causes lying at the back of so much incurable and chronic pathological disease at the present time, causes impossible to ascertain by any other diagnostic means; and of indicating treatment which will eliminate the fundamental cause. Whether physical normality is restored is another matter, as it may well be that the pathological processes have got to the point of no return and are out of control, i.e. of the etheric formative forces, and so cannot be reversed short of a miracle, though surgery may alleviate. But one never knows whether one has arrived there, and so radiesthetic help is at all times worth invoking.

For such treatment, as the reader knows, there is a wide choice of therapies, such as have been described in previous chapters of this book, in particular the ones I have called 'Unity',* all utilizing Vis Medicatrix Naturae in a consistent but great variety of ways, all of which have their place in the new medicine.

This applies particularly to Homoeopathy. For a hundred and fifty years, ever since the genius of Hahnemann first gave this great therapeutic innovation to the world, Homoeopathy has been the Cinderella of medicine. At no time has it had any general acceptance, and today it has even less than formerly. This is largely due to the fact that its peculiar contribution has never been properly understood. But it should now be plain that homoeopathic medicines work by virtue of the specific 'vital essence' – the Vis Medicatrix of each drug, which has been 'liberated' to a greater or lesser degree by the act of potentization (i.e. dilution and succussion) from its materialized form.

If one now adds to this the precision and control of drug and potency selection which Radiesthesia provides, Homoeopathy can become a science as well as the medical art it has been up to the present, and this may well produce a revolution in the whole science of medical therapeutics, which would be an incalculable boon to suffering humanity, and particularly to those to whom modern drug therapies are far worse than the disease.

For a long time to come modern materialistic medicine, which deals with the physical and pathological, will be required, but it should be supplemented increasingly by radiesthetic medicine, which deals with the realm of the formative ethers, i.e. the causal

* See Chapter VIII, p. 72 and Chapter XIII.

factors which in all cases underlie the physical. Both are complementary to and explanatory of one another in the contemporary
world, and, indeed, both are necessary, confronted as we are with
the present devastating degree and appalling amount of disease
in the soil, in the world of plants, in the animal kingdom, and in
Man himself.

If medical Radiesthesia can realize its true preventive possibilities, as well as its main function – the preservation of health
and wholeness – and materialistic medicine can realize that it has
only half the story and that it has left out the most important part,
the part which explains the whole – 'that disease,' as Dr Bach says,
'in its origin is not material' – then the emergence of the true
medicine of the future will become not only a possibility but a
fact.

This true medicine will indeed be new – to this age. People will
recognize that fundamentally disease of the body, as Dr Bach has
pointed out in his little treatise *Ye Suffer from Yourselves*, 'is an end
product, a final stage of something much deeper. It is entirely the
result of a conflict between our spiritual and mortal selves. So
long as these two are in harmony, we are in perfect health. But
when there is discord, there follows what we know as disease.
Disease is thus solely and purely corrective . . . it is the means
adopted by our own Souls to point out to us our faults; to prevent
our making greater errors; to hinder us from doing more harm;
to bring us back to the path of Truth and Light from which we
should never have strayed.'

As I started my pilgrimage with Dr Bach and his remedies, let
me end with him; as in the following quotation he sums up the
new medicine and its truth:

'The physician of tomorrow will have no interest in pathology
or morbid anatomy, for his study will be health. The prognosis of
disease will no longer depend on physical signs and symptoms
but on the ability of the patient to correct his fault and harmonize
himself with his spiritual life.

'Treatment will be essentially to bring four qualities to the
patient: first, peace; second, hope; third, joy; and fourth, faith.
All the surroundings will be to that end. To surround the patient

with such an atmosphere of health and life as will encourage recovery, and develop the desire to live a life more in harmony with the dictates of his soul than had been previously done.

'In addition to this, those beautiful remedies, which have been divinely enriched with healing power, will be administered, to open up those channels to admit more of the light of the soul so that the patient may be flooded with healing virtue.

'The action of these remedies is to raise our vibrations and open up our channels for the reception of our Spiritual Self, to flood our natures with the particular virtue we need, and to wash from us the fault which is causing harm.... They cure, not by attacking disease, but by flooding our body with the vibrations of our Higher Nature, in the presence of which disease melts as snow in the sunshine.

'Health exists when there is perfect harmony between Soul, mind and body.'

In the rise in the general level of consciousness, in our increased awareness of the supersensory world of being which will result, we shall know that health and wholeness are spiritual attributes, and our new being in its fulness will reorientate to those creative cosmic truths of life and living, which we have too long neglected, and should never have forgotten.

CHAPTER SIXTEEN

The Missing Dimension:
The Place of Psionic Medicine
in the Field of Medicine and Healing⋆

I feel that the most useful thing I can do in this opening address is to indicate what I believe to be the place of Psionic Medicine in the field of Medicine and Healing, and the wider fields of life in general.

We are now entering the last quarter of the 20th century, 25 years of supreme importance in the history and destiny of man – a time of crisis and great change – when important decisions for real progress or further decline will be made, depending on the degree and extent of understanding and appreciation of what is happening.

Thrown back on ourselves and our inner resources there can arise a new outlook, new values and ways of thought, which will enable us to regain, through the power of Christ, faith and belief in other spiritual dimensions with which this materialistic and over-intellectualised world has long lost touch.

So let me start with this quotation from Steiner's opening paragraph of his book *True and False Paths in Spiritual Investigation*. It reads: "Knowledge of the supersensible world, and our knowledge of the phenomenal world, the fruit of years of patient and diligent study, to which we owe the magnificent achievements of modern times, are complementary. For reality can be apprehended only by the person who is able to reinforce the remarkable discoveries which the natural and historical sciences have added to our stock of knowledge in recent times, with insight derived from the spiritual world."

This quotation applied to Psionic Medicine gives both the necessity and the raison d'être for its existence, as it is essentially an attempt to restore to modern medicine its indispensable and necessary counterpart: that aspect largely lost sight of in the materialistic – one might almost say mechanistic – trends of contemporary scientific medicine, limited as it is to knowledge of the physical body provided by sense-perception alone, augmented though it may be by

⋆An introductory lecture given to the Institute of Psionic Medicine at The Priory, Binfield, on July 16th, 1976.

all sorts of instrumentation of the greatest possible ingenuity and complexity, operated and controlled by brilliant intellects.

Thus Psionic Medicine, as its name implies, seeks to restore to materialistic medicine that missing dimension that it has largely lost – a dimension not only vital to the recovery of the Art of medicine, but which alone can give real meaning and understanding to its Science. If this dimension can be restored, then it will be possible once again to have a true comprehensive Science and Art of healing in a fundamental sense.

As a new dimension Psionic Medicine is thus not just an alternative or fringe form of healing but the starting point of the supersensible and spiritual complement, which will make sense of the whole, on all planes of consciousness.

But a primary requisite for this to come about, is that we take very seriously the ancient dictum "know thyself" – the attainment of self-knowledge and insight – as truth about the nature of Reality must now come increasingly from within, rather than, as hitherto, from the material world without, which the ancient seers designated as Maya – illusion.

This is not going to be easy, as we have entered a period in Earth life, as I have already said, of special spiritual conflict and crisis, when forces which would pervert the true destiny of the Earth and of mankind from being realised, will use, and are using, any and every subtlety and subterfuge, both psychic and spiritual, to confuse, mislead and bewilder. Only the utmost self-awareness and vigilant faith will protect and give insight to choose and act aright.

But given that we have advanced thus far in self-knowledge, we can begin to regain and reinterpret a great deal of lost knowledge and wisdom necessary for future spiritual progress, but which to modern minds makes nonsense, and in any case appears anachronistic. Also we can start to develop new faculties and occult senses, necessary for, first, the apprehension, and then the legitimate use of supersensible forces in the service of wholeness in practical life and living.

So let me at this point give a practical example of reinterpretation which bears directly on our psionic theme.

Some years ago I was asked to write a short ten-minute introduction to a discussion on "The Nature of Disease". At first sight it appeared to be an impossible task, considering that such a title would cover not only all human disease, but the disease of animals, birds, the soil, and the environment in general. But on reflection I thought it might be done if I could get down to first principles and basic concepts. This proved to be right, and the clue provided was this quotation from McDonagh.

"In the ancient period medicine was based on Philosophy, it remained one with the other sciences, and disease was approached through the front door of health – disease was viewed as being no more than extension of the imbalance of the four temperaments or constitutional types, and the cause of the extension was sought for in climate, race, sex, diet, environment, habits and occupation. Treatment consisted in attempting to restore the balance."

The ancient concept of disease was thus very different from our modern one of cellular pathology, as it was based on what was called "humoral pathology" – a doctrine referring all disease to the state and admixture of the four cardinal humours – blood (sanguine), black bile (melancholic), yellow bile (choleric) and phlegm (phlegmatic). This concept persisted throughout the mediaeval times and down to as late as the middle of the 19th century. In the light of modern scientific thought and research it appears complete nonsense.

And indeed it had its final coup de grâce with the publication in 1858 of Virchow's *Cellular Pathology,* which laid the foundation of scientific medical thought which traces every disease phenomena to changes in the cell. In this century it has developed into the vast complexities of modern pathology, microscopy, bacteriology and molecular biology. Diseases as a result have never been studied so profoundly and intimately in all their manifestations and pathological structure, i.e. changes in the cells, as at the present time.

But we may well ask whether all this vast and indeed invaluable knowledge has given us the clue to the *fundamental* nature of disease, which is in fact bound up with the unsolved problem of the nature of life.

Let me give you two modern definitions of disease:

(1) from *Chambers Encyclopedia.* "Disease may be defined as any impairment of mental and physical *health,* as result of heredity,

infection, tumour formation, injury, degenerative changes, poisoning or displacement of bodily structure."

(2) from the *Oxford Dictionary*. "*Morbid condition* of body, plant or some part of them, illness, sickness."

Note that the two key words in these definitions are "health" in the first, and "morbid condition" in the second. So in the attempt to understand the fundamental nature of disease, we obviously need to know what we mean by "health" and what in fact is a "morbid condition".

I examined these basic points in my book *Life Threatened;* here is a relevant passage (p. 132): "But has all this incredible amount of scientific knowledge brought us any nearer knowing what health is, or for that matter what disease is? One is considered normal and the other abnormal and yet both are natural processes, so we are still left with the problem as to what are in fact 'morbid conditions'?"

Let us go back to the humoral theory, was it as absurd as it appeared to be? Was it not possible that in the course of time it had become a meaningless distortion and caricature of something which once had made sense?

If we trace back the humoral theory we find the four humours – black bile, blood, yellow bile, phlegm – were derived from the four elements of Alchemy – Earth, Air, Fire and Water – which the alchemists claimed were the primary elements, which mixed in various proportions, formed all matter. These in their turn in occult tradition are the Etheric Formative Forces, the four supersensible *living* forces of the Cosmos, viz the Warmth Ether, the Light Ether, the Chemical or Sound Ether and the Life Ether – the active principles of which as Wachmuth says, "come to living expression in the phenomenal world."

The humoral theory now begins to make more sense, once we begin to get back to the original realities lying behind the nonsense.

"Health", according to this would be, as I defined it in my book *The Pattern of Health,* the free flow and harmonious and balanced interaction of the etheric forces. "Disease" would be an interference, for any reason, with this free flow and harmonious interaction.

This I believe is what McDonagh meant by approaching disease through the front door of health. Health is the norm, disease is a deviation from the norm to a greater or lesser extent.

But this still leaves us with the problem of the "morbid condition". Also the statement "health is the norm" tends to make one think that health is a static state, whereas in fact it is very much the opposite, and to understand this, as well as the morbid condition, we must introduce two further concepts – that of polarity and dynamic balance.

I have treated these at length in Chap. XVI "Polarity and Dynamic Balance" in *Life Threatened;* so I will try to summarise:

The body is a complex of polar forces of many kinds, primary, secondary and tertiary, in a state of precarious balance between the most fundamental, between the anabolic or building up forces, and the catabolic or disintegrating forces, between the earth or telluric forces and the cosmic formative forces, between the processes of cell growth and the formative process in man, to name a few.

If the dynamic balance between the totality of the polar forces can be achieved and maintained within normal limits, we have total health, or put another way, "Everything that we contain is held in a stream of change, in integration and in disintegration and in its disintegration becomes the bearer of the spiritual." But this balance can be thrown out, as we know, by all sorts of factors as listed by McDonagh, and in addition in these modern times by the ubiquitous and wholesale pollution of the biosphere. There is thus a constant and never-ceasing necessity for continual adjustment, which the body miraculously manages to do as a general rule, against overwhelming odds.

But for well being and wholeness this adjustment must be made and kept as far as possible at the point of dynamic balance. In other words the normal processes of either of the polar forces concerned *must* be interrupted or curtailed, neither must be allowed to overcome the other and go on to its final completion or end, which if it happened would, in terms of polarity, mean total imbalance or death. Normal processes of both must, for health, be stopped at the point of dynamic balance or a morbid process begins to develop.

So we can now define a morbid condition as a natural polar process which has been allowed to carry on, not only beyond the point of optimum equilibrium of formative forces, but beyond the limits of return, *without help from outside,* which, in this context, means appropriate treatment.

From the foregoing it is clear that two distinct phenomena are involved, that of morbid conditions, the right and proper field of pathological research and investigation as far as material medicine is concerned, and that of health, which by definition is the point of dynamic balance or norm, and is the right and proper field for study of what constitutes normality and wholeness.

These two fields are very different, well stated in this quotation from *The Peckham Experiment*: "Health is totally distinct from sickness, when subject to disorder, the individual obeys the laws of pathology. In health man observes a different natural law – the law of function – for health means living a full functional existence, in which development proceeds according to potentiality."

Having rediscovered the existence of the etheric world of the formative forces – the new dimension lying "behind" the physical material state, the question now arises as to how it is possible to detect and evaluate the etheric.

Obviously to detect supersensible forces, such as the etheric, special senses or faculties are required. If we were advanced enough to have developed our latent occult senses in the true way and with the right technique the problem would be easy of solution, but the vast majority of us have not as yet been able to do this and so the problem remains; but providentially there is a solution made possible by the use of the dowsing or radiesthetic faculty. Thus radiesthesia comes to our aid and provides the means whereby the etheric forces can be detected and assessed and information obtained for diagnostic and therapeutic purposes.

I believe that the rediscovery of the radiesthetic faculty in these modern times is not fortuitous, but that it has been vouchsafed to us by Providence to enable us to cope with the difficult and dangerous stage in human development which lies immediately ahead, for it gives indirect access to the supersensible worlds, more particularly to the etheric, thus raising our level of consciousness and extending our awareness and knowledge. The faculty should be regarded as a special and peculiar sense, halfway between our ordinary physical senses which apprehend the material world and our to-be-developed latent occult senses, which, in due course, will apprehend the supersensible worlds direct.

I published a booklet with Malcolm Rae under the title *The*

Radiesthetic (or Dowsing) Faculty: its role, scope and limitations in the modern world", available to anyone who wants a more detailed exposition.

But having now got the means to explore the etheric body it is necessary to develop a technique whereby assessment can be made of the findings: this Dr. George Laurence has developed and it is the technique which those of you who have sought training in Psionic Medicine have been taught. It was in fact described in the B.S.D. publication *Practical Dowsing* under the title "The Laurence Technique of Psionic Diagnosis and Treatment", and is based on an equilibrium of three force fields.

This technique enables qualitative assessment of the patient and his progress, and at the same time throws light on the physical-pathological findings of ordinary diagnostic methods or in other words uncovers the causal factors involved, thus adding spiritual science to material science. However it must always be remembered that the measurements are of the state of the etheric and not the physical, though for practical purposes these can be taken to coincide under normal conditions.

So far so good, but having found a special way of detecting supersensible energies one problem remains: in Steiner's words, "The one great question to be solved is how are we to put the spiritual etheric forces in the service of practical life?" Or in other words how in the present context is it possible to treat these unbalanced etheric states, and the answer lies in the practice and use of Homoeopathy both theoretically and practically.

The reason why Homoeopathy is the method of treatment par excellence, though not necessarily to be used exclusively, is because the act of potentization reduces the indicated remedy (healing substance) to what one might call a dematerialized state, so that one is, certainly in the higher potencies, dealing with what Hahnemann called "pure force – dynamically spiritual", so that the unbalanced state to be treated and the homoeopathic remedy are similar in essence.

Some recent research work on the preparation of homoeopathic remedies by employing magnetically activated archetypal patterns of remedies instead of the classical dilution and succussion method, would seem to indicate that when we talk about potentization we really mean, according to Rawson in his published scientific paper

Potentization and Research, that potencies are nothing more nor less than "information-transfer". In the Information Theory the unit of information is known as a "bit". The rationale of homoeopathic treatment on this view will be to provide and supply exactly the right number of "bits" of healing information – not too many and not too few – which the patient requires in order for the natural process of *Vis Medicatrix Naturae* to resume their orderly course and function, so that a cure in due course may come about.

It will not have escaped my listeners that ideally Psionic Medicine is primarily concerned with health and its maintenance, as it provides a means of ascertaining the norm – the point of dynamic balance and can detect at once departures from it which may temporarily occur. But as we live in a far from ideal world most people are alas in a state of chronic imbalance, i.e. a morbid condition, but here too Psionic Medicine can come to the rescue and find out the real course of this chronic lack of health, deal with it effectively with the appropriate indicated remedies, and so put the patient back on the road to health and well being.

And there I will end. But I should just like to add this: that I consider the theory and practice of Psionic Medicine in its ascertainment of the etheric body, is probably one of the best ways, anyhow for doctors and healers, to begin to regain new faith and belief, in supersensible and spiritual forces from their own practical clinical experience. Thus the way will be paved for the essential acceptance of spiritual science, of a spiritual world of reality lying in all its grandeur behind the phenomenal world of matter.

Chronic and Degenerative Disease
relative to its early detection, cause, prevention, and non-toxic treatment★

Let me preface this lecture with the following quotation from Rudolf Steiner's *Fundamentals of Therapy:*

"Man is what he is by virtue of body, etheric body, soul (astral body), and Ego (spirit). He must in health be seen and understood from the aspects of these his members; in disease he must be ob-

★A lecture given at the A.G.M. of the Psionic Medical Society on 2nd Oct., 1976.

served in the disturbance of their equilibrium; and for his healing we must find the remedies that can restore that balance."

The theme I have been asked to talk about this morning is so vast that it is essential, if we are not to get bogged down in a surfeit of fragmentary data, we try to discover some basic guiding principles which will simplify understanding of the whole.

We can, to start with, approach the problem from two different standpoints, either from that of disease – the usual one, or from that of health.

This latter I attemped to do in my foregoing lecture to the recent Conference of the Institute of Psionic Medicine which may well serve as a preamble to this talk. May I also commend to you, for careful reading and study, Carl Upton's brilliant exposition of this same theme, his opening lecture at the Conference entitled "Vital Dynamis", printed in full in the *Psionic Journal* (No. 11).

Those of you who heard or have read my lecture will remember that I said that McDonagh had suggested the approach should, in his phrase, be "through the front door of health", thus reversing the usual way of healing with the subject. In other words health is the norm, any polar deviation from which constitutes disease, to a lesser or greater extent.

As I shall be saying a good deal about McDonagh and his concepts in the course of this talk, it may be as well at this point, to say a few words about him, as I expect his many writings and theories may not be known to most of you here, though he wrote at least nine books on "The Nature of Disease" and also published annual reports, in his later years, of his considerable research work.

In my estimation he was one of the unrecognized geniuses who occasionally appear in Medicine. That his contribution has still remained largely unacknowledged is partly due to his heterodox views, but more particularly because he is extremely difficult to read, and still more to understand. And one's impression is that he himself did not fully appreciate the full significance of his findings, nor that in postulating what he called "Climate" and "Activity" as fundamentals, he was already moving out of material concepts and explanations.

This in the light of our present knowledge and understanding makes very clear the importance of his contribution to the nature of disease. In fact Dr. Laurence in a tribute to him said: "As far as I am concerned Radiesthesia has proved McDonagh's theory to me, and McDonagh's theory has enabled me to use Radiesthesia much more systematically and efficiently."

But to return to our theme. If health is the norm, obviously we must know what we mean by "health" if we are going to understand what we mean by disease. So to start off I define health as a functional state of dynamic balance, which like a gyroscope is continually adjusting back to the norm – the point of dynamic balance. From this it would follow that if for any reason this automatic adjustment breaks down and remains unbalanced, then disorder ensues; later, disease, and in the extreme degree chronic disease, degeneration, and finally death.

To prevent this happening, to preserve health and avoid disease it is necessary to know in more detail what is the nature of this state of dynamic balance, and I don't think we can do better than examine the question in the light of McDonagh's theories and concepts.

He postulates what he calls a primordial "Activity" by which matter is formed in an evolutionary spiral of development.

The spiral starts with the sub-atomic particles; in the second cycle the 92 elements appear; in the third the crystalline products, of which carbon and its derivatives are uniquely important, as round them the organic world is built. These three comprise the pre-colloid half of the spiral.

In the fourth cycle we find the colloids – the class to which protein belongs. This development leads to the fifth when the colloidal-protein is differentiated into the various structures of the vegetable world. Then the sixth, the animal phase, in which protein becomes the matrix of tissues and organs, of which Man and his physical body is the final and seventh creation.

In animals and human beings "Activity" makes a double cycle in the protein, producing a rhythmic alternating pulsation, first of expansion on the first cycle and then an equal contraction on the second. In health this goes on ceaselessly in the protein, and the ideal is thus for the physical body to be held in dynamic balance throughout life.

But if for any reason, and in modern life they are innumerable, this rhythmic pulsation is interfered with, disorder sets in; and if this imbalance persists outside normal limits, conditions of progressive deterioration will develop.

Thus, for example, to quote McDonagh: "disease arises when an invader releases an excessive amount of "Activity" from the storage depot in the protein – which is situated in the fourth part of the attracting portion – from which the anterior lobe of the pituitary gland originated.

"When too much 'Activity' is released – the protein first over-expands and later over-contracts. In the process of over-expanding 'Activity' is liberated, together with various constituents of the protein through excessive radiation. Over-contraction also results in the clotting time of the protein being shortened – with the production of viruses."

From this over-expansion and over-contraction arise many of the diseases with which we are familiar, both acute and chronic according to the degree and persistence of the imbalance, and the parts of the protein affected, from which the various organs of the body originated.

This over-expansion and over-contraction may be of the protein as a whole, but not necessarily, as each of the three sections may react in this way independently of the other two, and this determines what tissues and organs of the physical body exhibit clinical symptoms and pathological signs of disease and/or degeneration.

But to come back to "Activity". McDonagh never really defined what he meant by the term beyond saying it was, to quote him: "the primordial substance out of which the universe is being fashioned," but I feel we can be more specific, and legitimately equate "Activity" with the Etheric Formative Forces of the Cosmos, which are what form the etheric bodies of plants, animals and Man, and is the etheric body of each individual; in fact what may be called the life body, which in childhood controls growth and development, and which later is involved in the capacity of thinking.

We are now on more familiar ground, as the etheric is the usual level on which diagnosis and treatment in Psionic Medicine takes place.

Diagnosis thus consists in finding out the effect and degree of the disorganization of the rhythmic pattern, in the sense described above, of the protein of the body as a whole, and then what particular part of the physical body has been affected by the protein imbalance.

At the same time the causal factors must be ascertained, as the detection and elimination may well enable the etheric forces to restore dynamic balance, possibly without further treatment.

Early Detection

From this new standpoint let us look afresh at our theme, which brings us to early detection of the disordered state.

In a small book entitled *The Future of Medicine,* published in 1919, Sir James Mackenzie – the famous heart specialist – advanced the idea that there are four stages of disease; the pre-disposing state, the early stage, the advanced or chronic stage, and the final stage terminating in death. Modern medicine since his time has learnt a great deal about stages three and four, a little about stage two, but next to nothing about stage one – the pre-disposing stage; and yet the aim of medicine should be to prevent the diseased stage arising, and not to try to shut the stable door after the horse has already gone.

The reason for this lack of knowledge of this crucial stage is that up to this point there is still no damage to the tissues or cells, and no pathological changes either historical or morphological, only imbalance of the etheric forces, possibly showing a functional disorder, and indeed ordinary orthodox methods of diagnosis have no means of detecting such forces. Thus early detection is not made as a general rule.

But in Psionic Medicine we are employing a new diagnostic supersensible faculty – the Radiesthetic or Dowsing faculty – which can detect the nature and degree of the distortion of the etheric pattern by the special techniques which have been developed by Psionic Medicine. Thus early detection is possible of the very first departures from the norm – the point of dynamic balance – and at this stage normality can be completely restored. It is of course very rare to get patients seeking advice in such a very early stage of disorder.

It will be obvious what an immense advance this possibility of early detection would provide in the maintenance of health – the state of dynamic balance of the *whole* man, and the vast amount of organic disease or degenerative disorders which would be prevented from developing.

But even though this is now theoretically possible it is going to be increasingly difficult to implement practically, due to the sheer volume of toxic causes both external and internal with which humanity is now inundated and invaded by wholesale pollution in this technological age. Increasingly we shall have to deal with stages two and three, and this will be a combined effort of every form of healing procedure, especially and including modern medicine. But even here in these more advanced stages, although pathological changes in the majority of cases will have developed and be present, the radiesthetic faculty can still be used to ferret out the subtle *causal* factors lying at the back, which only with great difficulty, if at all, can be spotted by the ordinary diagnostic procedures of modern medicine. But if this *can* be done it changes the whole disease situation.

So let us now consider some of the main categories of these toxic factors.

Cause

First physical causes, such as nuclear fall-out. This obvious and well recognized menace results from nuclear radiation. But this is tending to recede from the public mind, as the high level radiation from strontium 90, calcium 137 and iodine 131, for example, is much less since the Test Ban Treaty has proved relatively effective, and so people feel safer and relax vigilance. But what is not recognized is that what is called the peaceful use of atomic energy is an even greater and growing menace, as the nuclear power stations of the world are pouring out low-level radiation, which cannot be controlled, in the form of tritium and carbon 14 – the radio-isotopes of hydrogen and carbon respectively. This means that wherever hydrogen and carbon are present (usually in conjunction with nitrogen and oxygen) in organic systems, they are now accompanied since 1954 by their radio-active isotopes in vastly increased amounts – in the case of tritium from the natural background, the count of 10 tritium units has risen to 6,500 T.U.*

Note that as a result, this depressing and alarming fact has come to stay: the hydrogen bonds holding together the intricate helix structure of D.N.A. can now incorporate tritium, and D.N.A. as is well known, is susceptible to radiation, and so is easily damaged, with an effect on function which can only be surmised at the present time, but over a period of time it may be much more deep seated and profound than has as yet been imagined.

*See – *Radiation and Nuclear Homoeopathy* by D.S. Rawson (M.A.(Oxon)).

To pass on to the chemical pollutants. Here we have a veritable Pandora's box of a host of synthetic products, ranging from chemical additives introduced in the processing of foods, which now run at over 2500 items and are steadily rising, to those used in horticulture and agriculture such as pesticides, insecticides, herbicides, artificial fertilizers, etc., many of which are taken up by vegetation or build up in the soil, and from there get into the rivers, streams and water supplies, increasing contamination to a greater or lesser degree.

One of the effects of this increasing use of these substances, and of the greatest significance for the future of mankind, is that, according to Rudolf Steiner, modern food, due to modern treatment of the soil, no longer contains the life forces necessary for the development of the human will. John Soper commenting on this in a paper entitled "The Need for a Change of Attitude to the Relationship between Soil, Food and Health" said: "This deadened earthbound chemical in our daily food may possibly suffice for a while to nourish our physical bodies and our deadened intellect, but when it comes to other parts of our bodies, the real genuine type of thinking, the feeling ability, the will, these too need to be nourished from food which contains the necessary forces and not so much substances". To which we can add this statement of McDonagh: "Far and away the most important factor is the *quality* of the food upon which plants, animals and Man are made to subsist, because it is inferior-quality food which is apt to render excessive the amount of 'Activity' which 'Climate' releases from the protein in which it is stored... Food upon which plants live is derived from the soil, and the quality of the life in the form of bacteria, fungi and protozoa in the soil, forming its so-called heart."

But in addition to all this there is an increase in recent years in toxic substances which can enter the food chains in other subtle ways and these in particular have been shown to be lethal to some forms of life and a menace to all. The notorious three are Lead, Mercury, especially in the form of methyl-mercury, and Cadmium, all produced from manufacturing processes, to which we should add Aluminium since this is used in vast quantities in cooking utensils throughout the civilized world, and to which 15% of people are sensitive and suffer accordingly. More metals are being added to the list ever year, and a non-metal – Fluorine – which if the powers-that-be have their way will add an unavoidable universal toxic factor.

No one knows what the constant consumption of this vast variety of chemicals day in day out will eventually do to the dynamic balance on which the health of humanity depends, but one can make a shrewd guess.

There is a further development of this chemical aspect in (strangely and ironically enough) the therapeutic drug industry; for as we all know, unexpected side effects may develop – comprising what is now known as iatrogenic disease, i.e. a condition produced by drugs given in correct therapeutic dosage to deal with the symptoms of a diseased condition, but which also produce toxic effects which may well be worse than the disease. In other words whatever the drugs may do therapeutically on a physio-chemical level they must obviously badly derange the normal functioning of the etheric forces in the dynamic balance of the human protein.

But in any case the suppression of symptoms which so often seems to be the main function of modern drug therapy obviously often interferes with the efforts of the etheric forces to restore normality and obstruct self-healing which is the only healing.

To such a pass have things come that in a recent survey it was found that a drug had contributed to an illness of some five out of every one hundred patients admitted to British hospitals, and as many as 30% of hospital patients suffer from some kind of unwanted effect. A further study involving 4000 families showed that more than 50% of the adult population and almost 33% of children take some kind of medicament every day. This therapeutic menace is brought home in a recent best seller *Medical Nemesis* by Ivan Illich.

All this chemical pollution in the physical body increases the over-contraction aspect of the rhythmic pulsation in the protein, and if continued, as it is in modern life, gradually increases all the degenerative diseases in spite of the body's inherent ability for self-healing.

Let us now move on to the role of bacteria – microbic invasion both from within and without as a cause of disease. This particular aspect of the departure from health in the form of infectious diseases etc. is not really such a menace as it has been in the past, owing to wise preventative measures embodied in the public health and sanitation legislation of the last century, including the provision of pure and potable water supplies. All this was made possible by the development of the science of bacteriology in the 19th century and in this century of molecular biology, though this latter would now appear to be leading us into most dangerous realms.

McDonagh made a special study of infections, especially Influenza, for they represented for him the acute phase of disease, when, due to an outside cause (which he called "Climate") the protein over-expanded and contracted, which gives rise to the various symptoms and signs of the illness, according to which portion of the protein has been affected.

A sub-acute stage usually follows the acute stage when certain portions of the protein do not return to normal and remain relatively over-contracted, and this process, reinforced by other internal factors such as intestinal toxaemia, in due course results in chronic over-contraction – this chronic phase is followed by actual degeneration. A further result of the intestinal toxaemia is that the normal bacteria in the bowel develop into pathological forms.

But it would appear that something else also happens which leads us directly to Hahnemann's Miasmic Theory of Chronic Disease, which Dr. Laurence by his psionic research has shown to be a definite fact.

Psionic analysis has revealed in so many cases that the causative factor in the sub-acute or chronic condition of the patient has been due either to an hereditary miasm or to an acquired miasm, or as Laurence preferred to call it "a retained toxin of acquired infection" from an earlier infectious illness, and that elimination of this miasm whether hereditary or acquired sets going the restoration of the patient back to health.

Laurence claimed that it was this unrecognised factor which prevented the restoration of dynamic balance in a great many conditions failing to respond to any form of treatment. For example, according to him the TK/TB miasms were primarily responsible in such conditions as asthma, eczemas, hay fever and other allergic conditions, chronic sinusitis, and pharyngeal or laryngeal troubles, migraine, mental illnesses of various sorts, mucous colitis, varicose veins, arterial degeneration, diabetes, and even Hodgkin's disease and leukaemia.

Upton in his paper "Vital Dynamics" also gives a list of other pathological conditions resulting from the miasms of syphilis and gonorrhoea.

What then is a miasm – that which is left behind after a clinically satisfactory and apparently complete recovery from an acute infection? At present we are not sure, but we are beginning to get some idea of its nature in the light of psionic research. Let me quote this from Carl Upton's lecture, "Vital Dynamics", which suggests that a miasm may exist in three modes. He says:

"If we take Measles as an example we recognise the miasmic state of Measles which is certainly not demonstrable at clinical or laboratory level, yet it has a profound influence on the constitutional dynamics often with dire effects. Then there is the recently demonstrated state of Measles as dormant virus, which can lead to serious consequences.* And there is the state of Measles seen in acute infections which is transient, but, it seems, may lead to the two other states which then show quite different clinical consequences which would not normally be associated at all with the usual infective episode seen in childhood. There is reason to suppose that this situation is not confined to Measles but may be true of all microorganic influences. It is significant also that one or other of these states may be dominant or recessive at different historical periods."

I suggest that in trying to find an answer to our query "What is a miasm?" we may also be helped, apart from Hahnemann, by what I consider most useful clues provided by the work and concepts of two outstanding medical research workers, one in the 19th century – Dr. Antoine Béchamp with his Microzyma Theory regarding the nature of living matter, and in this century Dr. Wilhelm Reich with his theory of Bions and cosmic orgone energy.

Béchamp's microzyma can be described, and I quote as "Actual units of bioblasts, ferments of the minutest perceptible order, capable of assimulation, growth and disease, and have to be regarded as elementary units of structure, standing between the cell and the ultimate molecules of living matter" and are ubiquitously present even in very old geological formations such as chalk, and according to Béchamp can constantly develop into various forms of bacteria according to conditions both outside and inside the body.

Unfortunately the scientific world accepted Pasteur's theories rather than Béchamp's in the development of the microbic theory of

*See "The Contribution of Psionic Medicine to Hahnemann's Miasmic Theory" by Dr. A.T. Westlake.

disease, and this has continued ever since, and Béchamp's outstanding researches have been largely forgotten and certainly neglected.

The remarkable story of how this all came about is recorded in a book called *Béchamp or Pasteur,* by Douglas Hume, which I hope some of you may have read.

Reich's contribution this century has likewise suffered a similar fate, all the more curious as Reich's concept of the Bion has a strong similarity to the Microzyma of Béchamp.

Bions, according to Reich, are invariably produced when matter is heated to incandescence and made to swell; they are also found, but more slowly, when any matter breaks down or disintegrates. Bions, to quote Reich "are microscopically visible vesicles of functioning energy and transitional forms from non-living to living matter. The Bion is the elementary functional unit of all living matter – Bions are constantly being produced, and can develop into protozoa or degenerate into cocci and bacilli."

There is here very obviously research work of a fundamental nature for the future, and its importance is clear to anyone concerned with the miasmic problem and indeed with the whole microbic theory of disease.

We are now left with what we may call the non-physical causes of disease – psychological, emotional, mental, including stress, and the whole field of psycho–pathology in general, but which nevertheless sooner or later can produce disorders and disharmony of the whole man, starting with what is now recognized as psycho–somatic conditions, which in turn may pass over into actual pathological disease and disintegration of the physical body.

I do not propose to discuss this aspect further except to make three comments: the first is that this whole field of the psyche has been invaded by modern materialistic thinking so that the cause of most psychological disorders is attributed to some actual traumatic shock, usually said to have been experienced in childhood and relegated to the unconscious, and only to be resolved by psychoanalysis or similar psychic therapies, or more recently by ambivalent drug treatment.

Secondly, and more serious, evil is regarded as having no reality. Modern man denies its existence, and psychiatrists have abolished it as a cause in mental and emotional break-downs. Thus this ignorance or unawareness of what is in reality a basic fact, lays modern society, vulnerable as we have already seen on other grounds, wide open to these influences, which St. Paul described "as spiritual wickedness in high places". I have no doubt myself that man's inhumanity to man in the modern cult of violence and murder, senseless destruction and vandalism, the lust for power, unbridled promiscuity, pornography and psychedelic drug taking, the use of black magic and devil worship, and demonic possession, and other corruptions on all levels, are manifestations of this evil, rampant, ubiquitous. We might also add the curious sort of imbecility which exhibits so often a sad lack of common sense and common charity in administration on all levels, and in the order of our daily lives and habits.

Thirdly, it is not generally recognized that man is not just an animated physical organism, subject entirely to the laws of matter, but that in fact he has three other "bodies" which obey spiritual laws; an etheric body derived from the universal cosmic ether, an astral "body", the body of feeling and thus consciousness, and an Ego which makes man a being distinct from animal, plant and mineral, a whole integrated being unique in himself. These latter two, the astral and the Ego, function normally on the supersensible levels and obey its laws. Whereas the etheric body is closely associated with the physical body to which it gives life, the other two are in a much looser relationship, and in fact it is essential it remains so, as if, for any reason the etheric control weakens and they, the astral or the Ego, penetrate deeper into the physical body and cannot withdraw as they should, then they cancel out the ordinary functioning of the etheric-physical, transforming it into abnormal functioning, and illness and disease follows on psychological and physical levels. This "illness" is normally prevented by the action of the etheric body which in health maintains the whole in essential dynamic balance.

So we see that the integrated function of the whole is far from being straightforward; very often on the supersensible level it is exactly contrary to what one expects on the physical.

Prevention

We now come to prevention. How far is it possible to avoid the threat to health and well-being with which we are surrounded in these modern times? The answer is that it is very difficult, and becoming increasingly so for everyone, especially the inhabitants of the urban conurbations.

A certain amount has been done by public health measures of various kinds, and indeed many of the pollution problems can only be attempts at solutions by concerted, co-operative action by local, regional, national or international bodies working with real knowledge and understanding, scientific expertise and disinterested enthusiasm for the common good. But all this presupposes a very different outlook and set of values than obtains today; and in any case few of us are in any position where we can influence, let alone initiate, any of the urgent measures which would enable us to find our way out of the polluted miasma of these times.

And so we are thrown back on ourselves and on individual responsibility for our way of life, and it is up to us to use what knowledge and intelligence we have to preserve our own integrity and wholeness, and to give informed guidance to all who look to us for help or for whom we have responsibility, and this certainly applies to doctors, teachers and parents. More especially does it apply to all those who understand the adverse psychic and spiritual perils which now confront mankind.

The true scientific knowledge is available if we seek it; it only requires the right motivation and use, and the true spiritual wisdom is also there for those who seek to be Christ-centred with and in their whole being.

On the physical–etheric levels the essence of prevention is to be able to detect the imbalance of the protein in its incipient stage of disorientation, then to find the cause, and here as I have already said one must not overlook, as it is not a cause one would expect, that this balance can be upset by the undue incursion of the astral and/or the Ego forces too deeply into the physical body. The cause found, then we must find the therapeutic means and remedies by which balance and harmony can be restored.

We must obviously be able to detect this imbalance before it has produced organic and structural damage, i.e. pathological changes to the physical body; or in other words we must be able to detect the changes which first take place in the etheric or life body of a human being. As this is a paraphysical dimension we require an addition to our ordinary physical senses in order to ascertain the information we require, and this special sense, as I have already said earlier on, is what is called the radiesthetic or dowsing faculty.

I believe this rediscovery of the faculty in this century for medical purposes is not fortuitous, but that it has been vouchsafed to us by Divine Providence to enable us to cope with the difficult and dangerous stage in human development which lies immediately ahead.

But we must be able to interpret and evaluate what the faculty reveals. This means that interpretative technique is required, and this has in fact been worked out by Dr. George Laurence whereby, using a diagnostic pattern, the deviation from the point of dynamic balance, i.e. health, can be determined in degrees, plus or minus, and the therapeutic remedy is what rectifies this departure from dynamic balance. The diagnostic pattern then becomes an indicator of the restoration to health by a true balance of the three forces involved – the patient, the causal factor and the right remedy – the simillimum. The true prevention is seldom possible or even attempted in these days, but there is one field which demonstrates its great value and commonsense if this possibility were more widely known. This is in the ascertainment and elimination of miasmic factors in would-be parents, so that children, subsequently born, will be free from hereditary miasms which may have for long periods been passed down each generation to cause a great deal of what is usually regarded as unavoidable chronic ailments and diseases.

This is now eminently possible, and has in fact been done, and so it would appear that for the first time in history this form of hereditary chain of diseases can be broken, to the greatest benefit of the individuals concerned, and the race.

I am sure other preventative possibilities will emerge in due course, but in any case we can get a greater insight of what in all cases is wrong; and although a great deal in modern life is not rectifiable at present, such steps as are possible can be taken to eliminate what can be dealt with.

Just as the discovery of the microscope and its technique for medical use made possible the science of Bacteriology in the last century, so in this, the rediscovery of the radiesthetic faculty will make possible, to a degree we cannot at present realize, the essential development of scientific spiritual medicine – the missing complement to modern scientific material medicine.

Non-toxic Treatment

This brings us to our last heading – non-toxic treatment. We have already considered the side effects of a great deal of allopathic drug treatment, which shows there is little co-operation with the healing forces of the body, and so it would be preferable and much more sensible to achieve results by direct co-operation without the adverse effects.

How do we define a non-toxic form of treatment? I suggest the following: a form of treatment which stimulates and co-operates with the etheric forces of the body to bring about dynamic balance, i.e. health and normality on all planes.

By this definition, synthetic allopathic drugs are mostly unacceptable except for emergency use to achieve some essential and necessary therapeutic result, when it is worth risking side effects for the overall result which is required. But apart from this, allopathic synthetic drugs are best left alone as a general rule.

But what then is available?

All down through the ages herbal remedies from many herbs and plants have been used effectively for curative purposes. This folklore medicine has also been full of superstition, but a good deal in a modern *materia medica* has sifted out the useful ones from the others. But the process has gone further in these modern times, as with a number adopted in scientific pharmacology the search has been for the active chemical principle involved and its isolation, but in the process the balance of the natural complex which nature has so carefully preserved may well be dispersed, and so the part is not so therapeutically good as the whole.

But useful as so many herbal remedies are, the treatment of choice in radiesthetics and psionic work is undoubtedly Homoeopathy; as by the process of potentization any substance used therapeutically is converted into a state which corresponds more closely energetically to the etheric to which healing belongs, and this can and does happen. As Steiner says in his *Fundamentals of Therapy*... "the physical organism alone could never call forth a process of self healing; it is in the etheric organism that the process is kindled. We are thus led to recognise health in that condition which has its origin in the etheric."

It would appear that potentization is in effect a process of dematerialisation by this process of dilution and succussion, as once the substance has been diluted to the 12th centesimal potency, a comparatively simple calculation shows that this exceeds the theoretical limits of 10^{23} imposed by Avogadro's Number.

But as we know, potentization goes on far beyond this to 30c, 200c, M (1000)c, 10M, CM etc. (often far more effective than the lower potencies) so obviously we are no longer dealing with matter, but a form of energy, and so we are in a different realm.

We must not forget, however, that the physical body also requires mineral substances, which normally should be supplied in a good balanced diet; but as so often happens when there is so much refinement of food, deficiencies occur, which must be made good, and this is usually rectified therapeutically by supplying the required minerals in the form of biochemics in low potency from 1x to 12x.

In this connection I should like just to mention the remarkable but ignored work of the Finnish physician Dr. Hans Kalm with his system of *Organotrophia as a basis for therapy,* which advances the supposition that "vital function of a cell or tissue begins to falter as soon as it fails to get but one Primary Element necessary for that cell to play its role in the physiological economy of the organ or organisms." He has apparently had excellent results when the chemical element lacking is supplied, as determined radiesthetically.

But in addition to homoeopathic, biochemic and element treatment we have a most efficacious non-toxic system in the Bach Flower Remedies, discovered and used by the noted Dr Edward Bach. This system is a most valuable ally to Homoeopathy, and consists of 39 flower and tree infusions prepared by a special sun and boiling method, plus the Radiation Remedy, making 40 in all. Their use is in the treatment of all manner of psychological and emotional and psychosomatic symptoms and disorders. It has by clinical experience been found that although they are usually used on their own, they work faster and better after all miasms and toxins have first been eliminated.

All this is not to say that there are not many other non-toxic auxiliary therapies such as "right living", including diet, Acupuncture, Chiropractic and Osteopathy, Colour and Musical therapy, Nature Cure and Hydropathy, and last but not least genuine Spiritual Healing, all of which claim to and largely do, stimulate, adjust and co-operate with the healing forces of the body.

Conclusion

And now to conclude. Thinking over what I have covered in this lecture, it is evident we are dealing with a new dimension both in the science and in the art of medicine; and it may be that to explore further hidden possibilities, a more profound thinking and comprehensive technique, beyond what we have so far been using, must now be added.

This is not to say our present concepts and techniques have been in any way inadequate, but that special means must also be available to detect and assess the more subtle and intangible cosmic forces which are also undoubtedly responsible for imbalance on the physical-etheric levels.

Possibly all that is required is to add the missing triangle to our present psionic pattern so as to make a complete pattern in the form of the Seal of Solomon. But how one would use such a pattern in this form for more comprehensive analysis is not clear, and so an entirely new pattern and technique may be requisite.

Pondering on this I wondered whether such a concept was possible. To my astonishment I found that it not only was, but that it had been anticipated and already realized tangibly for practical purposes. Using the radiesthetic faculty with the new technique enabled the causal factors to be traced back in sequence to their ultimate origin, and at this point the basic remedy is also found, which deals with all the other subsidiary causes en route. This basic remedy would surprisingly appear to be, in any given case, what Hahnemann called the simillimum.

But the use of this technique at the present time should be regarded as belonging to the very advanced stage of Psionic Medicine, only to be used for very special purposes, among which one would include difficult and very chronic cases; and so I only mention this in passing.

And now let me end with this quotation which I feel sums up what I have been trying to say. The quotation is from *Radiation and Nuclear Homoeopathy* by David Rawson. It reads:

"If the inner vision of Rudolf Steiner, such as is expressed in his book, *Man as a Symphony,* is regarded in the light of modern knowledge, the unseen effects are of equal importance to those that are experienced within the physical world.

"St. Paul in his *Epistle to the Romans* writes of the frustration within Creation when Adam's Sin pulled Nature down with it. But this in itself is not an irreversible process since according to Steiner, there is always the possibility that Man, will, of his own volition, accept the responsibility for the redemption of matter within the physical world. This can only be done by Man assuming the mantle of responsibility within the spheres in which he has influence and a measure of control. For, whilst there is hope that this responsibility will be accepted, then there is still the chance that both Man and Nature will be released from the bondage with which they are now encircled, for both are interdependent from an evolutionary point of view."

References

List of Lectures, etc., given to various Societies from 1947 to 1976, which provided the 'reports' from which the present book has been compiled.

B.S.D. = British Society of Dowsers

M.S.S.R. = The Medical Society for the Study of Radiesthesia

Titles of Lectures	Names of Societies	Dates
Christ's Healing Miracles in the Light of Radiesthesia	M.S.S.R.	March 1947
Wanderings in the Radiesthetic Field	B.S.D.	Jan. 1950
Vis Medicatrix Naturae	Congress of Radionics and Radiesthesia	May 1950
Further Wanderings in the Radiesthetic Field	B.S.D.	June 1951
The Oranur Experiment	M.S.S.R.	Jan. 1952
The Contribution of Radiesthesia to the New Medicine	M.S.S.R.	Nov. 1953
Towards Radiesthetic Accuracy; Further Clinical Examples	M.S.S.R.	Jan. 1954
Commentary on Lecture by Dr Griffith Evans	M.S.S.R.	Feb. 1955
Commentary on Lecture by Dr Laurence	M.S.S.R.	April 1955
Radiesthesia in the Light of Huna	B.S.D. Congress	June 1955
The Future of Radiesthesia	B.S.D. Congress	July 1955
Memorandum on a Medical Ecological Project		1956
Receptivity, Pattern and Wholeness	B.S.D. Congress	July 1957
The Pattern of Health	Guild of Health	March 1958
The Radiesthetic Faculty	B.S.D. Congress	July 1959
The Future of Homoeopathy: A Contribution	The British Homoeopathic Journal	January 1961
The Place of Psionic Medicine	The Institute of Psionic Medicine	July 1976
Chronic and Degenerative Disease	The Psionic Medical Society	October 1976

The Therapeutic Patterns (See Chapter XII)

In the first edition of this book the actual patterns mentioned were not described nor were there any diagrams. This omission was for reasons which appeared cogent and relevant at the time; but after ten years had elapsed and much change in attitude to such things had taken place, together with numerous requests for details about the patterns – their shape, construction and use – it was decided to publish, in the second edition, the patterns as originally drawn by the late W. O. Wood; together with working details of construction and therapeutic use in so far as these were explored. This, in fact, was only done with five out of the original seven – and of the five only three in any detail.

It must be borne in mind that these patterns appeared thirty years ago, and such further work on patterns, stemming from this original work, has shown that many factors not appreciated then now enter into both the design and use of what may be called the modern descendants of the original patterns. One such factor is the introduction of the golden mean, both in the design and therapeutic use—a factor of considerable importance.

Thus the original designs are now, in the main, of historical interest, though they still can produce effects. They have to some extent been superseded, as we did not appreciate at the time one fundamental principle both in construction and use, namely 'Essential Simplicity.' Thus the patterns were probably far more complicated, particularly in their use, than they need have been, and accumulated a great deal of what, looked at again, would appear to have been unnecessary. One of the results of this, and one principal reason for the abandonment of research into this form of therapy, was the amount of time required, and what could almost be called ritualistic technique which had to be observed in a single treatment.

Therefore, in the descriptions which follow, I have largely omitted all such accretions, as what we considered necessary at the time may not have been so, and in any case, with the advance of knowledge and experience since, the subject can now be approached far more directly and simply by any sincere person who may wish to experiment with these original patterns. For they still remain the foundation for this form of therapy and are an excellent introduction for the student to the whole question of pattern healing, which is going to play an increasing role in the future.

But it is important for the student to recognize that there would appear to be two main categories of patterns—those which relate to what may be called the Universal patterns, the proportions of which incorporate cosmic mathematics and are related to the life of the Universe and are therefore 'changeless' as viewed by man— and what may be called 'Man patterns' which will be directly related to his individual life and its duration, though they may persist beyond it if accepted and vitalized by other men.* But even then the results may be far less than were obtained at the time of their original creation, as recorded in Chapter XIII of this book. These therapeutic patterns of Mr. Wood appear to fall into this second category, which is the reason why I said earlier on that they are now mainly of historical interest only.

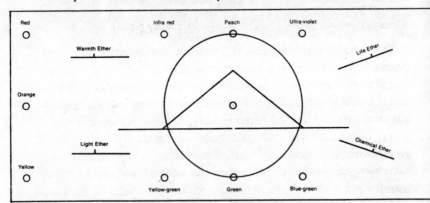

THE MASTER PATTERN

The complete set of these patterns consist of what is called the Master pattern, from which were derived three Static patterns, then three Dynamic patterns and, finally, one combining both Static

* This is bound up with what is called 'Valorisation.'

and Dynamic; though the evolution, it must be admitted, particularly of the later ones, is by no means obvious.

The Static series consisted of: 1. the static Diamond, 2. the static Celtic Cross; 3. the static Star of Bethlehem; the Dynamic series: 4. the dynamic Diamond, 5. the dynamic Celtic Cross, 6. the dynamic Star of Bethlehem, and finally, 7. the Composite.

These patterns should be made three-dimensionally in plywood, either full size, half size or even quarter size as they are far more effective than two-dimensional drawings.

In addition to the design itself the first two static patterns also employ actual Bach and Biochemic remedies for treatment purposes, which have to be radiesthetically determined and placed in the correct positions on the patterns. In the case of the third static— the Star of Bethlehem—some forty substances, some in homoeopathic potency, are an integral part of the pattern and to this extent become automatic. This becomes fully so in the dynamic patterns where the actual substance—Bach, Biochemic or other substances —are replaced simply by their names, and the only radiesthetic reading required is the length of treatment in any given case.

Various Uses of Therapeutic Patterns (as originally given)

(1) Static Diamond. 'Jack of all trades,' equivalent of 'Composite' on lower level, i.e., level of consciousness.

(2) Static Celtic Cross. Pattern for functional states in the etheric.

(3) Static Star of Bethlehem. Pattern for working directly on the physical state in cases of pathological disease.

(4) Dynamic Diamond. Works on the etheric body by colour or remedies.

(5) Dynamic Celtic Cross. For functional disturbances of the astral body.

(6) Dynamic Star of Bethlehem. Deals with disorders of the Ego.

(7) The Composite. Deals with the whole man, Ego, Astral, Etheric, Physical.

Record of Progress

Before starting treatment on any of the therapeutic patterns a radiesthetic analysis of the patient should first be made, according to any method the operator has adopted. This gives a general overall picture covering the main systems and organs of the body recorded in percentages, for subsequent comparison after the course of treatment has been completed.

THE STATIC SERIES

The Static Diamond

Full size, consists of a rectangular base, 3 ft. x 1 ft., with three diamonds:

No. 1: 3 ft. x 1 ft., bottom
No. 2: 2 ft. 3 in. x 9 in., middle
No. 3: 1 ft. 6 in., top

The top diamond, No. 3, has a 1 in. circle drawn in the centre.

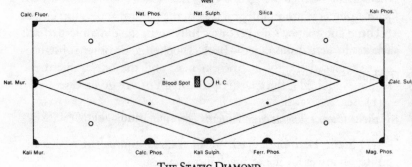

THE STATIC DIAMOND

The Diamond is an all-purpose instrument and has three main uses:

(1) As an Energizer of Bach and Biochemics.
(2) As a Stabilizer in conjunction with the Celtic Cross.
(3) For Colour Therapy.

The instrument, when in use, is orientated lengthways, North-South, and has twelve stations for the Biochemics around its edges, all 6x potency. Starting on the West side at the mid-line—Nat. Sulph., 6 in. North of the mid-line—Silica., NW corner—Kali Phos., Mid-way on the North side—Calc. Sulph., NE corner—Mag. Phos., 1 ft. along the East side—Ferr. Phos., East side mid-line—Kali Sulph., 6 in. South of the mid-line—Calc. Phos., SE corner—Kali Mur, Mid-way on the South side—Nat. Mur., SW corner—Calc. Flour., 1 ft. along the West side—Nat. Phos.

The Bach remedies are in three groups. Any of Group I are placed to the North of the mid-line on the top platform (diamond), viz. Vine, Oat, Olive, Oak, Gorse, Heather, Rock Water. Any of Group II are placed to the North of the mid-line platform, either side, or at the end (it doesn't matter), viz. Scleranthus, Vervain, Impatiens, Gentian, Chicory, Cerato, Clematis, Agrimony, Mimulus, Rock Rose, Centaury, Water Violet. Any of Group III are placed to the North of the mid-line on the bottom platform, either side, or at the end, viz. Elm, Cherry Plum, Pine, Larch, Willow, Aspen, Hornbeam, Sweet Chestnut, Beech, Crab Apple, Walnut, Holly, Honeysuckle, Star of Bethlehem, Wild Rose, Mustard, Red Chestnut, White Chestnut, Chestnut Bud. Also Rescue Remedy and Radiation Remedy.

In the central 1 in. circle on the top platform is placed Hexagonal Carbon if indicated.

The witness of the patient, blood or hair, etc., is placed on a glass slide immediately South of the central circle.

Technique for Treatment

(1) Ascertain radiesthetically what Bach remedies are required by the patient, also the required Biochemics, and whether Hexagonal Carbon is required.

(2) Place the Bach remedies on the appropriate levels, the Biochemics on their special positions and the Carbon on the centre.

(3) Find out, radiesthetically, the length of treatment, which should usually be between three and fifteen minutes.

(4) Then place the patient's witness (blood spot or hair) on the appropriate position, and time the treatment.

(5) At the end of the time, remove the Bach remedies and the Carbon, but leave the blood spot and the Biochemics in position.

(6) Repeat the treatment in twelve hours by replacing the Bach remedies and the Carbon for the indicated time, again removing at the end of the time, but still leaving the blood spot and the Biochemics.

(7) Next day, test to see whether the same Bach remedies are required, whether the same Biochemics and whether Carbon is still needed, and whether time is altered.

(8) Repeat treatment, and again in twelve hours.

(9) Repeat as for (7), and continue, if necessary, with the rhythm of treatment for six days, but on the seventh day, give no treatment and remove the blood spot from the Diamond, i.e., a total of six days' treatment.

The Diamond can be made half size or even a quarter size.

The Celtic Cross

The Celtic Cross consists of a cross

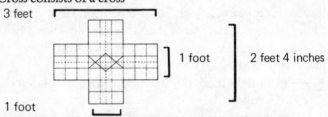

with four circles superimposed on the cross. First a large one of 24 in. diameter, placed centrally on the cross. Then one 16 in. diameter, centrally on this. Then one 8 in. diameter centrally on this. And finally, one of 1 in. diameter in the very centre.

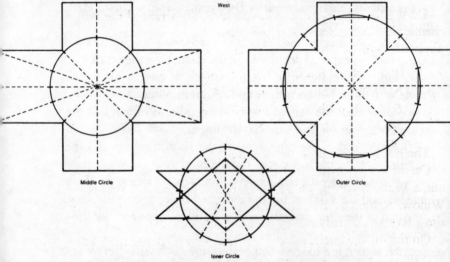

GEOMETRICAL CONSTRUCTION FOR DETERMINING BACH STATIONS ON ALL THREE CIRCLES OF THE CELTIC CROSS

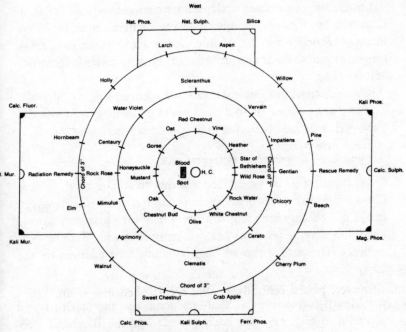

THE STATIC CELTIC CROSS

On the basic cross, i.e., the lowest level, are arranged the Biochemic positions exactly as on the Diamond, but they are now in obvious groups of three on the four arms of the cross:

West:	Nat. Phos.	Nat. Sulph.	Silica.
North:	Kali Phos.	Calc. Sulph.	Mag. Phos.
East:	Ferr. Phos.	Kali Sulph.	Calc. Phos.
South:	Kali Mur.	Nat. Mur.	Calc. Fluor.

The Bach remedy positions are arranged as follows.

On the lowest or outer circle, the twelve "trees": 1 Sweet Chestnut, 2 Walnut, 3 Elm, 5 Hornbeam, 6 Holly, 7 Larch, 8 Aspen, 9 Willow, 10 Pine, 12 Beech, 13 Cherry Plum, and 14 Crab Apple; also 4 Rescue Remedy and 11 Radiation Remedy.

On the middle circle, the twelve "healers": (1) Scleranthus, (2) Vervain, (3) Impatiens, (4) Gentian, (5) Chicory, (6) Cerato, (7) Clematis, (8) Agrimony, (9) Mimulus, (10) Rock Rose, (11) Centaury, and (12) Water Violet.

On the upper or inner circle, the remaining fourteen: (1) Red Chestnut, (2) Vine, (3) Heather, (4) Star of Bethlehem, (5) Wild Rose, (6) Rock Water, (7) White Chestnut, (8) Olive, (9) Chestnut Bud, (10) Oak, (11) Mustard, (12) Honeysuckle, (13) Gorse, and (14) Oat.

On the central 1 in. circle: Hexagonal Carbon.

The exact position of all these is given in the diagram, with the geometric method of arriving at the position in each case.

Technique of Treatment on The Celtic Cross

(1) It must first be ascertained whether treatment on the Celtic Cross is indicated. Very often, preliminary treatment must be given first, e.g., ordinary homoeopathic treatment for a toxic or miasmic condition may be necessary, or oral treatment with Bach or Biochemics. The patient should then be ready for treatment on the Celtic Cross.

(2) Now take each special 'rule' in turn, i.e., the Physical one, the Mental-formative, the Soul-emotional and the Spiritual, and ascertain in each case, the Bach remedy and the Biochemics required. Only one remedy should be indicated on each rule, but, in addition, on the Physical rule, one must ascertain whether Hexagonal Carbon is required, or not; and on the Spiritual, whether Rescue and/or Radiation remedies are required. So there might be in all, three Bach remedies, plus Rescue remedy and/or Radiation remedy, Hexagonal Carbon and one Biochemic (but occasionally there may be more Biochemics). (See Key to Rules.)

(3) The length of treatment must now be ascertained. This is important, as it is apparently possible to give an overdose and worsen the condition of the patient.

(4) All preliminary work having been done, the Celtic Cross is placed horizontally on a flat surface, with the long arms orientated exactly magnetic North and South. The Bach remedies already ascertained are now placed on the three circles in their correct positions, the Hexagonal Carbon, if indicated, on the central circle, and the Biochemic on one of the arms of the cross in the correct position. Also position Rescue remedy and Radiation remedy, if indicated.

The witness of the patient is now placed on a glass slide in the correct position, i.e., immediately South of the central circle, and left for the appropriate time, which must be carefully timed.

(5) The time up, remove everything, but replace the witness and the Biochemic on the Static Diamond for stabilization. The Diamond must be aligned North-South and the witness and the Biochemic put in their proper places. This is now all left for 24 hours, after which another treatment on the Celtic Cross is given, followed by 24 hours' stabilization.

(6) After the third treatment, i.e., on the third day, check progress radiesthetically, and retest on the Rules to see if there is any change in the remedies. Do this again on the sixth day, i.e., the second period of three days. This is followed by a day of rest. The witness is taken off the Diamond and no treatment of any sort is given.

This schedule is repeated the next and second week, and usually treatment can be stopped at the end of a fortnight.

When not in use, the Diamond and the Celtic Cross must be stood upright, as they do not then function.

The Special Rules

These rules are the sides of a square each 64 in., one North, one East, one South, one West, and all the Bach and Biochemics are arranged round the square. For example, on the East are the twelve Biochemics, on the South the soul-emotional Bach remedies, on the West the spiritual Bach remedies, and on the North the mental-formative Bach remedies. Each of these remedies has an exact place on the rules. As 64 in. is too long for practical use, the rules have been reduced to one-quarter size, i.e., 16 inches long, but it should be longer to provide room at one end for the witness. Mark the position of each number on each rule according to measurements given below.

To use them to find the remedy, take each in turn and face the rule towards the compass point—the last one is faced East, i.e., the sample or witness at the end is to the East, and the length of the rule pointing West, and so on, with the others.

Slowly pass the pendulum down each rule in turn, each being properly orientated. Stop at each numbered station and see if there

KEY TO RULES

(Note: The figures after each name give the position in inches of each remedy along the rules.)

	West SPIRITUAL	South SOUL-EMOTIONAL	North MENTAL-FORMATIVE	East PHYSICAL
(Witness)	Larch ¼	Water Violet 1	Oat ½	Nat. Phos. 1
(1)	Holly 1	Centaury 3	Gorse 2¼	Calc. Fluor. 3
(2)	Hornbeam 3¼	Rock Rose 4	Honeysuckle 3¾	Nat. Mur. 4
(3)	Radiation Remedy 4			
(3a)				
(4)	Elm 4¾	Mimulus 5	Mustard 4¼	Kali Mur. 5
(5)	Walnut 6	Agrimony 7	Oak 5¾	Calc. Phos. 7
(6)	Sweet Chestnut 6¾	Clematis 8	Chestnut Bud 7½	Kali Sulph. 8
(7)	Crab Apple 7¼	Cerato 9	Olive 8	Ferr. Phos. 9
(8)	Cherry Plum 8	Chicory 11	White Chestnut 8½	Mag. Phos. 11
(9)	Beech 10¼	Gentian 12	Rock Water 10½	Calc. Sulph. 12
(9a)	Rescue Remedy 11			
(10)	Pine 11¾	Impatiens 13	Wild Rose 11¾	Kali Phos. 13
(10a)				Hexagonal Carbon 13½
(11)	Willow 15	Vervain 15	Star of Bethlehem 12¼	Silicea 15
(12)	Aspen 15¾	Scleranthus 16	Heather 13¾	Nat. Sulph. 16
(13)			Vine 15½	

is any positive reaction by the pendulum. If there is, look up the number on the key below, and put the indicated remedy on its appropriate place on the Celtic Cross.

As I have already said, in our experiences only one remedy—apart from Radiation Remedy, Rescue Remedy and Hexagonal Carbon—on each level should be indicated.

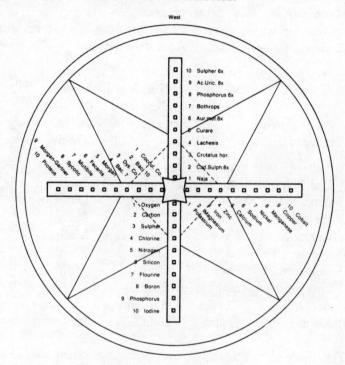

THE STATIC STAR OF BETHLEHEM

The Star of Bethlehem Treatment Instrument

The Star Instrument is constructed of 3/8 in. or 1/2 in. wood or plywood and comprises:

(1) A square 12 in. x 12 in. and four 'wings' consisting of a triangle with base 12 in. and perpendicular 20 in. long, which are fitted on to the sides of the square. The points of the triangles point NW, NE, SE, and SW. The total length is 52 in. from tip to tip.

(2) A cross with arms crossing at right-angles on top of the

square. Each arm of the cross is 22 in. long and 2 in. wide. The arms point North, South, East, and West.

(3) A small star at the intersection of the cross—the sides being exactly 1 in. This gives an angle of 10 in. from the horizontal. The points of this star point in the same direction as the big star.

Each layer is 3/8 in. or 1/2 in. thick.

There must be exact orientation in use.

On the cross are placed various remedies according to four classifications, at 2 in. intervals, starting from the centre.

West	*North*	*East*	*South*
"Poisons"	Metallic Elements	Non-Metallic Elements	Nosodes
All 6x potency except Uric Acid	All Turrenne Witnesses		All M. potency (Homoeopathic)
(1) Naja M	Potassium	Oxygen	Coccul. Co.
(2) Cad. Sulph. 6x	Magnesium	Carbon	Bac. 10
(3) Crotalus hor. M	Iron	Sulphur	Dys. Co.
(4) Lachesis M	Zinc	Chlorine	Bac. 7
(5) Curare M	Calcium	Nitrogen	Morgan
(6) Aur. met. 6x	Sodium	Silicon	Fecarlis
(7) Bothrops M	Nickel	Fluorine	Mutibile
(8) Phosphorus 6x	Manganese	Boron	Sycotic
(9) Ac. Uric 8x	Copper	Phosphorus	Morgon-Gartner
(10) Sulphur 6x	Cobalt	Iodine	Proteus

The whole of the Star and Cross, when set up, is surrounded by a trough 54 in. in diameter, 5 in. wide and 2 in. deep. This is filled with water to a depth of say 1-1/2 in. We were given to understand that this trough, with the water, is essential for the full functioning of the instrument—also to supply the missing element, Hydrogen, by the disintegration of the water into Hydrogen and Oxygen. Also it is said to give 'protection' from the 'radiation' which starts when the Star is orientated in a horizontal position, and extends twelve feet in all directions. Assuming this is so, the Star, when not in use, is dismantled, and the Cross stood up vertically. This may not be necessary or true, but I am leaving it in the instructions as this is how the Star of Bethlehem was first used. It is possible that a drawn circle just clear of the "wings" is all that is necessary.

Procedure in Setting Up the Star Instrument

(1) Put trough in position.

(2) Fill trough with adequate amount of water.

(3) Place square and cross in correctly orientated position inside the circle of the trough and add 'wings' (i.e., the triangles) in correct orientation, thus forming the complete Star.

(4) Place the blood spot of patient on a glass slide on the central star and leave for the indicated time, which must be ascertained radiesthetically. In the original use it was never less than one hour or more than 24 hours.

Before using the Star for treatment, it must be ascertained whether Star treatment is really indicated, also if it is, the patient must have some degree of understanding of the nature of the treatment, and know in general what is being done and give his or her consent, i.e., there must be conscious co-operation on the part of the patient.

At the end of the treatment, the blood spot is removed and placed on the Static Diamond for stabilization for the next 24 hours.

This completes the Star treatment, as only *one* treatment can be given on the Star, but this point requires reinvestigating.

Subsequent Celtic Cross treatment may be required.

THE DYNAMIC SERIES

The Dynamic Diamond

The dimensions are as follows: A rectangular base 40 in. x 16 in., first (bottom) diamond the same size, second (middle) diamond 28 in. x 11 in., and the third (top) 8 in. x 6-1/2 in. with a central square of one inch.

The colour stations are as on the Static Diamond round the sides of the rectangle, starting at the mid-point top side—Peach; then counterclockwise 6 in. from mid-point—Infra red; at the corner—Red; midway on short side—Orange; at lower corner—Yellow;

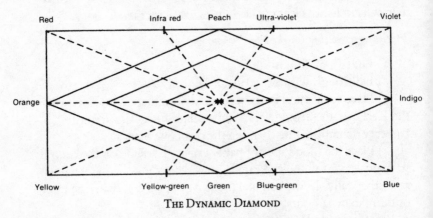

THE DYNAMIC DIAMOND

6 in. from mid-point lower side—Yellow-green; mid-point—Green; 6 in. from mid-point—Blue-green; corner—Blue; mid-point short side—Indigo; corner—Violet; 6 in. from mid-point—Ultra-violet; and so back to Peach.

If lines are drawn from these points to the centre, they will cut the three planes of the diamonds at definite points which gives the position of the colours on each of the three planes or levels. What colour is required, and which plane, must be ascertained radiesthetically, as well as the length of treatment. When this has been done, place the blood spot or hair on the exact position, and time. For example, Red on the Soul-emotional plane for X minutes.

This pattern was only used for colour work. What other uses it had were never explored and, indeed, we were not sure that it had any advantage over the Static Diamond for colour therapy.

The Dynamic Celtic Cross

This can be constructed of 3/16 in. plywood. It consists of six layers.

(1) A star, with four 'wings' and a central square
(2) A cross
(3) The large, or outer circle
(4) The medium, or middle circle
(5) The small, or inner circle
(6) The central circle

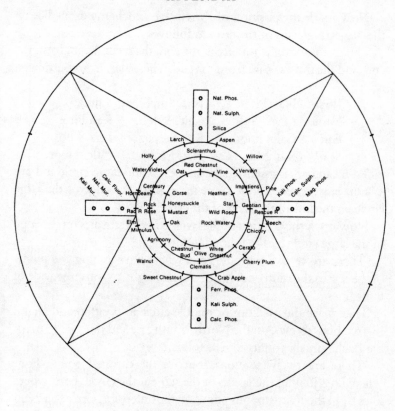

THE DYNAMIC CELTIC CROSS

There is also an outermost drawn circle, surrounding the whole.

(1) The central square is a foot square and each of the four 'wings' of the star is 12 in. x 20 in. This can be made in one whole forming the star.

(2) The cross is made of two interlocking pieces 32 in. long, 2 in. wide.

(3) The large circle is 18 in. diameter. When this is placed on the cross, each arm of the cross projects 7 in.

(4) The medium circle is 14 in. diameter.

(5) The small circle is 10 in. diameter.

(6) The central circle is 2 in. diameter.

(7) The outermost circle is 52 in. diameter, which is drawn on a table or on the ground, just clearing the points of the star.

Now mark the position of the twelve Biochemic remedies on the projecting arms of the cross as follows:

The first position is 1 in. from the end, the second 3 in. from the end, and the third is 5 in. from the end. The order, from outside in, is:

West:	Nat. Phos.	Nat. Sulph.	Silicea
North	Mag. Phos.	Calc. Sulph.	Kali Phos.
East	Calc. Phos.	Kali Sulph.	Ferr. Phos.
South	Kali Mr.	Nat. Mur.	Calc. Fluor.

To fix together, assemble the star, cross and large circle and put 5/8 in. brass screws about 1-1/2 in. in from the edge of the large circle on the line of the arms of the cross.

Now mark the position of the twelve Bach remedies on the edge of the large circle by the following formula:

'There are twelve stations. Four where lines joining the points of the star to the centre cut the circle, and eight 30° on either side of these lines.'

Then place the medium or middle circle in position and secure by two brass screws, on the North/South axis and proceed to mark the Bach remedies on its edge as follows:

'There are twelve stations, four on the cardinal points. Four where lines joining the points of the star cut the circle. Four where lines from the centre to four points on the outermost circle touching the points of the star 8 in. West and East of the North/South axis.'

Then place the small or inner circle in position and secure by two brass screws on the East/West axis, and proceed to mark the Bach remedies on its edge as follows:

'There are fourteen stations. Two cardinal East/West axis points. Eight points where a line from the centre cuts the outermost circle touching the points of the star 10 in. North and South of the East/West axis and vice versa. Four points where a line from the centre to the outermost circle 2 in. East and West of the North/South axis.'

The order of the remedies on each circle is the same as on the Static Celtic Cross.

Then place the central circle in position secured by a central brass screw.

The name of all the remedies must then be placed in position. These can be typed on gummed paper and then stuck in position.

In general all the names are placed with the tops of the letters pointing to the West; wherever possible the names are placed slightly away from the actual marked point on the edge of the circle.

To Operate It

(1) It must be ascertained radiesthetically whether treatment is indicated on this instrument, and unless it is it must not be used.

(2) If it is, then the consent of the patient must be obtained before treatment is started.

(3) Now draw a circle (i.e., the outermost circle) on the table or floor 52 in. in diameter and place the whole dynamic star inside with what was the West arm of the cross to the North (i.e., the whole instrument is turned 90°). Orientate this exactly magnetic North with a compass.

(4) If consent has been obtained then print the name (one they are commonly known by) and address of the patient on a piece of paper, about the same size as the other names, and place on a glass slide on the central circle, again with the top of the letters of the name facing West.

(5) The entire assemblage is now left for six hours. The whole process from the placing of the written name on the central circle is automatic and the time is the same for all patients.

(6) At the end of the time remove the patient's name from the central circle and burn the piece of paper. No further stabilization treatment is then required.

The Dynamic Star of Bethlehem and The Composite

No therapeutic work has, as far as I know, been done with either of these patterns, nor indeed any other research work, so these patterns are only included for historical completeness. It should be noted that the Composite was to be used in conjunction with an Infra-red radiation at the North pointing arm of the cross, an Ultra-violet source at the South pointing arm, and a white light at the Western arm. This may have had considerable significance but was never explored.

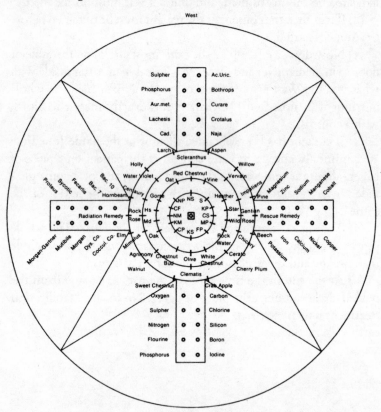

THE DYNAMIC STAR OF BETHLEHEM

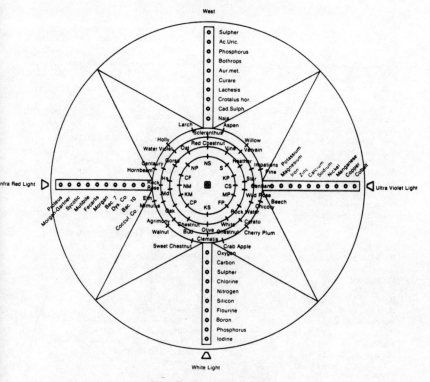

THE COMPOSITE PATTERN

Orientation When the Patterns Are Used for Therapy

All static patterns are to be orientated in the earth's magnetic field North-South.

All dynamic patterns are to be orientated at right-angles to the earth's magnetic field, i.e., East-West, the 90° rotation to be clockwise.

When not in use stand the patterns upright or, in the case of the Star of Bethlehem, dismantle the pattern at the end of treatment.

INDEX

INDEX

by pictures, 62
by wool, silk, oil, 64, 110
analytic and unitary, 70
laying on of hands, 44, 62, 65, 70, 105, 139
new conception of, 134
spiritual; *see* spiritual healing
of the whole man, 107
Health, ix, 1, 6, 116, 118, 132, 173, 176, 182, 197
High self, 79, 82, 88, 90
Homoeopathy, 20, 68, 72, 121, 133, 161, 174, 183
Horder Committee, 4
Hour-in-Time, the, 108, 140
Humoral Theory, 180
Huna, 76, 81, 89, 97, 144
Huxley, Dr Julian, 161
Hypnotism, 31

Iatrogenic Disease, 190
Injunction (legal), 59, 60
Insanity, 91
Insulin treatment, 84, 91
Intellectual knowledge, 167
Intuition, True, 86
Imagination, Creative, 109
Immunization against radiation, 58

Jensen, Dr Ernest, 16

Kahunas (Keepers of the Secret), 77, 80-85, 109
Kalm, Dr Hans, 199
Karma, 111

Laurence, Dr George, 121, 122, 183, 197
Lakhovsky, 35
Lehrs, Ernest, 137, 171
Lesourd, 17, 138
Leuret, Dr François, 100, 107, 140
Life Force, 27, 38, 61, 71
Lomi-lomi, 77, 81
Long, Max Freedom, 76, 111
Lourdes, 100, 101, 139
Low self, 79, 83, 89 *seq.*,

Maby, J.C., 96, 124, 127
'Man', 135
Mana, 79, 81, 82, 89, 91, 94
Magic, 76, 78, 79, 157
Magnetism, 29, 32, 34
Map dowsing, 83, 127, 158
Mass, The, 82
McDonagh, J.E.R., 6, 71, 87, 117, 143, 164, 179, 180, 181, 185, 186, 190, 192
Medical dowsing; *see* Radiesthesia
Medical Society for the Study of Radiesthesia, 16, 17, 70, 114, 155
Mesmer, Anton, 30, 37, 69, 83
Mesmerism, 31, 32
Miasmic theory of chronic disease, 122, 145, 163, 192
Mice, Mass death of, 52
Middle self, 79, 91, 95
Mind, 131

Renewal of, 97
Ministry of Healing, 139, 140, 142
Miracles, 84, 98, 100 *seq.*, 139, 142
New definition of, 101
Modern Medicine, 116, 121, 122, 142, 171, 173, 174
Monro, Dr Hector, 16, 17, 24
Morbid Condition, 180
Munia, 28, 37
Myognosis, 66, 91

National Health Service, 7, 8, 172
Nature Cure, 1, 16, 72
Nature of Disease Series, 116
Nervous ether, 35, 38
Neuberger, Dr Max, 25
Nicoll, Dr Maurice, 99
Nomenclature, x
Non-toxic treatment, 198
Nuclear energy, 47, 55

Obsession, 83
Oscilloclast, 4
Odyle or Odic Force, 31, 33, 38, 41, 68, 103
Oil (charged), 64, 105
Oranur experiment of, 46 *seq.*
DOR effects, 51, 55 *seq.*
Orgone; *see* Cosmic Orgone Energy
Orgone accumulators, 41, 42, 43, 48, 53, 58, 59, 72, 81
Orgonoscope, 41

Paracelsus, 28, 31, 37, 107
Pattern, 75, 130 *seq.*, 144, 146
Master pattern of health, 132, 135, 143
Pearse, Dr Innes, 6
Pendulums, 20, 82, 92, 94, 95, 128, 158
Pereti, Signor, 125
Pictures, 'Radiations' from, 62, 64, 96
Physical stimulation of low self, 83
'Point of no return', 161
Polarity, 66, 68, 81
Pollutant chemicals, 190
Pope Benedict xiv, 100
Possession by spirits, 108, 166
Potentization, 174
Psycho analysis, 37, 39, 83, 91
Prana, 38
Prayer, 85
Pre-matter forces, 96, 115
Pre-physical states, 161, 162, 163
Preventative medicine, A true, 3, 162, 173, 175, 195
Price, Weston A., 172
Protein, 117, 118, 119, 121
Drugs aggravating damage to, 71
Psionic Medicine 177 *seq.*
Pulsation, 42, 118

Quality of food, 6, 120, 172
Question and answer technique (Q & A), 127, 129, 133, 164, 166

INDEX

PUBLICATIONS REFERRED TO OR QUOTED IN THE TEXT

PUBLICATIONS REFERRED TO OR QUOTED IN THE TEXT